SOLOMON
&
SHEBA

SOLOMON & SHEBA

James B. Pritchard (ed.)

Gus W. van Beek
Lou H. Silberman
Edward Ullendorff
Paul F. Watson
W. Montgomery Watt

PHAIDON

Phaidon Press Limited, 5 Cromwell Place, London SW7 2JL

Distributed in the United States of America by Praeger Publishers, Inc.
111 Fourth Avenue, New York, N.Y. 10003

First published 1974

ISBN 0 7148 1613 2
Library of Congress Catalog Card Number: 72-79551

Printed in Great Britain by R and R Clark Ltd, Edinburgh

Contents

Introduction

James B. Pritchard

THE story of a visit made some three thousand years ago by a nameless queen of the Arabian kingdom of Sheba to King Solomon in Jerusalem has survived down to the present day in a mere thirteen verses of the First Book of Kings. In this, its canonical version, the story has been accepted as an historical event enshrined in scriptures sacred to Jews and Christians alike. A very slightly different version is found in Chronicles, and of course there have been differences regarding the proper interpretation of some of the original Hebrew, but the biblical story is considered canonically to be a literal, factual account.

Elsewhere, however, in extra-canonical writings and commentaries, the story has been elaborated upon in strikingly inventive ways. Over the centuries it has been borrowed, retold in languages other than Hebrew, altered to do service for a variety of ideas and institutions, and even become the subject of some superior works of art. While the story remained stable as it was transmitted in its biblical version, in Jewish, Arabic and Ethiopic writings it was altered to fit the purpose of the story-tellers and adorned with imaginative details that frequently reveal the character of the teller and his audience.

The modern reader of the biblical story of Solomon and the Queen of Sheba delights in it as did the reader in a distant age. The picture of courtly elegance and grandeur, the display of cleverness and wisdom, friendship between the two heads of state, the exchange of costly gifts, and the exclamation of surprise on the part of the queen upon seeing Solomon's wealth and witnessing his display of wisdom—these are images that kindle the imagination of simple and sophisticated alike. Yet questions present themselves to the twentieth-century reader. What, if any, historical evidence is there for the celebrated visit? Has modern archaeology uncovered the remains of the age of Solomon sufficiently to make credible the details of the story? What is known from other sources about the ancient kingdom of Sheba and its queens? What appeal did this romantic tale have that could account for its continuing popularity through three millennia? These are some of the questions that prompt our quest for the origin of the story and its long history in literature and art.

A shadowy history lies behind the earliest version we possess of the Queen of Sheba story. Very probably an oral tradition, forever beyond our reach, preceded the written account. Later the story may well have first appeared in written form in 'The Book of the Acts of Solomon', referred to in I Kings 11:41, but that book too

7

has not survived except for its title. Our most ancient witness to the tale is the account preserved in the Hebrew text of the First Book of Kings.

It is a simple, joyous episode from the Golden Age of Solomonic splendour, free from religious dogma and ponderous arguments. A queen from Sheba travelled by caravan laden with fabulously rich gifts to Jerusalem for the sole purpose of satisfying her curiosity about the famed wisdom and wealth of King Solomon. After the king had demonstrated his wisdom he proceeded to show his royal visitor the glories of his court. Its magnificence left her breathless—'there was no more spirit in her'. Confessing her earlier scepticism about the reports that had reached her, she declared that but half of the magnificence had been described to her. With a remark about the good fortune of those privileged to hear the wisdom of Solomon and a polite outburst of praise to Yahweh, Solomon's god, she made an incomparable present of gold, spices and precious stones. In return Solomon presented her with an unspecified gift and whatever she had asked besides. After this exchange the Queen of Sheba returned to her own land.

This is the straightforward account given in the First Book of Kings, Chapter 10:

[1]Now when the queen of Sheba heard of the fame of Solomon concerning the name of the Lord, she came to test him with hard questions. [2]She came to Jerusalem with a very great retinue, with camels bearing spices, and very much gold, and precious stones; and when she came to Solomon, she told him all that was on her mind. [3]And Solomon answered all her questions; there was nothing hidden from the king which he did not explain to her. [4]And when the queen of Sheba had seen all the wisdom of Solomon, the house that he had built, [5]the food of his table, the seating of his officials, and the attendance of his servants, their clothing, his cupbearers, and his burnt offerings which he offered at the house of the Lord, there was no more spirit in her.

[6]And she said to the king, 'The report was true which I heard in my own land of your affairs and of your wisdom, [7]but I did not believe the reports until I came and my own eyes had seen it; and, behold, the half was not told me; your wisdom and prosperity surpass the report which I heard. [8]Happy are your wives! Happy are these your servants, who continually stand before you and hear your wisdom! [9]Blessed be the Lord your God, who has delighted in you and set you on the throne of Israel! Because the Lord loved Israel for ever, he has made you king, that you may execute justice and righteousness.'

[10]Then she gave the king a hundred and twenty talents of gold, and a very great quantity of spices, and precious stones; never again came such an abundance of spices as these which the queen of Sheba gave to King Solomon. [11]Moreover the fleet of Hiram, which brought gold from Ophir, brought from Ophir a very great amount of almug wood and precious stones. [12]And the king made of the almug wood supports for the house of the Lord, and for the king's house, lyres also and harps for the singers; no such almug wood has come or been seen, to this day. [13]And King Solomon gave to the queen of Sheba all that she desired, whatever she asked besides what was given her by the bounty of King Solomon. So she turned and went back to her own land, with her servants.

The translation of the Revised Standard Version, quoted above, was made in 1952 from a Hebrew text with occasional reliance upon the Greek or another ancient version. Other translations differ slightly because of the nuances and ambiguities of certain Hebrew words and phrases, and because of variants in the readings of ancient manuscripts and versions. A few comments on crucial points may help explain the divergence of the several translators.

At the very beginning of the story the purpose of the queen's visit is said to have been the testing of Solomon with 'hard questions'. The Hebrew word is also used for riddles, the kind put by Samson to the Philistines in Judges 14:12, or conundrums of the type preserved in the Book of Proverbs. The Greek translation by a word related to 'enigmas' is accurate. The list of the queen's gifts to Solomon includes 'spices', but the word used here (*besamim*) is not restricted to the usual culinary items. It embraces in meaning anything that has a pleasing odour, such as perfume or incense. Arabia was famous for the latter. Some translations of the listing of the breathtaking display of Solomon's court differ from the 'cupbearers' of the version quoted above. An equally good case can be made for 'drinking-service', especially since 'cupbearers' would have been included among the 'servants' mentioned before them. An actual drinking-service of four pieces found in the Jordan Valley in the tomb of a wealthy woman who lived shortly before the time of Solomon may illustrate the reference.

One subtle overtone to the Hebrew version that is lost in the English translation should be mentioned, especially since it may have occasioned one of the more prominent elaborations that the story received. In verse 2 there appears a seemingly unambiguous phrase, 'she came to Solomon'. The Hebrew verb *bw'* used here generally means 'to come in'. Yet in more than a dozen places in the Bible it is used specifically for entering a tent or house for the purpose of sexual relations. Although the subject of the verb is generally a man, it is sometimes a woman, as in the sordid story of the daughters of Lot going in to their father (Genesis 19:34). Linked with this possible suggestion of an intimacy between Solomon and the queen is the phrase in verse 13, 'all that she desired', which was romantically interpreted in a Jewish legend as a desire on the part of the royal visitor for offspring by Solomon. Certainly nothing more substantial than these two suggestive phrases appears in the account to imply that there was other than a diplomatic encounter between the Queen of Sheba and Solomon. Yet, as we shall see, the scantiness of the evidence for a physical union between the two principals did not deter later story-tellers from elaborating on how the wise king managed to seduce the queen.

The magnitude of the queen's gift to Solomon of 120 talents of gold may escape the reader unfamiliar with ancient weights unless he is reminded that the quantity specified amounts to over four and a half tons (the equivalent today of about £2,800,000 or $7,000,000). One familiar with Hebrew literature is not surprised that at the end of verse 10 two verses are intruded about the fleet of Hiram that brought gold from Ophir. Obviously an editor inserted this extraneous remark because of the mention of gold in the Sheba story.

How far back into the past do these words from the Hebrew lead us? Although the setting of the story is the middle of the tenth century BC, the time of Solomon, the medieval Hebrew manuscript that served as a basis for the translation given above was actually written in the tenth century AD, two thousand years later. Are we then forced to accept a gap of two millennia of silence between the time of the event described and the writing of the earliest extant copy of a Hebrew manuscript that testified to it? Happily a Greek translation of the Hebrew narrative was made in the third century BC and later copies of it exist. The Greek text differs but little from the Hebrew version (it does have 'Happy are your wives' in verse 8, which was accepted by the translators of the Revised Standard Version, in place of the Hebrew reading of 'Happy are your men'). Apparently at the time that the Greek translation was made the Hebrew text stood much as it appears in the manuscript of the tenth century AD. Jewish belief in the sacredness of the canonical texts of the scriptures had obviously been an effective safeguard against change.

Another biblical account of the celebrated meeting is found in the Second Book of Chronicles, Chapter 9, verses 1–12. When this text, generally thought to date from the fifth to fourth century BC, is compared word for word with that in I Kings it appears to follow its earlier exemplar almost verbatim with no substantial differences. Yet in some very minor variants it is possible to detect the emergence of new views about such matters as the kingship in Israel, the pre-eminence of Solomon's wisdom, and the generosity of the king. The changes are slight, to be sure, but they are significant indicators of the views of the later age.

In verse 9 of the account in Kings the queen is quoted as saying that it was the Lord who had set Solomon on 'the throne of Israel'. But in the parallel passage it is 'his throne', that is, the Lord's, which Solomon occupies. To this view of the divine origin of the kingship suggested by the subtle change in the wording of Chronicles must be added the notion of the permanence of the institution. In the same verse in Kings the queen from a pagan land simply asserts that Solomon has been made king 'because the Lord loved Israel forever'. The Chronicler adds the phrase that describes the divine intent, 'and would establish them forever'. Such was the conviction of a later age.

Two other minor changes deserve mention. Slight though they are, they reflect important differences in nuance. In verse 7 of the account in Kings the queen asserts that Solomon's 'wisdom and prosperity' surpass the reports that had reached her. For the author of the later account in Chronicles, however, the source of her wonder was merely 'the greatness of your wisdom'. The impression is thus given that by the time of the writing of the version in Chronicles it was the wisdom rather than the wealth of the king that was predominant. This change in emphasis was achieved by the mere omission of a three-letter Hebrew word meaning 'prosperity'.

One addition to the story in Chronicles is important. The ending of the earlier story in Kings describes the parting generosity of Solomon thus: 'And King Solomon gave to the queen of Sheba all that she desired, whatever she asked besides what was given her by the bounty of King Solomon.' Yet in Chronicles the royal bounty included all that and more. By the simple addition of the words, 'besides what she had brought to the king', Solomon is pictured as having been in no way indebted to her for her gifts of spices, gold and precious stones. One wonders if Solomon is here described as actually returning the queen's gifts. An interpretation more fitting to oriental courtesy would be that he gave to her the equivalent of her presents to him. Yet apparently by the fifth century there was little question as to which was the greater of the two characters who met in Jerusalem and exchanged gifts and polite speeches. In Chronicles the tale had already begun the meandering course it was to take through the centuries.

The reference in the New Testament to the incident, while not specific in mentioning the land of Sheba from which the queen came, is nevertheless clear. The text for Matthew 12:42, repeated almost verbatim in Luke 11:31, reads:

> The queen of the South will arise at the judgment with this generation and condemn it; for she came from the ends of the earth to hear the wisdom of Solomon, and behold, something greater than Solomon is here.

The presence of this brief allusion to the visit of the queen in the Christian scriptures undoubtedly accounts, as we shall see, for the wide use of the incident as a subject in the Christian art and iconography of Europe.

One other first-century version of the ancient story should be mentioned and the important variants noted. The Jewish historian Josephus repeats the details of the story in Kings in an amplified paraphrase (*Antiquities*, Bk. VIII, 6. 5–6). Only once does he diverge significantly from the older accounts. The visitor is queen of Egypt and Ethiopia (named Nikaule in Bk. VIII, 6. 2) and there is no mention whatsoever of Sheba! The change in the locale for the home of the royal visitor from Arabia to the African continent may reflect the popular belief about the location of her home by the time of the first century AD. The less definite 'South' in the New Testament passages may also reflect this departure from the older tradition. It might also be noted that the 120 talents of gold mentioned in Kings as a part of the queen's gift to Solomon is reduced by Josephus to a more credible twenty.

Modern students of the history of the Bible and the ancient Near East are sharply divided on the question of the historicity of the story of Solomon and the Queen of Sheba. One opinion is that the story is largely the product of the imagination of an oriental story-teller, a tribute to his hero Solomon. In support of this view is the prevalence of superlatives characteristic of the folk tales, as a 'very great retinue', 'very much gold', a 'very great quantity of spices', and 'such an abundance of spices'. The vagueness of the title 'Queen of Sheba', without specific reference to her name or any mention of time or circumstance, it is argued, makes appropriate the designation of this story as a fanciful oriental legend. The vast distance that separates the capital of Sheba (if Sheba is identified as the ancient Saba in South Arabia, as it usually is) from Jerusalem, 1,400 miles of rugged desert, lends an air of improbability to the story. Furthermore, the theme of a pagan admiring or praising the achievements of Israel and blessing its god Yahweh is one frequently used for polemical purposes by writers in the Bible. There were such foreigners as Melchizedek, King of Salem (Genesis 14:18–20), the Pharaoh (Exodus 9:27), Rahab, the harlot (Joshua 2:9–11), and Naaman, the Syrian (II Kings 5:15), all of whom played the familiar role of the foreigner who testified to the greatness of Israel and its god. Thus, when these exaggerations and generalities are considered along with the author's obvious purpose of underlining the splendour of Solomon's court by an opinion from the outside, one of the verdicts of modern commentators is that the legend grew up without factual support from an actual incident in history. On the basis of internal evidence it has been argued that the account is a later addition to the more historically trustworthy material in the Book of Kings. R. B. Y. Scott has concluded, from a careful study of themes and wording of the Queen of Sheba story and related passages, that the extravagant descriptions of royal magnificence are found elsewhere in the Bible only in the post-exilic books of Esther, Daniel 1–6, and Chronicles. Consequently the account with which we are concerned is not only legendary but late in origin, separated by more than five hundred years from the time of Solomon.

Another view held by equally reputable historians of the ancient Near East takes issue with this dismissal of the story as a legend based merely upon a creative imagination. It is argued that archaeologists have discovered the capital of the ancient kingdom of Sheba, rich in natural resources which were traded throughout the world. There were at times famous queens of Arabia, who are mentioned by name in inscriptions. A long journey by one of them over the well-established caravan routes would not have been impossible. Professor John Gray, in his commentary on I and II Kings, goes so far as to venture the opinion that the visit 'was probably an historical incident', and John Bright in his *History of Israel* defends the traditional view as 'an incident by no means to be dismissed as legendary'. At the conclusion of his own archaeological work in South Arabia William F. Albright wrote of the Queen of Sheba story: 'In the light of numerous striking archaeological confirmations of episodes and references in the biblical story of Solomon, it does seem hazardous to treat this particular episode as though it were legendary.'

Our enquiry leads us first to examine the question of historical authenticity. During the past century archaeologists have probed the sites of the Solomonic kingdom in Palestine with the result that we now have a new vantage point from which to view the culture of the Solomonic era. In Chapter I we have attempted to describe the material remains of the tenth century BC which have emerged from the tells of the land and to set it alongside the picture of the kingdom of Solomon preserved in the Bible. At what points do the two pictures, the biblical and the archaeological, diverge? In what respects do they agree? These are the questions to be asked, and if possible, answered.

The land from which the queen is said to have come is the ancient kingdom of Sheba. Once only a name, Sheba (or Saba) is now known from hundreds of inscriptions and the researches of archaeologists in the realm of modern Yemen. In Chapter II Gus van Beek, who has himself participated in archaeological research there, describes what is known of that kingdom as well as what can be extrapolated about it from the archaeological findings of later periods. Known only as a distant and fabulous land by the writers of the biblical stories, Sheba is now disclosed as a land with a high culture supported by a lucrative trade in myrrh and frankincense. The routes for this trade are now traced. Is it possible that one of them leading north could have been the one used by the queen in her celebrated journey to Jerusalem? The reader may form his own opinion as to the credibility of the biblical narrative from new evidence only recently made available.

Our second task is to establish what use is made of the narrative in several cultural traditions. In the Judaic traditions the story of Solomon's meeting with the Queen of Sheba did not itself prove to be a favourite theme for story-tellers. Yet certain details from the story provided convenient points of departure for new tales. It was difficult for the creative Jewish mind to resist the impulse to supply the 'hard questions' or riddles, mentioned in the first verse of the biblical account, that were said to have been put to the wise king by his royal visitor. Three of these enigmatic questions along with the correct answers appear in the *Targum Sheni* of the Book of Esther, an Aramaic work that may be as old as the third and fourth centuries AD. Others appear in the *Midrash Mishle*, a midrash (i.e. a Hebrew exposition of the underlying significance of a Bible text) of the Book of Proverbs; and in the course of the centuries the earlier conundrums are repeated, explained and added to, sometimes with ingenious explanations.

A new character was introduced into the story. The 'cock-of-the-woods' (or hoopoe) is said in the *Targum Sheni* to have been first to bring Solomon news of the remarkable kingdom of Kitor (corresponding to the biblical Sheba), ruled by Malkath Sheba. The queen herself is variously pictured, sometimes hairy all over, so that a depilatory had to be devised to make her suitable for Solomon 'to lie with her' to beget Nebuchadnezzar. (Thus, by a remarkable synthesis of contradictions, the chief hero of the Jews becomes the father of their arch-enemy.) At other times she is said to have had hairy feet or goat-feet. But an even wider departure from the basic tradition is the equation of the Queen of Sheba with Lilith, queen of the demons, in the cabbalistic schools of the Middle Ages and in the folklore of the German Jewish communities of the seventeenth and eighteenth centuries. Such are the vagaries of the ancient, original story as it has been transmitted in the Judaic tradition in its winding course down to modern times. Lou H. Silberman leads us in Chapter III through the labyrinth of these writings.

One of the most interesting cycles of proliferation on the plot and details of the Queen of Sheba story appears in Arabic. The original core of the Hebrew story, with its emphasis upon the wisdom and wealth of Solomon, is almost completely transformed in the Qur'an. The Islamic version emphasizes the conversion of the queen to the worship of the true god instead of the sun-god of Sheba. But commentaries upon the Qur'an, and especially a work known as 'Stories of the Prophets', have found, in the relatively short passage of the Qur'an, suggestions for further enlargement with imaginative detail. Although these stories in Arabic, as well as those in Turkish and Persian, may strike the western reader as excessively fanciful, they do reflect better perhaps than a more pedestrian history the actual state of the human mind—that of both teller and listener—as it worked in the Near East throughout many centuries following the advent of Islam. They evidence the hopes and aspirations of the common man and constitute, as W. Montgomery Watt, the author of Chapter IV, suggests, 'the imaginative form in which men try to express and communicate their understanding of the world in which they live'. Even in the days of the flowering of Arabic scientific knowledge of astronomy, chemistry, geography and history, men were also humanists who could dream and aspire to freedom from the fixed limits of time and space.

It is in Ethiopia that this ancient legend has reached down to the present to serve the needs of an age three millennia from that in which it originated. For in the 1955 Revised Constitution of Ethiopia the two principals are revived and the claim is clearly set forth that the royal line 'descends without interruption from the dynasty of Menelik I, son of the Queen of Ethiopia, the Queen of Sheba, and King Solomon of Jerusalem'.

The source for this tradition is a repository of Ethiopian material preserved in the book *Kebra Nagast*. Here is what Edward Ullendorff calls 'perhaps the truest and most genuinely indigenous expression of Ethiopian national and religious feeling'. Although this collection reaches back to a mass of oral traditions, it was written down in the fourteenth century. But it was not until the middle of the last century that an actual copy was available for thorough study by western scholars. In this story, which will be related in Chapter V, there emerges the name of Makeda for the queen. Explicit too in the Ethiopian version is the account of the devious trick by which the King of Jerusalem was able to take the virgin queen and beget a son by her.

Comparing the Ethiopian version of the story with that of the Muslim sources one is aware of a vast difference in tone and feeling. The flights of imaginative detail characteristic of the Arabic versions of the cycle are replaced by a more rational accounting for the famous visit and the important results which emerged from it. Questions that normally arise in the more logical mind, but which are left unanswered in the Muslim accounts, are answered bluntly with detail that is concrete and reasonable. The old legend is seen moving into a more modern and a less mythopoeic age.

When we consider the history of the use of the theme of Solomon and the Queen of Sheba in Christian art it is clear that it went its own way uninfluenced by the traditions which arose in Jewish, Islamic or Ethiopic cultures. In Europe the meaning of the story took its own course as it expressed a changing theology and met the needs of the Christian communities. The Queen of Sheba was a type. She was pictured either as a prefiguration of the Gentiles who accept Christianity or as the Church. Eventually the connection was made between the visit of the queen to Solomon and the adoration of the Magi, who also are said to have come from a far country. With the rise of the Legend of the True Cross, the ancient theme was again seized upon and woven into the fabric of this distinctively Christian tale. Thus it was by allegory and typology that the story from the Old Testament was made to do service to the traditions of the New.

The wide panorama of Christian art, beginning with examples from the twelfth century and continuing down to the present, is surveyed and illustrated by Paul Watson in Chapter VI. While there is little in this vast display that throws independent light on the facts of the ancient story, there is a huge accumulation of evidence for the enduring popularity of a tale from the distant past.

PART ONE

The Archaeology

I

The Age of Solomon

James B. Pritchard

THERE can be no question as to the fact of Solomon's enduring reputation: he was remembered a millennium after his death as the king of Israel who ushered in an era of peace, prosperity and plenty, a time of magnificence, even of extravagance and luxury such as had not been seen before his day or paralleled afterwards. The brief phrase from the Sermon on the Mount in St Matthew's Gospel, 'Solomon in all his glory', epitomizes the age as it appeared to a writer who lived at a distance of ten centuries.

The Golden Age had not been due to happenstance. It had been achieved through the wisdom of Solomon. He was credited with the authorship of the Book of Proverbs and of the more cynical Book of Ecclesiastes. He had written, it was believed, the love poems of the Song of Songs as well as two of the Psalms (72 and 127), and the Wisdom of Solomon, a book which, although it was not included in the canon of Hebrew sacred scripture, was preserved in the Christian Apocrypha. Solomon occupied a unique place in the tradition of ancient Israel as builder, ruler over its most extensive kingdom, efficient administrator, shrewd diplomat who could make profitable foreign alliances, and above all as the wisest man in the history of his people. True, others in the long line of national heroes had been distinguished for bravery, piety, devotion to Yahweh, the God of Israel, generosity, but to Solomon was the power and the glory *par excellence*.

This appraisal of the Age of Solomon, current a thousand years after his reign, was dependent almost entirely upon the short account of his deeds found in the Book of Kings and in a later version in the Book of Chronicles. Solomon, chosen by his ageing father David to inherit the kingdom of tribes he had brought together, began his reign by the elimination of his political enemies at home and by foreign alliances abroad. He made the town of Gibeon his sanctuary, where he sacrificed and dreamed of the wisdom for which he later became famous. After a thorough organization of the national resources of Israel he began to build his palace, the house of the forest of Lebanon, the house for Pharaoh's daughter, and the Temple of Yahweh, the edifice with which the name of Solomon was to be firmly linked for centuries. By foreign trade, heavy taxation and forced labour Solomon was able to establish a kingdom of a magnificence that could astonish even a royal visitor from the enormously wealthy kingdom of Sheba. Yet with the accounts of the glory of his kingdom there are intimations of its weaknesses: his toleration of the religious practices of his foreign wives, and the political discontent among his subjects. Eventually upon his death his son Rehoboam inherited only a part of his father's kingdom, the state of Judah. Jeroboam, who had been exiled by Solomon, returned to reign over the larger and wealthier portion of the kingdom. The account in Kings and in Chronicles is that of the rapid growth of a fabulous kingdom and its sudden breaking apart into two rival states upon the death of Solomon.

In the first century AD there remained, of course, the setting: the land, with its districts and cities, which had been Solomon's kingdom, and which was familiar to those who read the ancient accounts. But of his famous buildings, including the Temple of Yahweh, not one stone was standing upon another. The tangible evidence for his kingdom had long since passed into oblivion. What the writer of the Gospel knew was what he could read in the Hebrew account of the glorious past and of the wise king who had brought it into being. The source could be accepted as trustworthy or rejected as romantic legend, but it could not at that time be tested by other sources, since there were no others to be had.

Today, some twenty centuries later, we are more privileged. We can see the Age of Solomon from newly recovered perspectives. It is ironical but true that the Solomonic Age has become clearer from a distance of three thousand years than it had been for those who saw it at closer range. What is the new vantage point?

Simply put, new sources have been discovered for writing the history of the time in which Solomon lived. The first and most important is the documentation for the ancient Near Eastern world, of which Solomon's kingdom was but a small and at the time relatively insignificant part. Thousands of written documents in long-forgotten languages can now be deciphered and read with accuracy. Neighbours alluded to in the more parochial biblical history—Egypt, Phoenicia, Aram, Philistia and Assyria—have emerged from their obscurity. They are no longer mere names within the biblical text, but well-defined peoples, each with its own history, religion and material culture. In short, the world to which Solomon belonged, the world alluded to in the Bible, has been clothed with reality through the discoveries of scientific archaeology and decipherment of ancient texts. This is an achievement of only the past century and a half.

When we move from the surrounding world to the very area over which the kingdom of Solomon is said to have extended, again we find our knowledge has increased. Archaeologists have recovered from the mounds of ancient cities in Palestine clues for reconstructing life as it was lived in his day. The rich detail of the picture includes actual fortifications, water systems, houses of patricians and peasants, articles of everyday life and a variety of relics. The archaeologist has intruded into the intimate life of the past. All of this recently discovered data can now be used to check, supplement and at times correct the traditions which were once the sole source for history.

Geography and Chronology

Solomon's kingdom, according to the Bible, was considerably more widespread than that said to have been taken in the conquest by Joshua and occupied during the days of the Judges. And, in fact, its boundaries encompassed more land than those of any of the successors to Solomon on the throne. Its outline is roughly that of a rectangle, measuring 100 by 300 miles, along the east coast of the Mediterranean, extending from the River of Egypt in the south to Qadesh on the Orontes River in the north, with the exclusion of the two narrow coastal strips occupied by the Philistines and the Phoenicians. The author of the Book of Kings staked out the boundaries along general lines: 'Solomon ruled over all the kingdoms from the Euphrates to the land of the Philistines and to the border of Egypt' (I Kings 4:21). The area of the state was slightly less than that of Portugal.

While the land was not extensive, it was varied. The desert in the south, the Negeb, was dry and barren, a veritable wilderness. The plateau of Transjordan, consisting of Edom, Moab, Ammon, and Gilead, could grow grain and part of it was forested. In the mountainous spine that ran from north to south there were figs, olives and pomegranates, as well as grapes; and in the tropical climate of the Jordan Valley, more than a thousand feet below sea-level, there were date palms. It was a land that could hardly, by absolute standards, be called rich in natural resources. It was a 'land of milk and honey' only in contrast to the arid areas of Sinai and the deserts of Transjordan. Compared to the fertile basins of the Nile and the Tigris-Euphrates it was poor indeed. It is difficult to estimate with any accuracy how many people this land supported in the days of Solomon but one experienced archaeologist has ventured a guess that the Israelite population in the second half of the tenth century BC reached 800,000.

The dates for the Solomonic empire are only slightly less certain than the definition of its borders. A remarkable consensus exists for the dates of his reign, far greater in fact than that for such prominent ancient Near Eastern kings as Hammurabi of Babylon or Menes of Egypt, for both of whom there are contemporary documents. The famous seventeenth-century Archbishop Ussher, whose work on biblical chronology was for long accepted as standard, placed the death of Solomon at 973 BC. More recent calculations are somewhat lower, extending from 933 to 922 BC.

The date for the death of Solomon has been arrived at by pegging the reliable list of regnal years for Israelite and Judaean kings in the Bible to a listing of the

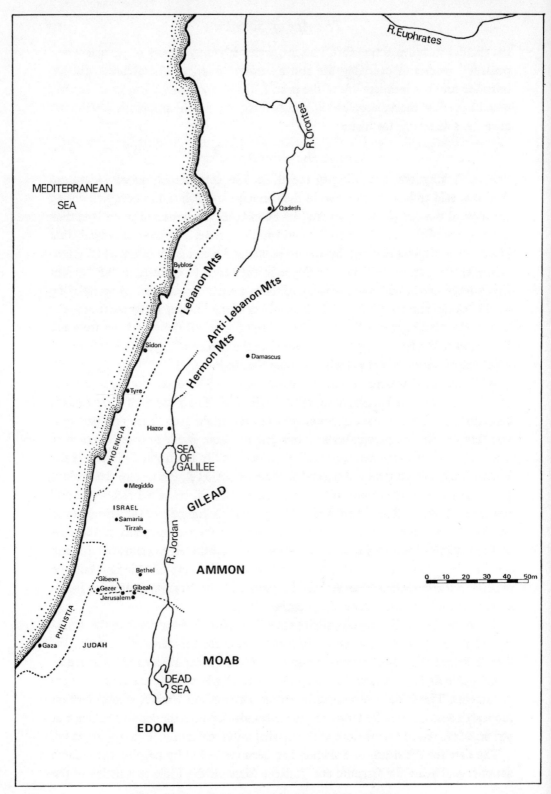

Fig. 1. Map of the ancient Near East in the tenth century BC

years of reign for Assyrian kings found on cuneiform tablets. Events in which Israelite and Assyrian kings participated appear in both biblical and Assyrian records. Happily the Assyrian regnal years can be adjusted to our system of reckoning years in the era before Christ through the record of an eclipse of the sun, an event which by astronomical calculations is known to have taken place in the year 763 BC. The record of this natural event, considered as a divine omen by astrologers of ancient Assyria and faithfully recorded, is the nexus that enables us to fix the date within a relatively narrow margin.

Yet exactly when he began his rule is open to some serious question. In I Kings 11:42 the figure of forty years is given for the length of his reign. The suspicion that this number is only an approximation arises from the fact that his father David is also credited with a forty-year reign. Not only in the Old Testament is such a period a normal expression for a lifetime or generation, but in the ninth-century inscription on the Moabite Stone this is the period given for the time Israel occupied the land of Medaba. From these and other indications the reference which allots forty years to Solomon may possibly be considered as a synonym for a full generation, and only an approximation of the regnal years. One can only guess that Solomon ascended the throne of Israel shortly before the middle of the tenth century BC.

Neighbours of Israel

Egyptian history during the tenth century BC is relatively undistinguished in its leaders and their military exploits. How far Egypt had slipped from being the dominant world power it was during the 'age of imperialism', as the New Kingdom (approximately the sixteenth to thirteenth centuries) has been called, is reflected in the story of Wen-Amon's visit to Phoenicia about a century and a half before the time of Solomon. Wen-Amon had been sent to Byblos by Ne-su-Ba-neb-Ded, the ruler of the Delta of Egypt, to get lumber for the barge of the god Amon-Re. Arriving finally at Byblos Wen-Amon presented his request to Zakar-Baal, the prince of the city. The latter had the boldness to answer the request made by the emissary of a once great world power with the blunt words: 'As for me—me also—I am not your servant! I am not the servant of him who sent you either.' It was only after Wen-Amon had sent to Egypt for a payment that the Prince of Byblos provided the timber for the royal barge of the Great God of Egypt. Obviously the days of Egyptian power in Asia had long since come to an end. Asiatic goods once available as booty or as tribute had now to be paid for in advance. From Egyptian sources there is no indication that the power of Egypt had increased by the time of Solomon. The once great power to the south of Israel was no longer a menace as it had been to the inhabitants of Palestine in earlier days.

The other traditionally major power of the Near East, Assyria, was, in the tenth century, similarly without territorial ambitions or the means for achieving them.

Slightly over a century before the accession of Solomon to the throne of Israel, Tiglath-pileser I (1114–1076 BC), king of Assyria, had been able to boast:

> I went to Lebanon. I cut [there] timber of cedars for the temple of Anu and Adad, the great gods, my lords, and carried [them to Ashur] . . . I received tribute from Byblos, Sidon, and Arvad. I crossed over in ships [belonging] to Arvad. . . . I killed a narwhal which they call 'sea horse', on high sea.

From the preserved records of Assyrian expansion westward to the Mediterranean it appears that two centuries were to pass before another king, Ashurnasirpal II, would duplicate the triumphal adventure of Tiglath-pileser I and clean his 'weapons in the deep sea'. From all we know about its history, Assyria was concerned with its own domestic problems during the tenth century, too weak to provide a threat to those who lived beside the 'Great Sea'.

Phoenicia, more particularly the powerful city state of Tyre immediately to the north of Israel, was the foreign power with which Solomon is said to have had closest and most direct contact. Just when Phoenicia began to play its famed role as the dominant sea power within the Mediterranean and beyond is as yet obscure. Probably the Phoenician ships began to ply their trade after the defeat of the 'Peoples of the Sea' by Ramses III in the twelfth century. Certainly by the end of the twelfth century Sidon was a busy port, to judge from a remark of Zakar-Baal, the Prince of Byblos, to Wen-Amon that there were fifty ships in that harbour.

But it was the city of Tyre that eventually became dominant, probably about the beginning of the tenth century, as a major sea power and colonizer of islands and promontories throughout the Mediterranean basin. Its king was Abibaal, the father of the more famous Hiram I, the Phoenician monarch with whom Solomon is said in the Book of Kings to have had commercial relations both in building and in shipping.

Farther to the north on the Phoenician coast Yehimilk reigned as king of Byblos, another important city state of the tenth century. What we know of him is confined to a short building inscription discovered at Byblos in 1929. The text credits Yehimilk with restoring all the ruins of the houses of Byblos and ends with an invocation: 'May Baalshamen and the Lord of Byblos and the Assembly of the Holy Gods of Byblos prolong the days and years of Yehimilk in Byblos . . .'

Among all the neighbours of Solomon the Phoenicians were the most active in trade and commerce. They are known for their skills, such as navigation, the production of a stable purple dye from the murex, metal-working and other crafts, and for the ability to sustain themselves in a few coastal cities that were shut off from the rich natural resources of the hinterland by the barrier of the Lebanon range. On occasion they did fight in defence of their cities, but wars of conquest are noticeably absent from what records we possess for the course of Phoenician history. Primarily they were a people of trade and commerce.

When the Phoenician cities found themselves threatened by the powerful armies of the Assyrian kings of the eighth and seventh centuries they were able to work out a *modus vivendi* with their more aggressive neighbours. We know, for example, that King Esarhaddon of Assyria made the following treaty with King Baal of Tyre:

> If a ship of Baal or of the people of Tyre is shipwrecked off (the coast of) the land of the Philistines or anywhere on the borders of Assyrian territory, everything that is on the ship belongs to Esarhaddon, king of Assyria, but one must not do any harm to any person on board ship, they should *li[st]* their names [and inform the king of Assyria] . . . nobody should harm their ships . . .

From what we know of the major powers of the ancient Near Eastern world in the tenth century they were too weak or too preoccupied with domestic problems to reach out for conquest or tribute, as they had done frequently in the past and as they were to do later, to the land over which Solomon ruled. The urban centres which figure prominently in the biblical narratives about Solomon are Jerusalem, his capital and the scene of his most extensive building operations; Hazor, Megiddo and Gezer, cities Solomon is said in I Kings 9:15 to have built; and Gibeon, where he offered burnt offerings and was said to have dreamed his famous dream, in which God appeared to him and promised to give him whatever he asked. Solomon humbly asked for understanding and discernment of judgement in governing the people of Israel. God therefore granted him the gift of great wisdom, for which in the popular and proverbial imagination he is still most commonly renowned (I Kings 3:5–14). Each of these cities has been identified and subjected to archaeological excavations. What lay buried has revealed a wealth of information about life in the tenth century: architecture, crafts, the use of writing, artistic conventions, trade and commerce. There is no dearth of data on what life was like in the Palestine of the tenth century, thanks to the careful exploration of dozens of sites which were occupied in that period.

One of the most extensively excavated cities of ancient Palestine is a mound called Tell el-Mutesellim, the Megiddo of the Old Testament, or Armageddon, as it is referred to in the New. (Armageddon probably derives from the Hebrew *Har Meggido*, 'mountain or hill of Megiddo'. It is cited in Revelation 16:16 as the place where at the end of the world the kings of the earth, under the leadership of demons, battle the forces of God. Megiddo is situated on a strategic pass commanding the road from Egypt and the Palestinian coastal plain to Galilee, Syria and Mesopotamia. From the fourth millennium BC to the fourth century BC it was the scene of many important battles—as it was again in the First World War. The text of Revelation seems to imply that it had become a symbol of the final battlefield where

God's armies will defeat the forces of evil.) During the years 1925–39 archaeologists from the Oriental Institute of the University of Chicago peeled off layer after layer of the mound to disclose what remained of the city that stood there in the tenth century BC. As the science of archaeology has developed and new methods have been devised the early conclusions of the American excavators have been checked and revised by a team from the Hebrew University led by Yigael Yadin in the 1960s.

It is tempting to ascribe to King Solomon of Israel, as indeed many have done, a particular stratum, that numbered IVB-VA, counting from the top downward and using the Roman numerals for major occupational levels and the letters A and B for sub-divisions within them. Yet it must be made clear that not a single reference to Solomon has been found at Megiddo. No inscription names him and no specific find can be definitely related to any biblical reference. The label of Solomonic, so often glibly given to walls and other constructions at Megiddo, is supported solely by the statement in I Kings 9:15, that Solomon built, among others, the city of Megiddo.

Even though archaeology has produced at Megiddo no specific link with Solomon of the Bible, other important figures of ancient Near Eastern history have been attested. A fragment of a stela of Shishak, the Egyptian king of the Twenty-Second Dynasty, who recorded on the wall at Karnak an account of his expedition to Palestine, is tangible evidence for a tenth-century occupation at Megiddo.

Fig. 2. General plan of the city of Megiddo (American Schools of Oriental Research, *The Biblical Archaeologist*, 33, 1970, p. 70)

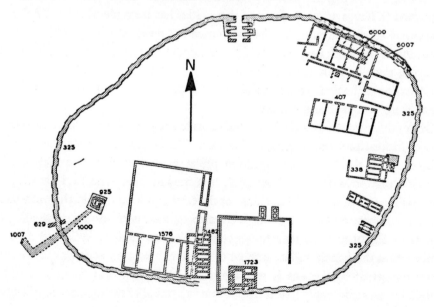

1. Sarcophagus of Ahiram, the most distinctive monument of Phoenicia (Service des Antiquités, Beirut)

2. Aerial view of Tyre from the north, showing the peninsula which was originally an island and was joined to the mainland by Alexander in 332 BC (Institut français d'archéologie, Beirut)

3. General view of the mound of Megiddo (Oriental Institute of the University of Chicago)

4. Reconstruction drawing of the Palace of Megiddo, Building 1723 (Oriental Institute of the University of Chicago)

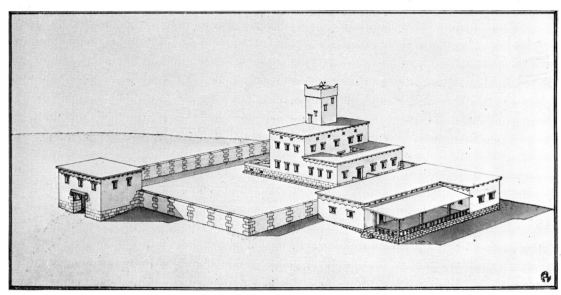

5. Aerial view of the eastern end of Hazor, at the end of the 1957 season of excavation (Professor Y. Yadin, Hebrew University, Jerusalem)

6. Canaanite temple at Hazor, the closest parallel to the Jerusalem temple plan of the tenth century (Professor Y. Yadin)

7. Tenth-century gate at Gezer (Hebrew Union College)

8. The mound of Gezer from the north (Hebrew Union College)

9. Aerial view of Jerusalem, taken before the recent development of the city (Elia Photo-Service, Jerusalem)

10. Shipping of timber by sea on a relief of Sargon II (Louvre, Paris; Photo Marburg) ▶

11. Ostracon from Tell Qasile mentioning 'Ophir gold', *c.* 700 BC (Museum Haaretz, Tel Aviv)

12. An attempt to reconstruct the Jerusalem Temple (*Biblical Archaeologist*: Harvard University, G. E. Wright and F. Albright)

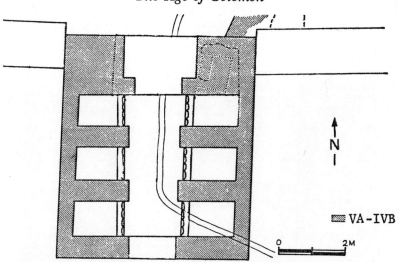

Fig. 3. Plan of the city gate at Megiddo in the tenth century BC (*BA*, 33, 1970, p. 85)

Furthermore, a lower stratum, VIIA, contained objects bearing the names of Ramses II and Ramses VI, which date this layer to the twelfth century. Thus with specific epigraphic evidence such as this, as well as artefacts and architectural detail with parallels elsewhere, we can, on quite objective grounds, be certain that in the intervening layers we are dealing with the actual remains of a people who lived in the tenth century BC, the Age of Solomon, king of Israel.

The city of Megiddo was small, measuring about thirteen acres in area (Fig. 2). It was protected partly by the elevation provided by the dozen or so cities that had been built on the same site and then destroyed or abandoned—a new city was built directly on the debris of the earlier—and partly by a casemate or double wall that encircled the city.

A six-chambered gateway at the north provided access to the city (Fig. 3). To enter the walled-in area one had to traverse a narrow passageway, 66 feet long, along which were built six rooms, three on a side, in which armed guards could be posted. As many as four double doors, hinged at the piers that extended teethlike into the passageway, would have blocked the entrance of attackers. This gateway was not only a means for providing the maximum security in time of attack, it was a city monument, a place where people met for business and administrative and judicial decisions, as is reported in the description of Absalom, Solomon's half-brother (David's favourite son and heir apparent, until he was killed while leading a rebellion against his father), sitting at the gate in II Samuel 15:2. Prototypes of this gateway can be traced back for hundreds of years. The plan of this particular defensive measure was sufficiently effective to have been copied, as we shall see below, at least twice.

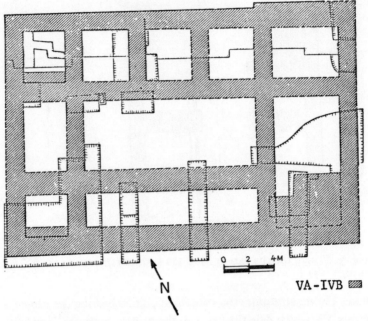

VA-IVB

Fig. 4. Plan of Palace 6000 at Megiddo (*BA*, 33, 1970, p. 73)

Within the bulwark of the tenth-century city of Stratum IVB-VA at Megiddo stood several large public buildings, one of which (6000) has been called a palace because of its large size and intricate plan (Fig. 4). It is rectangular in shape and measures 69 by 92 ft. (about 21 × 28 m.). A central hall or court is completely surrounded by rooms: five on the north, one on each of the east and west sides, and a small room and entrance hall on the south.

In the southern sector of the city two other public buildings have been recovered. One, called by the excavators 1723, is well built with thick walls and measures 71 by 75 ft. (about 22 × 23 m.; Ill. 4). It could well have served as a fortress or small palace. To the west there was found a larger structure, 1482, with more rooms arranged on an entirely different plan.

Vital to any defensive system is a protected access to fresh water. At Megiddo the spring was at the base of the mound outside the city wall. The builders of the tenth-century city had provided a protected access to the vital water source in the form of a narrow passageway, a little more than three feet (about a metre) wide (629 on the plan in Fig. 2), that pierced the city wall on the south-west side and led to the spring. The walls of the passage are built of well-dressed stones laid in the familiar header-and-stretcher pattern. A roof once covered the passageway to make it a tunnel for the defenders of the city in time of siege.

The largest mound of ancient ruins in Palestine is Tell el-Kadeh, some eight miles north of the Sea of Galilee, long identified as the site of the biblical city of

Hazor. This rectangular mound of more than two hundred acres was first trenched by John Garstang more than fifty years ago. But it was not until 1955 that its history began to be systematically recovered by Yigael Yadin, who cut into this extensive tell at a number of selected sites. He and his colleagues dug there until 1958 and then returned in 1968–9 in an attempt to solve some of the problems of the city's history that had been raised by the earlier excavations.

Not only is Hazor said to have been taken by Joshua but it is listed as one of the cities built by Solomon. The excavators have found twenty-one city levels, extending from about 2500 BC (Stratum XXI) down to the Hellenistic period of the second century BC (Stratum I). Through this long period of more than two millennia the city was destroyed and rebuilt many times. The first settlement was on a restricted area of about thirty acres; in the eighteenth century BC it burgeoned to include an area of more than two hundred acres; in the thirteenth century BC the great city of Hazor was destroyed, never again to be rebuilt to such proportions. After two centuries of limited settlement, a tenth-century city, Stratum X, came to occupy the western half of the thirty-acre higher mound at the south of the site. Although much of this occupation is yet to be uncovered, the samplings made by Yadin have revealed a clear picture of the type of defences employed. The city was surrounded, as was Megiddo in the tenth century, by a casemate wall that averaged about sixteen feet (about five metres) in width (Fig. 5). The shell, built of well-laid stones, consisted of an outer wall five feet (1·5 metres) thick, and an inner wall about four feet (1·1 metres) thick. Between these two lines of fortification is a span about eight feet (2·4 metres) wide divided into oblong rooms that open into the inside of the city.

The most interesting feature of the rampart at Hazor is the gate to the city. Two towers built outside the line of the casemate wall provided a commanding position for the defenders. On each side of the gateway there are three rooms set between

Fig. 5. The city wall and gate at Hazor (*Israel Exploration Journal*, 8, 1958, p. 84)

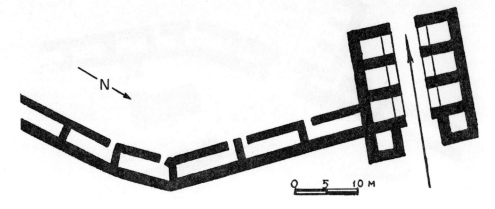

the four piers that jut out to protect the narrow entranceway. Not only is the plan identical to that of the gate that stood during the tenth century at Megiddo, but the measurements are approximately the same.

The mound of Tell Jezer, the ancient Gezer, has shed considerable light upon the history of the tenth century, despite the fact that it was extensively excavated at a time when few of the techniques of scientific archaeology had been devised. Beginning in 1902 and continuing through to 1909, R. A. S. Macalister dug nearly two thirds of the tell, amassing a tremendous amount of material to document the life of this city over a period of some 3,000 years. On one of his plans appears a complex of walls labelled 'Maccabean Castle'. After Yigael Yadin had found the six-chambered gate at Hazor, he looked at Macalister's plan and thought he could recognize a familiar pattern of walls, one side of the six-chambered gateway characteristic of the tenth-century defences at Megiddo and Hazor. Yadin dotted in the other side of the gate complex as he judged it to have been on the basis of the other two tenth-century examples and published his hypothetical plan in 1958. (Fig. 6).

When an American team went to Gezer in the 1960s to take up the excavations where Macalister had left off in the early days of Palestinian archaeology, they found that the 'Maccabean Castle' was indeed the tenth-century gate to Gezer and that, as Yadin had guessed, it was like those at the two other sites in providing access through the familiar casemate wall associated with them. The actual plan of the fully excavated gate at Gezer, published in 1971 (Fig. 7), shows the similarities in the architectural features of the three important cities, Megiddo, Hazor and Gezer.

Fig. 6. Macalister's plan of Gezer with projected east side of gate dotted in (*IEJ*, 7, 1957, p. 84)

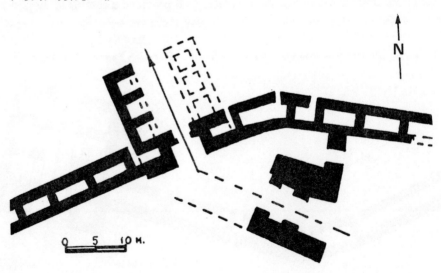

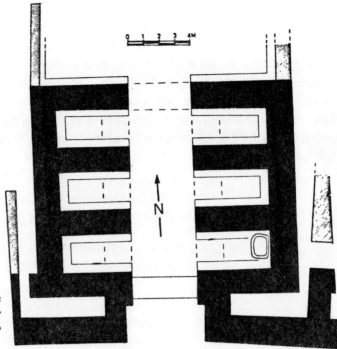

Fig. 7. Plan of city gate at Gezer after recent excavation (*BA*, 34, 1971, p. 114)

While city gates, fortifications and palaces are particularly attractive to the archaeologist, the less monumental remains serve better to indicate how the average Israelite of the tenth century BC lived. Stratum III of the excavations at Tell el-Far'ah, probably the ancient Tirzah, has provided a sample of living quarters for the common people (Fig. 8). Houses of several rooms built around a central courtyard were found to stand along narrow streets. Entrance was from the street

Fig. 8. Israelite houses of Stratum III at Tirzah. (D. W. Thomas, *Arch. and Old Testament Study*, p. 376)

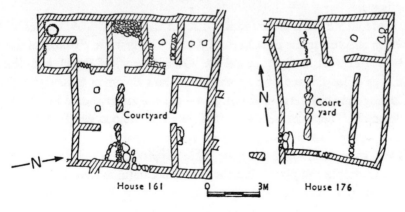

Courtyard

Court yard

House 161   House 176

to the court, where the family cooking was done, and from which access was gained to the several rooms that served as sleeping quarters and storerooms. Both the irregularity of the plan and the poor methods of construction attest the simplicity of domestic life as it was lived in the tenth century.

It was not, however, a period of illiteracy. The tenth-century archaeological finds are not limited to architectural remains and mute artefacts. Actual writing in Hebrew has been found. A small inscribed stone, measuring $4\frac{1}{2}$ inches long, found in 1908 at Gezer by Macalister, has been judged to have been a mnemonic ditty for children:

> His two months are (olive) harvest,
> His two months are planting (grain),
> His two months are late planting;
> His month is hoeing up of flax,
> His month is harvest of barley,
> His month is harvest and *feasting*;
> His two months are vine-tending,
> His month is summer fruit.

And the period also produced some genuine literature. In the 'Court History of David', which we will discuss below, we almost certainly have a contemporary historical account, unchanged by later theological or polemical writers.

The Biblical Narratives

Thus far we have quoted uncritically certain statements in the Bible about Solomon and his age. We must now raise questions as to the value of these biblical quotations as historical sources. How old are they? Do they reach back to the age in which Solomon lived? Why were they written down and composed into a narrative? Are they all of equal historical value? These are some of the questions with which we must deal. We can attempt to utilize the answers to them, along with the extra-biblical and other archaeological data, to produce a history of this age in the life of ancient Israel.

Just about all we know from the Bible about the Age of Solomon lies within a mere eleven chapters in the First Book of Kings. The first two chapters of this book really belong to what has been called the 'Court History of David' and deal with the last days of his life and give an account of how Solomon came to the throne; the following nine chapters—I Kings 3–11—are the major source for the reign of King Solomon. Those chapters constitute less than 10,000 words in the English translation, approximately two pages in a daily newspaper.

This relatively small segment of the Bible is particularly rich in anecdotes and details about people and places. But the author is careful to state in I Kings 11:41 that his is an account dependent upon a more primary and more detailed work,

'The Book of the Acts of Solomon', a source which, alas, has not survived. Thus it is intimated that this preserved history which we possess is one stage removed from the primary record. The account in Kings is a compiled history, not a primary source, and the reader is referred, as it were in the footnotes, to a lost document for more detailed information and additional facts which the author of our document did not include.

What then is the point in time from which our history as it now stands in I Kings 3–11 was written? For more than a century now scholars in the field of biblical studies have seen in the narratives about Solomon phrases—one might call them clichés—which first became current in ancient Israel during the religious revival of King Josiah of Judah in the second half of the seventh century BC, the period of national crisis a few decades before the great catastrophe of the Babylonian Exile. It is the language of this period, and not that of the Age of Solomon, that appears in the text of the dreams and prayers of Solomon in I Kings. Thus, it has long been observed that the biblical narratives about Solomon reflect the later age in which they were composed as much as they mirror the time in which the principal subject lived.

The prominence given to the Temple and its construction—several chapters on this one building as contrasted to the single sentence recounting Solomon's building of the cities of Megiddo, Hazor and Gezer—may well be due to the prominent place that this sanctuary, once a royal chapel but later a national shrine, came to occupy in religion at the end of the seventh century BC. Among the many buildings constructed by Solomon in the tenth century the Temple had grown, as it were, by the seventh century until it towered in importance over all the other achievements of the pre-eminent builder. The hope that Yahweh would not allow the destruction of his Temple became in the times of trouble virtually an article of religious faith. It was this trust in the Temple as a guarantee to national security that the Prophet Jeremiah attacked in his bold address in 609 BC. He declared: 'Do not trust in these deceptive words: "This is the temple of the Lord, the temple of the Lord, the temple of the Lord"' (Jeremiah 7:4).

The need for national security in the seventh century when Israel was threatened by the Babylonians is obvious, and the hope that Yahweh would not permit his house to be destroyed obviously played no small part in the author's selection of the narratives that described the building of Yahweh's house by Solomon as the most important achievement of the tenth-century king. In retrospect the construction of a relatively small building, measuring a mere 35 by 104 feet (11 × 32 m.), took precedence over that of other buildings in Jerusalem, the strengthening of the fortifications of the city, and even over the building of the important cities of Megiddo, Hazor and Gezer. Such is the distortion of a subsequent age, the hindsight of history. It would have been strange indeed if the resulting seventh-century document failed to reflect the times in which it was composed and the place which Solomon's Temple had come to occupy in the community of ancient Israel just before the Exile.

The popular—even folkloristic—character of the history of Solomon's Age is equally apparent. References to prominent world figures outside the borders of Israel, such as the Pharaoh of Egypt, the Queen of Sheba, Hiram of Tyre (Hiram was a common Phoenician name), are vague. Contrast the references in the following more annalistic accounts of the Kings of Israel and Judah, to Shishak, Sennacherib, Tiglath-pileser, Necho, all of them specific enough to remove any doubt as to what ruler of what neighbouring power was meant. The history of Solomon's Age was composed for a popular audience that had little curiosity concerning the specific reference to the names of important personalities outside its own tradition.

The biblical accounts of the Solomonic Age abound with references to gold and pure gold. The author was impressed with the lavish use of this precious metal in his description of the Temple and its furnishings in I Kings 6. Not only the Sanctuary of the Temple is said to have been overlaid with 'pure gold', but the floor as well. Similarly treated were the cherubim (i.e. the guardians of the sacred place), the carved doors of the Temple, and chains of gold are said to have been drawn across the wall before the Sanctuary.

The cultic equipment is said to match the lavish decoration: a golden altar, a table of gold, ten lampstands of pure gold; flowers, lamps, tongs, cups, snuffers, basins, pans, dishes for incense and even the door sockets were of gold (I Kings 7: 48–50). And although the Temple predominates in the description it is not the only building on which Solomon is reported to have lavished such ostentation. The House of the Forest of Lebanon is described as having 200 shields of gold, each weighing 600 shekels (a total of over 2,000,000 gold dollars in current value) as well as 300 shields of beaten gold (I Kings 10:16–17).

Since it was obvious that Palestine was a relatively poor land and gold was not indigenous to the area, the author took pains to identify its source. Ophir, a distant land reached by the navies of Solomon and Hiram (I Kings 9:26–28, and referred to again in Chapter 10, verse 11 in the context of the Queen of Sheba's visit), was identified as the place from which the gold had come. In one verse the figure of 420 talents—over 24,000,000 gold dollars in value—is mentioned; in another, it is said that 666 talents—more than 38,000,000 gold dollars—flowed into the treasury of Solomon each year (I Kings 10:14). Yet there is nothing to indicate what was exported in exchange for this gigantic income.

How concerned the author was about the measure of Solomon's wealth is even more apparent when we compare this account of his age with that of the Court History of David in II Samuel 9–20 and Chapters 1–2 of I Kings. The Court History has been almost universally acclaimed by biblical scholars not only for its literary excellence but for its candid objectivity. Here there is but one mention of the precious metal: the crown of Milcom, king of Ammon, conquered by David's forces, contained one talent of gold (II Samuel 12:30). In the Court History of the king who conquered the vast kingdom over which his son Solomon ruled this one talent, as far as we are told, constituted David's entire assets of gold.

When one passes from the pages that describe the glory of Solomon to those that contain the accounts of the reigns of his successors on the throne in Jerusalem there is relatively little said about the gold of the Temple. It no longer glitters as it did in the narratives about the Golden Age of Solomon. Shishak is said to have taken away the shields of gold (I Kings 14:26), while Asa (I Kings 15:18), Johoash (II Kings 12:18), Jehoash, King of Israel (II Kings 14:14), Ahaz (II Kings 16:8) either dipped into the Temple treasury for gold to pay off an invader or looted it. But no specific inventory of objects or amounts is recorded; the references are vague. The sole exception is the mention of 30 talents of gold given by Hezekiah to Sennacherib as tribute (II Kings 18:14). At the very end of Judah's dynastic history, in the crisis of the invasion of the Babylonians, mention is made of the booty of gold from the Temple (II Kings 24:13, 25:15). Yet in all these instances the references are laconic and lacking in the extravagant detail which is so characteristic of the writings about the Solomonic Age in I Kings 3–11. One has the feeling in reading the accounts of the deeds of the lesser kings that the imagination which the writer about the Age of Solomon had allowed free rein has been considerably restrained.

Another of the author's major themes is the respect which Solomon's peers showed to him. Solomon, according to the author of I Kings 3–11, was not a vassal of the neighbouring kingdoms, as were some of his successors, but an equal who commanded respect and even admiration. The Egyptian king gave him a daughter in marriage and a generous present in the form of the city of Gezer; the alliance with Hiram of Tyre was one between two equals; and the Queen of the distant Sheba marvelled at Solomon's wealth and wisdom. The choice of material to be included in this short biographical document was apparently made on the basis of a theme which is stated in inclusive terms:

> Thus King Solomon excelled all the kings of the earth in riches and in wisdom. And the whole earth sought the presence of Solomon to hear his wisdom . . . Every one of them brought his present, articles of silver and gold, garments, myrrh, spices, horses, and mules, so much year by year . . . And the king made silver as common in Jerusalem as stone, and he made cedar as plentiful as the sycamore of the Shephelah
>
> (I Kings 10:23–25, 27).

It is reasonable to suppose that hyperbole such as that mentioned in the above summary extended to the listing of other resources. The round figures of 40,000 stalls for horses (I Kings 4:26), 12,000 horsemen (I Kings 4:26), 1,400 chariots

(I Kings 10:26), 30,000 men sent to Lebanon (I Kings 5:13), 80,000 hewers of stone in the mountains (I Kings 5:15)—may have served more as an impressionistic support for the writer's thesis than as a count or census.

From these examples it may be concluded that the picture of the Age of Solomon presented in the Book of Kings has become understandably obscured by the author's own aims, those of a writer who wrote for a later generation with its own religious needs. One might say that the exaggeration that appears in I Kings 3–11 is but a tribute which a later writer presented to the builder of the Temple, which at the time of writing was the hope of a nation for survival, the dwelling place of the deity who alone could save his people from political disaster.

Despite the predominance of exaggeration and the lack of specific detail, such as the names of some of the most important of Solomon's contemporaries, there remain some valuable clues for the historian concerned with the Age of Solomon. There are occasional hints, for example, that Solomon was not without his problems even with his wealth and wisdom. Hadad of the royal family of Edom, a traditional enemy of Israel to the east, had found refuge in Egypt, married into the royal family there, and apparently returned to his native land full of hostility for Solomon (I Kings 11:14–22). Rezon, the first king in Damascus known by name, hated Israel and waited for an opportunity to even up an ancient score from the days of David (I Kings 11:23–25). And even more menacing was Jeroboam. Once an officer of Solomon, he had defected to Egypt, where he had found refuge in the days of Shishak and possibly encouragement for his plans for the coup which he later carried out after the death of Solomon.

Nor was all well in the realm of religious affairs. The generous policy of tolerance pursued by Solomon allowed complete freedom of religion to those brought into his court from other and pagan lands. The former exclusiveness of the early settlers from the desert was eroded in the new age of internationalism. Solomon, the builder of the house of Yahweh, is also credited with the building of a high place to Chemosh, the Moabite god, as well as for Molech, the god of the Ammonites (I Kings 11:7). Even the worship of Astarte of the Sidonians was allowed in Israel. Information such as this about the wise and wealthy hero, while it may explain to the reader why his kingdom did not survive him, does nothing to gild the picture of his greatness. This discordant note raises the suspicion that here there may be a hard historical fact in the narrative and that it can throw light on the age and its religious practices.

In a similar vein are the references in the story to Solomon's use of forced labour, the corvée. Although the result of his building programme is greatly admired, the means by which it was achieved is frankly stated: heavy taxation and slavery. In these two policies the king is shown to be despotic. The sequel to the story of oppression is that of the dissolution of the kingdom. Nowhere is the despotism of

Solomon more apparent than in the remark of Rehoboam in his confrontation with those of the northern kingdom of Israel who sought relief from the excesses of his father: 'My father made your yoke heavy, but I will add to your yoke; my father chastised you with whips, but I will chastise you with scorpions' (I Kings 12:14).

With this policy decision of Rehoboam in the crisis of succession to the throne of Solomon the glory that had been Solomon's came to a sudden end. The kingdom was divided into two parts, each of which had to struggle for survival until they both came to an end and their inhabitants were carried away into exile in a distant land.

We are now faced with two decidedly different impressions of the Age of Solomon. Neither is as complete or as precise as we should like. But each has its own character and is within certain limits consistent within itself.

Archaeology has been able to recover sizeable portions of three cities of the tenth century BC, cities prominent enough to have been mentioned in the Bible as cities which Solomon built. Each is extremely modest in extent: Megiddo is no larger than 13 acres; Gezer measures approximately 27 acres; and the area of the higher mound at Hazor, half of which was encircled by the tenth-century casemate wall, is only 30 acres. These 'cities', even by the ancient Near Eastern standards represented in Babylonia and Assyria, were far from what one might call urban centres; they were more like villages. The buildings within them were small in size and far from palatial. Within walls of roughly cut stones there were floors of beaten earth or plaster. Artefacts of bone, stone, clay, an occasional metal tool or weapon, suggest a cultural level which was apparently lacking in both artistic sophistication and wealth. As yet no evidence has been found for the use of chariotry or for the metal trappings for the harness of horses. As for gold and other precious metals, its occurrence is limited to an occasional earring or other article of personal adornment. From the tenth-century level, Stratum IVB-VA, at Megiddo not a single gold item is recorded by the excavators among the hundreds of entries within the catalogue of finds. The general impression gleaned from a survey of the archaeological remains that have come from the tenth century—and they are considerable—is that cities were built on a small scale, that buildings were simple and modestly constructed from materials locally available, and that the standard of living was far from luxurious when compared to that prevailing in other parts of the ancient Near Eastern world. Solomon is mentioned in no Egyptian, or Mesopotamian, or Phoenician document. Only from the Bible do we learn that he lived.

In contrast to this picture of life in the tenth century is that derived from I Kings 3–11, a life that might be termed a 'Golden Age'. Mentioned are huge amounts of gold, ivory carvings, bronze in abundance, woods imported from distant lands, chariots and horses, and international trade with distant and exotic lands. Everywhere the accent is upon opulence and extravagance measured in large but round figures. While in some respects the picture of grandeur is specific and dimensions of buildings are given, there is a noticeable lack of specific information about the principal characters. When accounts of the maritime adventures are given there is little specific data about the lands to which ships sailed except the names of two places, Ophir and Tarshish. In fact, references to geography outside Israel and Syria are either vague or non-existent. Such is the broad, glittering picture of the age given in the biblical account.

The divergences that exist between these two impressions of the Age of Solomon may be lessened, if not entirely reconciled, by one of two explanations. The first is that the sampling which archaeology has provided is not representative. For example, the tenth-century levels of the city of Jerusalem remain untouched. But even if the archaeologist could get below the heavy overburden of debris and the more modern sacred buildings it is likely that little of the reported treasures could have survived the looting that followed the destruction of 586 BC by the Babylonians. Precious materials that once were the pride of the Age of Solomon would have long since been salvaged for other uses or taken as booty. Proof for the wealth of the Temple, as it is described in the Bible, is not likely to be produced by archaeological effort.

Another explanation for the discrepancy is that our only literary source for the Age of Solomon is late and to some extent legendary. It was composed—using a more ancient document as source to be sure—for a specific purpose, which was not that of the antiquarian or the historian. It had as its aim the strengthening of a popular belief in the importance of the central shrine of ancient Israel, the Temple in Jerusalem, which was built in a golden age of prosperity and peace, the sure tokens of the deity's favour. Its builder was the extraordinarily wise king, one whose wisdom was manifest and confirmed in unrivalled prosperity. Unmistakably the divine favour had been bestowed upon the age that had produced the Temple and upon the king who was primarily responsible for building it. It then followed that in a time of crisis—such as that which Israel experienced in the last days of the Assyrian Empire—the restoration of the central shrine to the place it had occupied some three centuries earlier would achieve results similar to those gained at the time of its building. In the rewriting of this chapter from Israel's past of plenty and prosperity a slavish conformity to the annals had no place. The crisis of the end of the seventh century loomed too large to allow the writer to indulge in the pedantry of unimaginative history. The age long buried beneath three hundred years of history could be recovered in the vivid terms of popular imagination and folk memory. It is the version written in the age of national crisis and not the one referred to as the 'Book of the Acts of Solomon' that has survived.

Thus far we have tried to show that we stand in a favoured position for viewing the Age of Solomon. To the once sole source in the Bible has been added that of archaeology, which has laid bare the civilization of the people who lived on the land in the middle of the tenth century BC. Yet this augmentation of the source material presented us with problems that did not before exist: the disparity between the cultural poverty of Palestine in this age and the impression of grandeur and wealth presented by the biblical account. This inconsistency in our accounts could be resolved by the dismissal of all the biblical material as pure idealization of the past and without historical value. Or it might be lessened by the admission that parts of the narrative have more value for historical reconstruction than others. It is the latter that seems to be the more prudent course. Let us look very briefly at some of the details in the Book of Kings that seem from the present state of our knowledge— and more information is bound to appear as archaeological discoveries continue— to be consistent with other data.

The general picture of the international climate in the times of Solomon given in the biblical account is in accord with what we have come to learn about the ancient Near Eastern world of the tenth century BC. The traditionally great powers, Egypt and Assyria, were either too weak or too absorbed with domestic problems to constitute a threat to Israel. The time was propitious for the growth and development of a smaller power lying between the two great empires. Released from the fear of attack a small power such as Israel could turn its attention to domestic economy and the construction of public buildings that could serve as a source of pride and a symbol of national unity. This, apparently, Israel did in the peaceful years which circumstance allotted to her.

In particular the biblical accounts of the contract which the builder of the elaborate public buildings in Jerusalem had with Hiram, king of Tyre, are highly credible and fit into what we have come to learn about Phoenicia as a power dependent upon world trade for its economy. The export of cedar was basic to its economy, and literary as well as archaeological sources attest to the reputation of its metal-workers. That the nationalistic writer of the seventh century responsible for editing the accounts of the Age of Solomon should have been willing to credit foreign workmen with the fashioning of the house of Yahweh is added reason to respect this tradition as historically accurate.

Most prominent among the achievements of Israel's wise ruler in the Book of Kings is his building programme, particularly that of the Temple in Jerusalem. That the long and detailed description in Chapters 6–7 is the work of a priest and not of an architect is apparent to anybody who has tried to sketch or reconstruct this famous building: one has but to look at the many attempts, from that of Stade in 1887 to that of Stevens and Wright in 1955, to be convinced that the description

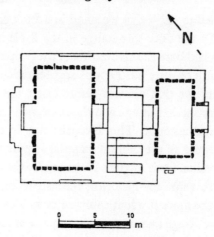

Fig. 9. Plan of Hazor Temple (*Encycl. of Arch.
Excavation in the Holy Land,* p. 162)

in the Book of Kings can be depicted in quite different ways, one of which can be seen in Ill. 12.

The ground plan of the building, however, is not difficult to sketch. It was an oblong building, measuring 35 by 104 ft. (11 × 32 m.) on the inside, divided into three rooms, with an entrance beside which stood two columns on the shorter side. This general plan for a sacred building has long been known from a small temple discovered at Tell Tainat in North Syria. But more recently a similar plan has come to light much nearer Jerusalem. In 1957 a three-room building was discovered at Hazor and it was clearly identifiable as a temple by a rich assortment of cultic objects found in the inner room, or Holy of Holies (Fig. 9). Little of the upper part of the building has been recoverable but the ground plan is clear. It consists of three rooms, a porch on which stood two columns, a main hall and a Holy of Holies within, and the overall measurements are 56 by 82 ft. (17 × 25 m.). A temple was first built on the site some centuries before the one described above and destroyed in the thirteenth century BC. Obviously the religious tradition was Canaanite and the building discovered in 1957 represented an age-old, traditional method for constructing a religious shrine in the land. With the similarity in general plan of the Canaanite structure to that of Solomon's temple in Jerusalem one can hardly avoid the conclusion that while the latter was devoted to a god foreign to the land of Canaan, the building constructed for his worship conformed to an architectural scheme which had roots deep in the history of religious worship in the land.

The description of the methods of taxation and forced labour employed by Solomon fit well into the history of the rebellion that effected the division of his kingdom upon his death. The information on Solomon's tolerant attitude towards foreign cults is highly credible in the light of the prophetic protests against apostasy in the two succeeding centuries, those of Elijah in the ninth and of Hosea in the eighth. And the tradition of the alliance with Phoenicia for the barter of timber and for sea-borne trade is well within the framework of what we know of the history of Israel's northern neighbour.

Such was the background to the story of the visit made by the famous Queen of Sheba to the wise and wealthy Solomon.

II

The Land of Sheba

Gus W. van Beek

THE biblical narrative tells us little about the culture of Sheba, whose nameless queen visited the court of Solomon. The fact that the state had a monarch suggests that Sheba was a kingdom, little different in political organization from the contemporary states to the north—Egypt, Israel, the Phoenician city states and Assyria—and we can reasonably infer that a somewhat comparable bureaucracy administered the land. The fact that the ruler was a queen is not surprising in view of the prominent role played from time to time by women in ancient Near Eastern governments. Assyrian inscriptions from the reigns of Tiglath-pileser III and Sargon II mention Zabibe and Samsi, two queens of Arabia, in the second half of the eighth century BC; Egypt had already experienced a most effective woman ruler in the person of Hatshepsut of the Eighteenth Dynasty; and Israel had had its charismatic female leader in the person of Deborah. Furthermore, in both Egypt and Israel, queens had been extremely influential in the affairs of state through advising or sharing leadership with their king-husbands.

The account in Kings, as well as those in Job, the Psalms, Isaiah, Jeremiah and Ezekiel, all suggest that the economy of the kingdom of Sheba (or Saba) was based on caravan trade in spices, gold and precious stones, which brought in considerable wealth. Such a trading economy—and indeed the safe journey of the queen herself and her retinue over some 1,400 miles of desert—presupposes the existence of a strong political state and a highly organized economic system, whose sway or influence extended far beyond the borders of the kingdom. Classical authors, notably Strabo, Diodorus Siculus and Pliny the Elder, add to the economic picture in describing the vast wealth that flowed into southern Arabia as a result of this trade. But such accounts tell us little about South Arabian culture in general and Sabaean (Sheban) culture in particular. It remains for the archaeologist to fill in the enormous blank areas, and this task has just recently begun.

As yet no part of the Queen of Sheba's capital city—Marib in eastern Yemen—has been excavated in sufficient depth to reach levels dating from her time, the tenth century BC. Indeed, so far, in a very small area of only one town site in the entire south-western corner of Arabia have deposits from the period of the Queen of Sheba been uncovered; that site, Hajar Bin Humeid, some forty miles from Marib, has revealed a cultural continuity and a chronological framework stretching from about the eleventh or tenth century BC to the early centuries AD. Excavations at other sites, however, have brought to light more detailed information about South Arabian culture between the seventh century BC and the third century AD: Marib and Huqqa in Yemen, Timna and its cemetery Heid Bin Aqil in Wadi Beihan, Hureidha in Wadi Amd of the Hadhramaut, and ancient Sumhuram (modern Khor Rori) in Dhofar Province of the Sultanate of Muscat and Oman. And intensive surface surveys in Wadi Tiban near Aden, in the Hadhramaut, and in Nejran have provided an overall view of the history of human habitation and patterns of settlement in southern Arabia from the Old Stone Age to the present.

While digging has been concentrated in the remains of periods somewhat later than the tenth century BC, we can extrapolate backwards to the time of the Queen of Sheba, and describe with some confidence the culture of her period. Her reign must have fallen during the formative period, or very near it, when the foundations of Sabaean culture were laid. There, as in Egypt, Mesopotamia and Greece, an indigenous core of cultural tradition persisted from early times throughout its history. While allowances must be made for cultural evolution and for ideas and accoutrements acquired from many foreign lands, the major aspects of this cultural tradition were surely in existence when the Queen of Sheba ruled. Through the study of the later, we can surely understand the earlier.

But before considering the broad outlines of South Arabian culture, we must turn to the geography. The political unity, economy and culture of the state were greatly influenced and, in a large part, determined by the location, topography and environment of the land. An exceptionally important factor for the development of Sabaean culture is the comparative isolation of the country which, in retrospect, worked to its advantage. Located in the south-western corner of the Arabian peninsula, with boundaries roughly corresponding to those of modern Yemen, Saba (Sheba) was more than 1,400 miles as the crow flies south of Palestine. The terrain in between is a barren, almost waterless desert, consisting of rugged mountains near the coast, and a broken, sand- or rock-covered tableland to the east of the mountains. This enormous region is extremely difficult to cross unless one is well provided with camels and experienced guides. The coasts of the Gulf of Aden and both sides of the Red Sea are treacherous with coral reefs, offer very few watering places, and were often infested with pirates in antiquity, as we know from classical authors. These conditions made travel by land and sea between Saba and the great empires to the north hazardous in the extreme and had the effect of isolating southern Arabia. Such isolation enabled the Sabaeans to fashion their civilization in security, safe from the military devastation visited regularly on northern countries. It was not until the fourth century AD that the region was conquered by foreigners: whatever foreign influences entered Saba during its floruit came through Sabaean-dominated trade. None of these influences was

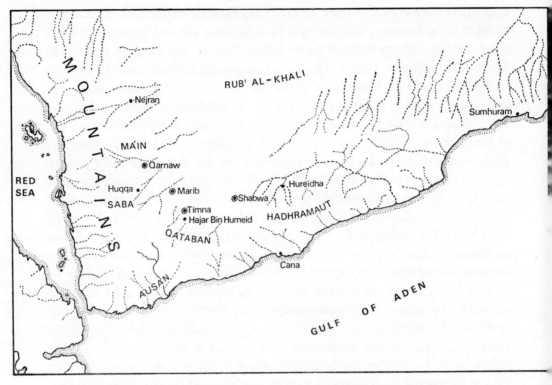

Fig. 10. Sketch plan of southern Arabia showing major archaeological sites and approximate locations of the ancient kingdoms

imposed; all were selected by the Sabaeans themselves. There is, therefore, no Egyptian, Assyrian, Babylonian, Early Persian, Hellenistic, or Roman period in southern Arabia. Sabaean culture is Sabaean throughout, and it affords almost laboratory conditions for the study of cultural development.

The land itself is beautiful in its diversity, and in the characteristics of its several zones. The coastal plain is narrow, hot and humid; its sandy soil is so salty that even potsherds do not survive. In recent centuries, and possibly in antiquity as well, it has been a malarial zone, and has never supported a large population. Immediately to the east, a chain of mountains paralleling the coast rises precipitously to heights of 5,000 feet in the south, and more than 10,000 feet in the north. Interspersed between the mountains are a number of upland valleys and plains which, like the astonishing terraced slopes of the mountains themselves, are intensively cultivated today. This zone receives considerable rainfall from the south-west monsoon during the spring and early summer, and torrents of water pour down the watersheds. While the mountains and their plains are the most intensely populated region of modern Yemen, there is as yet no evidence of occupation in this zone before the seventh or sixth century BC; travel through these mountains has always been difficult. The mountains gradually descend to a rocky tableland, broken by innumerable wadies. Nowadays much of the region is covered by sand and in some places by fields of dunes, but in antiquity the sand had not advanced so far westward from the Ramlat Sabatein. The climate is rigorous, with high daytime and low night-time temperatures but little humidity and virtually no rain. Here, run-off water from the mountains to the west floods the wadies, compensating for the meagre rainfall and making irrigation agriculture feasible. Travel was possible by ass or the favoured camel, whose minimal water requirements and large, padded feet are especially suited to sandy and silty terrain. It was on the tableland, and more specifically in the silt-floored wadies, that Sabaean civilization originated and thrived.

The date of Sabaean settlement of this region still cannot be fixed precisely, although its outer limits must be between about 1600 and 1200 BC. The former date is derived from linguistic considerations which indicate that the migration took place *after* the development of alphabetic writing. The latter is the present minimal date, based on available archaeological indications, for the establishment of the first high culture in southern Arabia.

The Sabaeans and their fellow South Arabs developed ingenious irrigation techniques which are without parallel in the ancient Near East. The systems employed in both the Nile Valley and the Tigris–Euphrates Basin utilized perennial rivers, and were solely concerned with the distribution of readily available water and concomitant flood control. In southern Arabia, there are no perennial rivers; there are only wadies, i.e. valleys that are dry throughout most of the year, and that carry water only when heavy rains in the mountains create flash floods (*seil*) during a few weeks each year. The South Arabs of necessity devised a system to distribute the flood as quickly and as widely as possible. It consisted of earthen dams to deflect the *seil* into primary canals, from which water was distributed by sluices and both secondary and tertiary canals to the fields.

The system varies in design according to the demands of the topography of the different wadies. At Marib, an enormous dam faced with stone was erected near the narrow mouth of Wadi Dhana. The *seil* pouring through this defile was deflected through stone sluices at each end of the dam into two huge canals from which hundreds of smaller sluices diverted a portion of the water into smaller canals, and these distributed it to the fields. Nowhere were the dams intended to impound water in a reservoir: for example, the sluices on either end of the famous dam at Marib could not be closed off; they were solely intended to carry the flood as rapidly as possible to the fields.

The fields between the dam and the mound of ancient Marib, some eight kilometres to the east, are covered with small mounds which contain the remains of secondary and tertiary sluices built of rubble, and possibly some of the smaller canals. The fields themselves are now cut by rectilinear erosion which deepened the original canals, so that one can now determine the lines of these canals by studying aerial photographs of the erosional pattern of the silt. This system seems to have irrigated no less than about 4,000 acres (1,620 hectares).

Wherever the water table was less than about eighty feet below the surface, well irrigation was used to supplement the flash-flood system, making cultivation possible on a reduced scale throughout the year. In all probability, many vegetables were grown in plots irrigated by wells, while cereals were chiefly grown in the fields irrigated by flash floods. That these systems provided adequate food for the population is proved by classical authors who regarded the land as self-sufficient. *The Periplus of the Erythraean Sea*, for example, includes no foodstuffs in its lists of commodities off-loaded in South Arabian ports.

As yet only the first steps have been taken in reconstructing the agriculture of ancient southern Arabia. All that is known at this time is derived from seed impressions in clay vessels. Most ancient pottery from this region was tempered with straw and seeds which were probably picked up from nearby threshing floors. In firing, of course, the straw and seeds burned out, leaving their imprints in the clay. The following cereal grasses have been identified: teff, broomcorn millet, barley and a possible occurrence of oats. Of these, probably only teff requires comment. This cereal is widely used in Ethiopia today for making bread, and its occurrence in South Arabian pottery suggests that it may have been a principal source of flour in antiquity. Other useful plants include the grape, cumin, flax, garden sorrel and sesame. Flax suggests that linen clothing was worn by the South Arabs as was the case in Egypt, and, together with cumin and sesame, it may also have provided oil. In addition to the obvious importance of these plants as food, several of them probably figured in the pharmacopoeia of the ancient Near East.

Sabaean wealth, however, was derived from the production and distribution of frankincense and myrrh. In the first century AD Pliny the Elder described the Sabaeans as the wealthiest race in the world because they sold that which was of the lightest weight for the highest price and bought nothing in return. Diodorus Siculus elaborates on the same theme:

This tribe [the Sabaeans] surpasses not only the neighbouring Arabs but also all other men in wealth and in their several extravagancies besides. For in the exchange and sale of their wares they, of all men who carry on trade for the sake of the silver they receive in exchange, obtain the highest price in return for things of the smallest weight. Consequently, since they have never for ages suffered the ravages of war because of their secluded position, and since an abundance of both gold and silver abounds in the country, ... they have embossed goblets of every description, made of silver and gold, couches and tripods with silver feet, and every other furnishing of incredible costliness, and halls encircled by large columns, some of them gilded, and others having silver figures on the capitals. Their ceilings and doors they partitioned by means of panels and coffers made of gold, set with precious stones and placed close together, and have thus made the structure of their houses in every part marvellous for its costliness; for some parts they have constructed of silver and gold, others of ivory and the most showy precious stones or of whatever else men esteem most highly. For the fact is that these people have enjoyed their felicity unshaken since ages past because they have been entire strangers to those whose own covetousness leads them to feel that another man's wealth is their own godsend.

(III 47:5–8)

So valued were these commodities, Pliny tells us, that at Alexandria, where raw frankincense was processed, workmen in the factories were required to strip and submit to a search before leaving the premises. As we know from the Wise Men's presents to Jesus (Matthew 2:11), frankincense and myrrh were ranked with gold as gifts suitable for a king. We are also informed by Pliny that Nero heaped a full year's production of frankincense on the funeral pyre of Poppaea, his wife. It is possible to calculate the annual value of southern Arabia's trade in these substances from different citations by Pliny. He stated that Rome's trade with Asia amounted to 100,000,000 sesterces annually. Elsewhere, he noted that the annual cost of trade with South Asia was 50,000,000 sesterces, leaving about 50,000,000 sesterces as the yearly value of trade with Arabia. Most of this went on the purchase of frankincense and myrrh.

Frankincense and myrrh are gum resins which are exuded from the bark of trees, frankincense from *Boswellia carterii* and *Boswellia frereana*, and myrrh from *Balsamodendron myrrha*. The trees are tapped and the gum resin slowly flows out, hardening on contact with air (Ill. 15). It is then scraped off, packed in bags, and shipped to processing centres. These trees grow only in southern Arabia and in neighbouring Somalia (Fig. 11). Frankincense trees are restricted to Dhofar in South Arabia and to the eastern part of Somalia, while myrrh trees are found in the mountains bordering the southern coast of Arabia to the west of Dhofar, and in the western hills of Somalia. Presumably their restriction to these areas is governed by a peculiar combination of soil, elevation and rainfall. The result was that the South Arabian states enjoyed an absolute monopoly on the production of these substances.

Frankincense and myrrh had many uses in antiquity. Frankincense was a basic ingredient in most offerings given to the gods. In Roman times, it was heaped on funeral pyres to yield a sweet odour that would be pleasing to the gods, although Pliny, in one of his more cynical moments, said that this custom was to cover the smell of burning bodies. Myrrh was used in preparing bodies for burial; Nicodemus, for example, wrapped the body of Jesus in linen with a mixture of myrrh and aloes (John 19:39–40). But myrrh was chiefly used in making cosmetic lotions. Queen Hatshepsut of Egypt is said to have rubbed myrrh oil on her legs, and a six

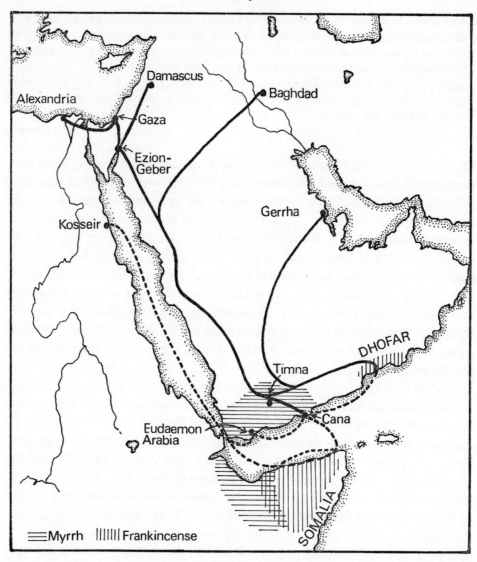

Fig. 11. Sketch plan showing the approximate zones in which frankincense and myrrh grow in southern Arabia and northern Somalia, and the major shipping routes by both land and sea developed to distribute these substances

months course of beauty treatment utilizing oil of myrrh was given to Esther as part of her preparation in the Persian King Ahasuerus' harem (Esther 2:12). Three famous lotions are mentioned by ancient authors: Egyptian, 'Megaleion', and stacte; in the first two, myrrh was the principal ingredient, while stacte was pure myrrh oil. Both frankincense and myrrh were prominent in the *materia medica* of the ancient world. Frankincense was used in antidotes for hemlock and other poisons, for pains in the side and chest, for haemorrhoids, and for paralysed limbs, ulcerations and abscesses. Myrrh was prescribed for ear, eye and nose ailments, for haemorrhoids, to induce menstruation, for malaria and dropsy, and in plasters for broken heads. These are some but by no means all of the medicinal uses of frankincense and myrrh, according to Assyrian records and to Celsus in *De Medicina.*

The demand for these substances gave rise to a lively trade and to the development of both land and sea routes (Fig. 11). From Dhofar, frankincense was transported by sea to Cana, or by land to Shabwa via the Hadhramaut. From Cana, the major land route went to Shabwa, Timna, Marib, Ma'in, Nejran, and northward to Yathrib (modern Medina), and Dedan (modern El-Ola). At Dedan, one route branched off to cross the desert by way of Teima to Mesopotamia. At some point in what is now northern Saudi Arabia, a major route turned westward, crossed the Wadi Arabah, the Negeb, and terminated at Gaza, the major incense emporium on the Mediterranean Sea. Another route continued northward along the King's Highway through Rabbath-Amon (later Philadelphia and modern Amman) to Damascus and northern Syria, with branches to Jerusalem and Bethel in Israel.

To guarantee the safe passage of these precious commodities along the caravan routes, either the South Arabs had to control all tribes or groups through whose territory the road passed, or they had to negotiate treaties with these people, paying duty or customs to each group. Because of the enormous distances covered by the caravans, it seems unlikely that one state could maintain hegemony for very long over all tribes along the way. Thus negotiated agreements for passage were probably arranged in most, if not all, periods. Indeed, Pliny explains that the high cost of these substances at Mediterranean ports resulted in large part from taxation en route.

The earliest information about trade with the incense region is found in Egyptian records. In the Fifth and Sixth Dynasties (*c.* 2440–2175 BC) of the Old Kingdom and during the Eleventh Dynasty (*c.* 2133–1992 BC) of the Middle Kingdom, trips were made to Punt (the Egyptian name for southern Arabia or Somalia) to obtain incense and other exotic products. The most famous of these expeditions occurred in the Eighteenth Dynasty during the reign of Queen Hatshepsut (1503–1482 BC), who graphically portrayed the land of Punt, its people and products—including myrrh and myrrh trees—in reliefs in her mortuary temple at Deir el-Bahri near Luxor (Ill. 14).

Next we learn of Solomon's expeditions to Ophir, whose products suggest that it is probably to be identified with Punt. Solomon's fleet, built and manned by Phoenicians, perhaps obtained a concession to call at ports under Sabaean control to take on water (there are few water holes on either coast of the Red Sea) and cargoes as part of an agreement with the Queen of Sheba. Since Solomon controlled the largest land empire in the Near East in the tenth century BC, including all termini of the major trade routes used by Sabaean caravans, it seems likely that he may have assured freedom of passage for Sabaean trade in return. It is therefore plausible to interpret the Queen of Sheba's visit to Solomon as an economic mission whose primary purpose was the conclusion of a trade agreement governing both land and sea routes, rather than as a meeting of mutual admiration as suggested by the Bible.

During the first century BC and the first century AD classical authors, notably Pliny the Elder and the anonymous author of *The Periplus of the Erythraean Sea*, described in some detail the sea routes, sailing times, and the commerce of each port along the Red Sea, the Gulf of Aden, and the Indian Ocean. The ships which plied these routes were based in Egyptian ports and sailed on regular schedules which were governed by the prevailing wind system. Ships destined for Indian ports departed from Egypt no later than July and called at the Arabian ports of Muza, Ocelis, Eudaemon Arabia and Cana. At that point, they had three routes to choose from. They might sail around the east end of Arabia, visiting the Persian Gulf ports first on the Arabian side and then on the Persian side before proceeding south along India's west coast; they might hug the Arabian coast for three days and then sail into the open sea directly to north-western India; or they might bear for the open sea heading off-wind immediately after leaving Cana, go around the southern tip of India, along its east coast, and on to the west coast of Indo-China. They returned in December or January with the winds associated with the north-east monsoon. If they left India too late, they wintered at Moscha where they traded merchandise for frankincense, then sailed along the coast of Arabia to Egypt when favourable winds returned.

A portion of the Red Sea fleet specialized in the incense trade. These vessels could leave Egypt as late as September and visit the ports on the northern coast of Somalia, turning northward to Cana after leaving Cape Guardafui, and then calling at the Arabian ports on their return voyage to Egypt.

All of this bustling commerce was part of the normal scene in ancient Saba, and there can be no doubt that it had its beginning during the reign of the Queen of Sheba, if not slightly earlier. It brought not only an unparalleled level of prosperity to the kingdom, but also put the geographically isolated Sabaeans in almost constant contact with the mainstream of ideas running through the great civilizations of the ancient Near East and the Mediterranean basin.

Owing to the lack of written documents in Saba our reconstruction of its civilization and cultural institutions can only be based on the material evidence recovered through archaeological research. This evidence is limited to architecture, art, minor arts and environment, and while it enables us to describe these in considerable detail, it does not permit us to make definitive statements regarding the more abstract features of the culture, such as social structure, kingship, law and religion. In considering these latter, we are limited to inferences from the material culture, and while much of what is inferred is probably correct, it must be remembered that we are operating in the world of speculation where ready proofs do not exist. With this caution firmly in mind, let us turn to the material world of the Sabaeans.

On the north side of the Wadi Dhana, Marib, the capital city, was surrounded by a large alluvial fan which, during the flood season, was covered with green fields of waving grain. To the north-west and north, a sloping ridge of black volcanic rock provided both a real and a picturesque border for the green of the foreground, while to the east and south, the gold of the sands and the brown of the occasional rocky knoll rolled in receding waves to the horizon. The city itself was constructed of a yellowish-white limestone.

In its general appearance, Marib probably differed little from the great cities of Syro-Palestine and Mesopotamia. Its size was probably comparable, since it measured approximately one kilometre long by half a kilometre wide at its greatest extent. During the time of the Queen of Sheba it may have been somewhat smaller. (Archaeological soundings have not yet been made around the circuit of the mound to determine precisely the history of habitation in each sector.) Its monumental architectural style utilized straight lines and flat, often receding planes. Even piers were square or rectangular in section and were surmounted by capitals without curving lines. Recessed niches with their sometimes successive receding planes emphasized the straight line and created an interesting interplay of light and progressive shadow tones. Symmetry was also a hallmark of the style with both structural design and decorative elements carefully balanced. Except for the use of ornamentation, Sabaean buildings in many ways resemble the clean functional lines of much of western architecture in our own time.

It is likely that Marib was a walled city, although its walls are nowhere exposed. A possible parallel structure, however, is the oval enclosure wall of the great Marib temple, the Mahram Bilqis, located across the Wadi Dhana at a distance of about three kilometres from the mound of Marib. This is one of the strongest fortifications known in southern Arabia, consisting of an inner and an outer wall, tied together by a series of bonded cross-walls. The resulting cavities or chambers are now filled with loose rubble, but some may have originally been open and served as store-rooms. Such walls are known as casemate walls, a design common in the Levant, for example, in Gibeah of Saul, in Solomonic constructions at Megiddo and Gezer, and in later Omri-Ahab fortifications at Samaria. There, casemate walls are probably Phoenician in design and possibly in construction, and date between the late eleventh and ninth centuries BC.

The fortification wall of neighbouring Timna, the capital of the kingdom of Qataban, was battered or sloping and constructed of rubble, which may have originally been covered with a smooth plaster face. This wall was preserved to about ceiling height of the buildings abutting on the inner face of the wall. Above this point, the wall may have risen vertically somewhat higher still. The enclosure wall at Ukhdud in Nejran was built of ashlar which was laid with varying competence in different sections. The overall plan was square with a series of irregularly arranged and spaced offsets on each side. This wall is unusual in that it was no more than two courses thick anywhere in its length, and formed the rear or side walls of the houses inside. Apparently each householder built the section of wall which formed part of his house, and this accounts for both the irregularity of design and the variety of construction skills. While all of these walls were well built, with the probable exception of the still unexposed, putative oval wall at Marib, they lacked the mass of the defensive walls of northern cities, where warfare was an almost annual occurrence. Indeed, the relative weakness of the defensive enclosures suggests that stronger walls were not necessary because the region was comparatively peaceful and had little fear of attacks.

The only excavated gateway of such a fortification system is the South Gate at Timna. This gateway consists of two rectangular towers which flank the flagstone-paved entrance passage. Built of enormous irregular blocks and randomly coursed slabs, the towers stand in marked contrast to the small block construction of the wall, and are not bonded to the wall ends. A stairway led to the upper storeys of each tower. The entrance was closed with two massive doors whose lower pivot holes were preserved *in situ*, and a deep recess in one side held the beam that was used to bolt the doors. On either side of the passage, and built against the opposing towers, were two benches, probably used by soldiers and by the elders of the city who, in typical ancient Near Eastern fashion, conducted business and civic affairs in the gateway. The walls of the towers were covered with inscriptions, some of which describe the construction of the towers with appropriate dedication to the gods.

Like the Sumerians, Assyrians and Babylonians, the South Arabs provided much information about the construction and repairs of their monumental structures. Names of kings and their fathers or sons, names of builders, extent of construction, and lists of gods to whom the work was dedicated were inscribed on both single blocks and in long running texts covering many blocks and sometimes several courses of the structure (Ill. 17).

To judge from partially exposed buildings at Marib, the South Arabian city was laid out in an orderly manner within the limits imposed by the shape of the mound surface. While it lacked the rather formal urban planning and symmetry of the Greco-Roman city, Marib was probably divided into small plazas, industrial and market sections, and civic and residential areas, all separated by relatively wide streets. So it is with Timna, where an open square just inside the gateway gave access to two streets lined with shops, and civic and residential structures.

These buildings were all constructed of stone, reflecting the stature and affluence of the capital city. Small towns, on the other hand, were built entirely of mud brick, or with an occasional stone structure, and with narrow meandering lanes, not unlike present-day small towns in southern Arabia. The masonry employed in these structures ranges from enormous, roughly-shaped gabbro blocks to finely cut limestone ashlar. In the early periods, the ashlar was dressed with drafted or smooth margins and a pecked face. This style has a long complex history which must be briefly described if we are to understand how the South Arabian style came about, and, at the same time, the technical processes involved. In the first stage, the edges of the block are cut back to form a smooth margin, but leaving a rough boss projecting on the face (Ill. 17). The drafted margins enabled the mason to lay the blocks with straight bedding and rising joints on the face. This is the prototype of 'rusticated' masonry, which has been popular periodically from Roman times to the present. The Phoenicians used this style only below ground level where it could not be seen. Once laid, the bosses of all blocks above ground level were trimmed off with a flat chisel, which left a smoothed or shaved face in Phoenicia, or a single or multi-point chisel, which yielded a pecked surface in southern Arabia. This style of dressing seems to have originated in Phoenicia, and a number of examples are known from Israel dating to the tenth and ninth centuries BC.

From Phoenicia it passed to Mesopotamia, South Arabia and Greece and while it never found great favour in Mesopotamia or Greece, the simpler rusticated style was widely used in Roman structures. It was in southern Arabia that it achieved its greatest popularity and had its longest duration. The earliest known examples appear in the oval wall of the Marib Temple (Ill. 17) at Timna, and probably at Sirwah where they go back to the middle of the seventh century BC; it is possible that when earlier strata of the Marib mound are excavated, examples will be found dating from as early as the reign of the Queen of Sheba. This style of dressing was used both in town buildings and in purely functional structures such as the sluices of the Marib Dam. As centuries passed, it became sloppier in execution until the beginning of the Christian Era when the design was incised on veneer wall panels as a purely decorative device.

Some of the early buildings are constructed with recessed niches in the outer walls. The Timna Temple (*c.* sixth century BC) is a good example of the use of such recesses to relieve the monotony of the long, otherwise unbroken walls of the buildings. This structure has a total of eight niches on three sides, and possibly had others on the fourth side which were subsequently covered by later construction. Many buildings were probably decorated with more elaborate recessed niches consisting of several stages with a row of square blocks in the deepest stage. These blocks are interrupted at intervals by a horizontal design consisting of a louvred panel and a row of dentil-like projections immediately below. While no examples of this style of recessing have been recovered as yet in full-scale architecture, it was widely used to decorate wall panels and plaques, the sides of incense burners, furniture legs, and solid stone chests, in obvious imitation of South Arabian building façades.

The closest parallels in full-size architecture are the false stone windows in the peristyle hall of the Marib Temple (Ill. 16). These windows are recessed to a depth of 10 cm., and are carved to resemble wooden lattice-work. The louvre-dentil motif appears in full size. It is repeated twice in each window, once above the imitation lattice on the recessed window panel itself, and again on the lintel above the window. Altogether there are sixty-four windows in the hall, and they also appear on the outer surface of the one wall that has been cleared. But there they are placed 70 cm. below and without regard for the spacing of those inside, which suggests that their function was solely ornamental rather than symbolic. While the hall does not pre-date the middle of the fifth century BC, we may reasonably expect the existence of prototypes in the preceding centuries, so that somewhat similar windows may have been used in buildings of the time of the Queen of Sheba.

Considering the great quantity of sculpture that has been found in the few excavated sites in southern Arabia, it is reasonable to suggest that there was probably more sculpture in this region than in any other country of the ancient Near East and Mediterranean world with the possible exceptions of Egypt and Rome. The reasons for this emphasis on sculpture are probably to be found in the uses to which sculpture was put, and in the subtle psychological and philosophical view of man that characterized the culture. Virtually all sculpture was made for votive purposes. Almost every piece so far discovered was found either in a tomb or a temple where it had served as a memorial to one who had died or as a dedicatory piece to a god or gods. Such usage severely limited the choice of subjects, poses and scenes. There are virtually no views of daily life and the multitude of man's activities that received emphasis in Egyptian art and to a lesser degree in Greek art, and such examples as have been found are late and poorly executed. Poses are invariably stiff and formal, whether standing or seated. Throughout there is a kind of archaic formalism which must have developed very early in the culture and remained to the end. At no time did there emerge a spirit of free expression such as occurred in the Golden Age of Greece.

Yet within these limits, a South Arabian style developed that emphasized the personality of the individual. To the ancient South Arab, it was the face that best expressed the individuality or the personality of a man. Similarly the name of the person also gave him a separate identity and, at the same time, membership in a family or clan. The South Arabian sculptor, therefore, accentuated the head and face, and the person's name, which was inscribed on the statue base, while showing an almost complete disregard for the body. Faces emphasize individual features, and no two are alike. The body, on the other hand, is often omitted altogether, but if it is used at all, it is poorly modelled and seems only to serve as a link between the base and the head.

Let us examine these figures in greater detail (Ills. 18, 19, 22). All faces were rendered in a standardized style, although the features were individualized. Eyes are large, wide open, and staring. For the most part, they were inlaid with separate stones or paste, but some are carved from the stone itself. The nose is straight, slender, and sharply ridged on top. The small mouth is rendered with lips closed and slightly curved in a half-smile. Cautery marks are often cut into the cheeks, perhaps as a clan identification. Eyebrows are usually incised and, like the cautery marks, often filled with paste or plaster. Ears are small and well-formed, the lobes sometimes pierced for earrings. While the hair is occasionally rendered by carving, it was normally made of plaster, the very softness of which produced a more life-like realism that contrasted with the smooth polished stone face. In some instances, traces of pigment on the plaster hair show that it was painted, but most heads now show only the rough tool marks which once served to key the plaster. The female head shown in Ill. 22 exhibits all these characteristics, and is the finest example of stone sculpture to come out of southern Arabia. The holes on both sides of her neck were probably drilled for the attachment of a delicate gold necklace, which was found in the same tomb. She was found in the Timna Cemetery, and probably belongs to the first century BC.

Male heads usually have beards, rendered by a series of pecks or small drilled holes; in style, the beard sweeps downward in a thin line from the sideburns following the jaw-bone, and resembles that worn by many Yemenis today. Moustaches sometimes appear without an accompanying beard.

When the entire figure is carved, the body is almost formless and stocky (Ills. 18, 19). Arms and legs are very thick and heavy, with the forearm extended and the hand holding a staff or offering. On female statues, breasts are always small. No aged people are represented, and presumably custom indicated that all figures should be presented as virile men and young women. Indeed, most bodies are identical and could be interchanged without making the slightest difference. On the best seated statue that has come down to us (Ill. 19), the body, from breasts to feet, is smaller than the head itself, giving a very dumpy appearance to the figure.

Statues, and especially heads, as well as stelae, were mounted in stone boxes. These boxes had pivot holes in the upper and lower corners, indicating that they were equipped with one or two doors which were probably made of wood. A square vertical hole was cut through the upper front edge for inserting a peg to hold the doors shut, and sometimes a small horizontal hole was drilled through the front of this edge into the peg hole, so that a pin might be inserted to prevent the peg from slipping through. This upper front edge was sometimes inscribed with the personal and family name of the deceased. Some heads were cut flat on top, presumably to fit them in available boxes.

The South Arabian sculptor chiefly utilized calcite (alabaster) for both sculpture in the round and reliefs. Calcite abounds in this region, and is a superb material for sculpture because it is beautifully veined, translucent, easily carved and capable of a lustrous polish. A fine-grain limestone—approaching lithographic limestone in its characteristics—and marble were occasionally used.

Relief sculpture was commonly carved on recessed panels and stelae. In the former, the figure stood on about the same plane as the border of the panel, and relief was achieved by cutting away the background to recess the back surface. On stelae, the uppermost plane was usually the figure and the stele surface was cut back slightly below it.

Relief sculpture also stressed the upper part of the figure, and sometimes this is all that is represented. Although smaller in size than most statues, figures carved in relief were often surprisingly detailed in the rendering of the head and garments. Indeed, the drape of the garments was much more meticulously worked on reliefs, showing that the sculptors were sufficiently talented to achieve considerable realism in their work when they chose to do so. The subject matter of reliefs was basically the same as that of sculpture in the round. Some early reliefs on stelae owed their inspiration to North Syrian styles, and are not only intrinsically valuable but are also important as evidence of ancient trade and the transmission of ideas and designs. A man holding a staff on a relief from Timna has the same pose and dress as figures on northern reliefs of the seventh and sixth centuries BC. Indeed, this pose was used as early as the twelfth century BC at Megiddo in Canaan, and was surely current at the time of the Queen of Sheba.

An unusual type of relief is the 'face plaque' (Ill. 20), in which highly stylized, almost geometric facial features were cut on square or rectangular slabs. The eyes were rendered by U-shaped, eye-shaped, round or square forms; the nose was indicated by a long slender ridge; and the tight lips by a small square or rectangle. A border on the same plane, and sometimes inscribed with the name, normally enclosed the features. Some plaques preserve traces of red paint on the face and border (Ill. 20), indicating that many or possibly all were originally painted. Here, as with figures in the round, no two face plaques were made exactly alike, suggesting that they were regarded as a kind of stylized portraiture. It may be that they were made for families who were unable to afford larger more realistic reliefs or statues in boxes.

In few ancient cultures were bulls more sensitively and more realistically carved than in southern Arabia (Ill. 25). This was no doubt due to the fact that the bull with its crescent-shaped horns symbolized the moon god, one of the principal deities in the pantheon. Considerable care was given to the proportions and to such details as the folds of the upper eyelid, the muzzle, the nostrils and the mouth, all of which were rendered with exceptional realism. For the most part, these bull heads were carved on stelae and rectangular plaques, and only a few statues in the round are known. By way of contrast, stone lions—which probably represented the sun god—were quite stylized. Many of their features resemble those of Hittite and North Syrian lions, especially the squarish, open mouths and teeth, which suggest some cultural influence from that region.

Ibexes were also very often sculpted, presumably because they too symbolized the moon god with their graceful arching horns. They were often used to form a border around large votive inscriptions. On those plaques, the ibexes were shown crouching, each one occupying a square box-like area and placed one above the other. Their horns were represented as much larger and more curving than in reality. There is also a number of large blocks with rows of ibexes shown in a frontal view and standing side by side (Ill. 23). These ibexes are quite abstract; the more easily recognizable features are the ridged horns and knob-like eyes; the muzzle, beard and chest were rendered sketchily on successively deeper planes, while the legs were represented by two parallel bands extending from the sides of the head to the base. Owing to the size and cutting of these blocks, it is probable that they were used as the coping of buildings or piers. Free-standing ibexes— usually in combinations of two side by side—were also carved on small blocks of alabaster; such pieces were probably votive offerings, although they are not inscribed.

Another popular motif—thus far only known in reliefs—consisted of groups of cherubim facing a date-palm tree. These mythical creatures with lion bodies, large bird wings and human heads generally stand with one foreleg on the ground and the other resting on a frond of the tree. Usually this motif was repeated several times along the top border of those inscribed plaques whose side borders were decorated with the crouching ibexes.

The South Arab artisans also excelled in metallurgy, especially in the technology of bronze. That bronze sculpture and plaques were made locally is proved by the many vitrified clay crucibles with drops and ridges of copper adhering to all surfaces that were found in the excavations. The earliest important bronze found is a statue of the youthful Phoenician deity Baal Melcarth—counterpart of the Greek Herakles—wearing a lion skin. The statue, which is about two-thirds life-size, is highly stylized in the modelling of the figure and garments. The name Ma'adkarib is incised on the left shoulder, and a boustrophedon inscription (i.e.

alternate lines written in opposite directions) extends from the shoulder to the bottom of the skirt; though only partially decipherable, it states that the statue was dedicated to the moon god, Ilumquh. The inscription also informs us that the statue was gold, which seems to indicate that it was originally gilded with gold leaf which was later scraped off. In style the figure is distinctly Near Eastern, and probably Phoenician, and represents the wide circulation of motifs in the region. It was found in the peristyle hall of the Marib Temple one metre above the floor, and belongs to about the sixth century BC.

Another spectacular bronze group is composed of two lions each with a male baby rider (Ill. 24). The babies hold the subjugated lions by means of a chain in one hand which is attached to the animal's collar, and carry a stick or dart in the other hand. The back forepaw of each lion is extended and raised as if it had originally rested on some object. The gaunt, supple bodies of the lions, their beautifully modelled heads and manes, their sinewy legs and huge paws, and the realistically fat bodies and faces of the babies make them among the finest ancient bronzes in existence. Both lions stand on bases with identical South Arabic inscriptions giving the names of the craftsmen—Aqrabum and Thuybum—who refurbished the building to which these pieces were once attached. Dating from *circa* 75 BC, they were found in the debris just outside a building known as House Yafash at Timna. The motif probably symbolizes the supremacy of the moon god, represented by the male babies, over the sun god, represented by the lions, and was meant to protect both the house with which they were associated and passing caravans with their rich cargoes. Though considerably later than the Queen of Sheba, these lions nevertheless illustrate both the content of religious thought as it developed in Saba, and the astonishing skill of the Sabaean sculptor who worked in bronze.

Among the minor arts and crafts, pottery is the least technically developed of all local products and the poorest in quality. The reasons for this backwardness are to be sought not in the ineptness of the South Arabian craftsman, but in the local custom and the economic orientation of the culture itself. First of all, in southern Arabia greater use was made of other materials—namely sacking, stone, and metal— than of clay for making containers. Consider the containers used for the major export products, frankincense and myrrh. Since these substances are light, dry and not fragile, heavy clay jars or wooden boxes were unnecessary for their storage and shipment, and indeed would be heavier than the products carried in them. It would have been quite unprofitable to load a camel, which can manage loads of approximately 450 lb., with 375 lb. of commercially valueless clay vessels carrying only 75 lb. of frankincense or myrrh, when 425 lb. of incense could be transported in no more than 25 lb. of sacking or leather bags. Moreover, sacks could be loaded and carried much more easily than clay jars or wooden boxes on a camel, or they

13. The southern sluice of the Marib Dam. The line of this canal is indicated by the wall.
At the base of the tower are a number of vertical stones which probably represent the
facing of the earthen dam and indicate where the dam abutted on this sluice structure

14. Measuring myrrh in the Land of Punt. From Queen Hatshepsut's mortuary temple reliefs at Deir el-Bahri

15. Frankincense 'tears' forming on a tapped tree in Dhofar

16. Some of the 64 false windows in the peristyle entrance hall of the Marib Temple. Holes in the walls mark places where stone or bronze votive plaques were attached

17. A portion of a long building inscription on the oval wall of the Marib Temple. This text, written boustrophedon by a priest, Taba ʿkarib, is a dedication of the wall from the inscription upwards, of children, slaves and palm groves, mentioned by name, and is dated *c.* 500 BC. This portion of the wall is constructed of ashlar dressed with drafted margins and pecked centres. The cross walls of this casemate wall show in the upper right centre of the photograph (Photo Jamme)

18. An alabaster statue of a woman named Gaba'um Han'amat. Her head is flat on top either to fit her into a box or to receive hair worked in plaster, and her arms are adorned with two bracelets each. From the Timna Cemetery

19. One of the few seated figures in the round. The proportions of the body are entirely out of scale with those of the head. Her waist is poorly defined, and her knees are indicated by a ridge just above the feet. From the Timna Cemetery

21. Relief of a woman, incorporating Syro-Hittite designs of the twelfth to seventh centuries BC. This South Arabian copy was found in the Timna Cemetery

20. 'Face plaque' in the form of a stele. Traces of red paint are preserved around the eyes, nose and borders of the plaque. From the Timna Cemetery

22. The finest South Arabian head known. Carved of alabaster, her eyes are lapis lazuli set in paste, and her hair is worked in plaster. From the Timna Cemetery

23. Frieze of standing ibexes probably used as a coping design for a building or a large pier. This block is one of several found at Timna, and another is a corner block with the row of ibexes continuing around the side

24. The Timna lions and male riders, a superb example of ancient bronze sculpture. The group probably symbolizes the subjugation of the sun god to the moon god

25. A typical South Arabian bull head in alabaster. From the Timna Cemetery

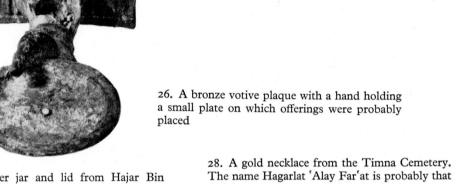

26. A bronze votive plaque with a hand holding a small plate on which offerings were probably placed

27. An alabaster jar and lid from Hajar Bin Humeid

28. A gold necklace from the Timna Cemetery. The name Hagarlat ʿAlay Farʿat is probably that of the woman to whom it belonged

could be stacked more densely and much higher on a ship. If such lightweight containers were used in South Arabia's major industry, it seems likely that their use became more common in the South Arabian home and shop, with the result that clay pots were not utilized in such quantities for storage purposes as in other countries of the ancient Near East. Indeed, in southern Arabia today, goat-skins and sacks are employed much more frequently in the home and store than elsewhere in the Arab world.

Then, too, it is almost axiomatic that the number of clay vessels used in an ancient society is in inverse proportion to the affluence of that society, since prosperous people have a preference for more costly stone and metal vessels. This is especially true in those regions where suitable stone and metal abound. In both respects southern Arabia was indeed fortunate, because alabaster and steatite were plentiful in the region. *The Periplus of the Erythraean Sea* lists alabaster (calcite) as an export from Muza (probably ancient Mocha), indicating that quantities of the stone in excess of local requirements were available. Indeed, according to this source, Muza was the only port exporting alabaster in the entire Red Sea and Indian Ocean region. Steatite was quarried in the mountains of the Wadi Beihan area and probably elsewhere as well. Although the source of copper in antiquity is not yet known, the quantity of artefacts made from it indicates that it too was plentiful in the region. The quantity of such raw materials in the hands of skilful craftsmen inevitably led to the production of an abundant supply of fine and costly vessels for use in wealthy households. As a result, the potter's craft neither made use of known mass-production techniques nor attracted skilled craftsmen here as it did in the cultures of the Fertile Crescent.

However, even though pottery is not common, it is not without interest. Indeed, the very fact that the archaeologist is not overwhelmed by tremendous quantities of sherds enables him to study the ware more intensively than is possible elsewhere, and thereby to wrest more cultural information from it.

By the time of the Queen of Sheba, South Arabian pottery had already developed those special characteristics that were to remain with it throughout the first millennium BC. Clays were poorly prepared and were commonly tempered with chopped straw, ground steatite, or a mixture of different rocks, some of which were natural inclusions in the clay and others of which were added by man. Of the pottery from the time of the Queen of Sheba, approximately 80 per cent was tempered with chopped straw, 15 per cent with ground steatite, and 5 per cent with mixed rocks. Straw temper is a hallmark of early (Neolithic to Early Bronze Age) pottery in the ancient Near East and the very extensive use of straw in southern Arabia caused many archaeologists not working with stratified deposits to assume that this ware is earlier than it actually is, when in fact straw tempering continues into the Christian era.

All South Arabian pottery was hand-made in all periods; the potter's wheel was never employed in forming vessels. Yet, as in the pre-Columbian period in the New World, this was no bar to the production of elaborate and highly sophisticated forms, many of which imitate metal or stone prototypes. All large pieces were made in pipe-like sections which were piled on one another when leather-hard, attached by slip, and sealed by rubbing the joint. Curiously enough, few forms have handles and most vessels stand on a ring base which is sometimes so high that it becomes an attached stand. The vast majority of bowls are exceptionally large with diameters ranging from 30 to 45 cm., suggesting that food was eaten from large common bowls, rather than from smaller individual bowls as was the custom elsewhere in the ancient Near East. The lack of water or wine jugs and pitchers suggests that skins were used as liquid containers, and the paucity of small jugs and bottles probably indicates that perfumes and ointments were kept in stone or metal containers, a few examples of which have been found.

Most of the pottery that would have been seen by the Queen of Sheba was covered with a dark red slip before firing, and occasionally with an additional red wash which was applied after firing. Burnishing or polishing with a smooth object, such as a pebble or bone, imparted an interesting interplay of shiny and matt lines and zones to the surface. In this early period, deep bowls and jars were commonly burnished with a combination of vertical and horizontal strokes which further enhanced the form of the vessel. It is interesting to note that the use of red slip occurs in southern Arabia at precisely the same time that it appears in western Iraq, northern Syria, and throughout the Levant, indicating that this style of finish enjoyed a wide popularity in the ancient Near East through the early centuries of the first millennium BC. Furthermore, the combination of vertical and horizontal burnishing was most common in the Levant during the tenth and ninth centuries BC, at the same period that it achieved its greatest popularity in southern Arabia. The occurrence of these traits points to a close relationship between South Arabia and the lands to the north, and probably indicates cultural borrowing from this region, and more particularly from Syro-Palestine, at the very time that our nameless queen ruled Sheba.

The most common decorative devices used on pottery in the tenth to ninth centuries consist of rows of knobs and monograms, the latter either in relief or incised. Both knobs and monograms in relief were made separately and attached to the vessel when it was leather-hard. The knobs—which may imitate rivets on metal prototypes—have their closest parallels in knobs on bowls and jugs of the same period from Palestine. Monograms undoubtedly served as symbols of ownership as well as ornaments.

As noted above, stone vessels abound in South Arabian sites, and while most of the extant examples belong to later periods, the lack of obvious typological development suggests that similar forms occurred earlier. The most common are hemispherical bowls carved from steatite. As a rule, these bowls have two roughly cut ledge handles near the rim, and are finished with a wide smooth flat band, composed of irregularly shaped facets just below the rim, and rough diagonal tooling over the remainder of the outer surface. Such bowls were probably used as cooking pots.

Finer and more delicate are the small alabaster cosmetic jars, usually complete with a lid. The most common form has a broad flat or slightly convex base, sides curving inward to a small mouth, and two handles on the shoulder representing miniature stylized bull heads. The interior was drilled and the rim was undercut with a flat chisel to increase the interior diameter. The flat or arching lid usually has a small pierced lug handle, and a grooved edge on the under surface so that it would fit snugly into the jar. The finest whole alabaster jar found to date is shown in Ill. 27, and though later in time than our period, it illustrates the level of skill of the stone worker.

Only a few pieces of South Arabian jewellery have been recovered in controlled excavations. Beads were made from chalcedony, agate, carnelian and glass, and do not differ in form from those found elsewhere in the Near East. Small bronze spherical pendants, hollow inside perhaps for carrying a small pebble, were probably worn around the neck and rattled as the person moved. The most spectacular piece is a gold pendant with a portion of the chain and beads preserved (Ill. 28). The pendant is crescent-shaped and bears the name of a woman, incised in South Arabic, Hagarlat 'Alay Far'at. Between the upturned arms of the pendant is a

Fig. 12. Burnt bone furniture inlay with two birds on opposite sides of a tree. Holes were drilled in the edges at the corner as well as through the face for attachment. 79 mm. wide. From Hajar Bin Humeid

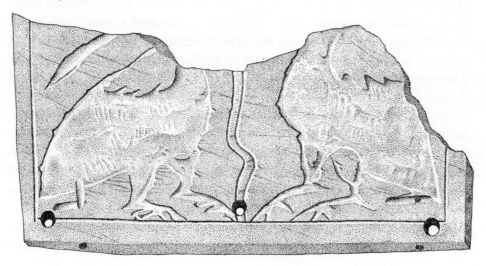

smaller circular pendant with the face of a woman in repoussé. Fragments of bronze mirrors and alabaster cosmetic palettes indicate that the South Arabian lady was very much aware of her beauty and took pride in her appearance.

Inlays of bone attest to the existence of attractive furniture and boxes into which such pieces were set. The best example of such inlays is one of burnt bone shown in Fig. 12, in which two birds whose heads are missing stand on opposite sides of a tree, eating its fruit. In view of South Arabian wealth, it would not be surprising if early Phoenician ivory inlays are some day found when more sites have been excavated. With regard to other furniture, we have only a few pieces represented on stone reliefs. One is a large chest with elaborate recessed panelled sides, standing on stylized bull-shaped legs, and with a turned stretcher between the end legs, probably dating from some time during the first century BC or first century AD. Cross-legged stools and tables, resembling modern folding furniture, appear on one late Sabaean relief. On others, high-backed, armless chairs complete with footstool, and a bed similar to Greek and Roman couches are shown. Of these pieces, only the stone chest is uniquely South Arabian, and we can reasonably assume that Sabaean furniture of the tenth century BC was not unlike that of other nations in that period.

The language used by the Queen of Sheba is called Sabaean, one of the dialects of ancient South Arabic. Other dialects were used in the neighbouring kingdoms of Ma'in, Qataban and Hadhramaut. None of these dialects is used today, having been replaced, following the conquest of Islam, by North Arabic, which belongs to a different branch of the Semitic language family. South Arabic is the oldest member of the south Semitic branch, the major modern survivor of which is Ethiopic, which was derived from South Arabic in antiquity.

Sabaean was written with an alphabet which consisted of twenty-nine consonants, more than any other Semitic language. The origin of its script is still somewhat obscure, but it perhaps derives from one of the earliest Semitic scripts, the Proto-Sinaitic script of about the seventeenth century BC, with some Canaanite influence. It seems to have split off from its northern progenitors no later than the thirteenth century BC, by which time consonants in such dialects as Canaanite and Hebrew had begun to coalesce.

The South Arabic script appears in an elegant monumental style and in a cruder graffito form. The monumental script is characterized by symmetrical, somewhat elongated letters formed with clean and simple lines (Ill. 17). This style was used in inscriptions on buildings, sculpture, reliefs, and on utensils and tools of everyday life such as stamps, incense burners and pots. That it was in use by the time of the Queen of Sheba is certain, since it already appears in contemporary pottery inscriptions. Through the centuries the script evolved, becoming increasingly ornate with the addition of serifs and the splitting of strokes that make up the letters. But in the first half of the first millennium BC, its well-proportioned letters have a beauty and grace that exceed that of any other script from the Mediterranean world, including early Greek. The graffito script is much more irregular and variable, owing no doubt to the fact that such inscriptions were hastily written without the benefit of good tools, and by people who were not professional scribes.

Known South Arabian inscriptions now number more than ten thousand, but they are not as informative about the history, economy and culture of the region as one would wish. Monumental inscriptions are usually concerned with building, votive and funerary texts, while graffiti chiefly consist of names painted or scratched on walls and rocks, not unlike those found on public structures today. There are only a few texts known that record historical events, and no annals, economic texts, laws or mythological reflections have as yet appeared. It has been possible, however, for South Arabian epigraphers to develop a chronology of the rulers of the various South Arabian kingdoms, although there is still considerable disagreement as to details. This chronological arrangement is based on the occurrence of royal names in building and other dedicatory texts and on the typological classification of the letter forms of the texts according to the various stages in the palaeographic evolution of the script. Names occurring in graffiti are being studied to determine the changing fashion in names, and the relative popularity of names in each kingdom and other territorial and ethnic subdivisions. Many of the graffiti are found on isolated rocks and in places sheltered from the wind, suggesting that they were probably carved by shepherds and caravaneers, as well as the occasional traveller. If this suggestion is correct, it would indicate a high percentage of literacy in the population, higher than today in fact, when shepherds and caravaneers are almost never able to read and write.

No temple or religious text from the time of the Queen of Sheba has as yet been found, and most of what is known of the contemporary religion is derived by inference from later religious structures and from dedicatory inscriptions. As in most contemporary Semitic cults, the Sabaeans and other South Arabs worshipped stars and planets, chief among whom were the moon god, variously known as Sin, Amm, Anbay or Ilumquh; the sun god, called Shams; and Athtar or Astarte. There is no reason to doubt that this pantheon was also revered by the Sabaeans in the tenth century BC. Indeed the Queen of Sheba may have served as a priest, or even the chief priest, of the faith, since the title of the early rulers—Mukarrib, which probably means 'priest-king'—denotes a significant role in the cult. Presumably there was a body of mythology and a calendar of religious holy days and festivals as in Mesopotamia and Canaan where somewhat similar cults were in vogue.

The earliest temple known is the Mahram Bilqis, meaning the precincts of the Queen of Sheba, at Marib. The oldest parts of this structure go back to the seventh century BC, but its substructure may incorporate remains from still earlier centuries. As it now stands this temple is a large complex consisting of a peristyle hall, which opens on a large area enclosed by an oval wall. The hall featured a large, paved, open court, surrounded by a stone-roofed ambulatory supported by 32 square monolithic piers about 16 feet tall (4·95 m.). The walls are decorated with false lattice windows carved from stone (Ill. 16). Piers and walls must have been covered with votive plaques of bronze and stone, judging from the numbers found in the debris and from the many attachment holes cut in the stone. There must also have been a number of free-standing votive statues in bronze and alabaster set on bases around the hall and in the court. At the south end of the hall, a doorway led to the oval enclosed area. Set in the floor of this doorway was a large bronze basin, filled with water, through which the faithful walked before entering the oval area. The basin was presumably kept full of water from an overhead reservoir, and a channel carried the overflow water across the open court of the hall through the opposite entrance. It is interesting to note that every South Arabian temple excavated to date has either a water reservoir or a well near the entrance to the temple proper, suggesting that some form of ablution was involved in the rites of worship.

The interior of the walled oval area has not been excavated so that the nature of the structure or structures within this area remains unknown. Other major temples—at Timna and Hureidha—are no more helpful in clarifying the details of worship, since their interiors were destroyed to floor level or below in antiquity.

Nor have we tombs from so early a date as the tenth century BC. From the seventh century on, however, burials were made both in caves and in stone-built mausolea; the former were customarily used in regions such as the Hadhramaut where the neighbouring sandstone or limestone cliffs are sufficiently soft to cut caves and ledges, and the latter in hard rock and open regions. At Marib, adjacent to the oval enclosure wall of the Mahram Bilqis on the east side, is a mausoleum constructed of well-cut limestone on an almost square building plan, whose roof was supported by four monolithic piers like those of the peristyle hall. Around the walls are tiers of ten burial compartments for a total of sixty bodies, and at least two chambers below the floor.

Each compartment has vertical slots in the sides, into which stone or wooden closing panels were secured. Whether these compartments were used for inhumations or served as ossuaries is not known; the fact is that few bones have been found in any South Arabian tombs—except the cave tombs of Hureidha—but this may be due to ancient plundering. Grave goods were put in the tombs, and offerings were placed outside the burial chambers, indicating a belief in an afterlife, and the continuing reverence for the dead by the community. We can reasonably assume that these burial customs and beliefs existed at the time of the Queen of Sheba, and perhaps one day archaeologists will be fortunate enough to find her own tomb.

While her tomb and documents of her time have yet to come to light, and while remains of the tenth century BC are still largely unknown to archaeology, the recovery of a small amount of contemporary evidence together with a considerable amount of material from only three or four centuries later enables us to reconstruct a general outline of the Queen of Sheba's culture with considerable probability. She would have lived surrounded by the accoutrements of an affluent civilization: a thriving trade that brought unparalleled prosperity; an irrigation agriculture that provided ample subsistence; a distinctive architecture in stone that was second only to that of Egypt in the ancient Near East in its execution and variety of ornamentation; a richness in metallurgy and stone carving as well as an abundance of artists and artisans who pursued these vocations; a high degree of literacy among the people, who had a keen appreciation of the importance of a written language and of their beautiful alphabetic script; and an art that is representational in a symbolic archaic manner. This unique civilization had its roots in the high cultures of the north, but its growth took place in the isolated region of the south-west corner of Arabia. There it developed in its own way and largely at its own pace in the peace and security of its isolation. Yet the Sabaeans were never out of touch with the intellectual and artistic trends of the great empires of the Near East and the Mediterranean world, because of their fabulous commercial activities which chiefly centred on the exotic products of their land.

PART TWO

The Legend and its Diffusion

III

The Queen of Sheba in Judaic Tradition

Lou H. Silberman

ALTHOUGH Solomon in all his glory provided a theme to which the legend-spinners of Jewish communities turn often and with diligence, the story of his meeting with the Queen of Sheba—an episode one would expect to be elaborated on with especial delight—was not, in fact, much used. On the contrary, the *haggadot*—the legends—of the Jews all but ignored this royal encounter. Indeed, a passage in the Babylonian *Talmud* seems, when incorrectly although not infrequently so interpreted, to deny the queen's very existence. But though the visit itself aroused little interest in the story-tellers, the queen's 'hard words' to Solomon, mentioned but not quoted in the First Book of Kings, were puzzled over and varying guesses as to what they were multiplied with the passing years. Even more, an Aramaic paraphrase of a verse in the Book of Job (Job 1:15) and the mention of 'the gold of Sheba' in Psalm 72 became starting points for a meandering stream of thought that eventually transformed the Queen of Sheba into Lilith, queen of the demons, who strangled infants in their cradles, could be summoned with magic charms, and as a succubus coupled with men.

There are very few texts that in any way report the details of the visit of the queen to Solomon. The longest and most elaborate of these is found in the so-called *Targum Sheni*—the second *targum*—to the Book of Esther. This work, although it is called a *targum*—that is, an Aramaic translation of a scriptural text—is in fact far from that. Indeed, it is not even a more or less close paraphrase as some other *targumim* are, but is a free rewriting of the Book of Esther in which the author has combined legends and his own imaginative inventions into a novella that goes far beyond the tale that scripture tells. Scholars disagree as to its date. Some attribute it to the third and fourth centuries AD; at least one suggests a date as late as the eleventh century; a recent writer, without being more specific, hears in it 'the sound of the dolorous life of the Jews of the Land of Israel in the days of Christian domination', apparently meaning before the Arabic conquest in the seventh

65

century. All, however, agree as to the place of composition—the land of Israel—for the Aramaic reflects the dialect of the west.

What is the story of the Queen of Sheba's visit to Solomon doing in a novella based on the Book of Esther? This necessitates a further comment on the structure of the *Targum Sheni*. It is built upon verses from the Book of Esther, each providing the opening line for a section of the novella. The second chapter begins with the second verse of Esther: 'In those days, when the king Ahasuerus sat on the throne of his kingdom in Shushan the capital', and, picking up the mention of 'the' throne, develops from there. The throne was not *his* throne, the author understands the presence of the definite article and the absence of the possessive pronoun to mean. It was, he writes, 'the throne of Solomon, which Hiram, the son of a widow of Tyre, had made with great skill'. With this as a beginning, he tells first of Solomon and his greatness; then, in the next chapter, of this throne which Solomon had had made and how the wicked Nebuchadnezzar had plundered Jerusalem, burned the Temple, carried the people into captivity, and taken the fabulous throne as booty. Then follows a description of the lamentable fate of the throne, carried from one land to the next by one conqueror after another, in a chronology whose disarray is compounded by the author's eagerness to include the most notorious names and several additional legends, until at last Cyrus the Persian seated himself upon 'the throne of Solomon, the like of which there was not in all the kingdoms'.

Having come back to Solomon, the author provides a paradigm for Ahasuerus' banquet, recounted in the Book of Esther, describing a great feast which Solomon gave for 'all the kings of the East and of the West'. Not only were the kings summoned but 'the wild beasts, the birds, the reptiles, the devils, the demons, and the spirits' who danced before him 'to show his greatness'. When the roll was called, all had assembled but the cock-of-the-woods (hoopoe). Solomon was not to be thus insulted and gave the order that the bird be brought before him under threat of death.

It is with the coming of the cock-of-the-woods into the king's presence that the story of the Queen of Sheba's visit begins, for it is the cock's excuse that brings the kingdom of Sheba to Solomon's attention. The bird cleverly diverts the king's wrath by recounting a journey that brought him to a country whose capital city was Kitor. The name, as Paulus Cassel (whose text, translation of, and notes to the *Targum Sheni* are most valuable) indicated, is related to the Hebrew word *ketoret*, 'the smoke of incense', and refers, of course, to the frankincense for which Saba was famous. The cock-of-the-woods mentions the wealth and luxury the incense trade brought to Saba, and Cassel's notes quote Strabo who wrote: 'On account of abundance of servants, the inhabitants are lazy and careless in their manner of life' and who reported that the king of Saba ('who presides over the court of justice and other things') was not permitted to leave the palace, for if he did, 'the people would at once stone him, in consequence of a saying of an oracle'.

The *targum* says that this land 'whose silver lies about like dung in the streets' and whose ancient trees are 'watered from the garden of Eden' was ruled by a woman whose name was Malkath Sheba. These words may be translated 'Queen of Sheba', but the grammatical construction suggests that this was not understood by the *targum* to be her title but her proper name. It is interesting to note here that in medieval Jewish texts the reading is often 'Malka' Sheva', to be translated Queen Sheba, the second word thus being understood as her proper name, the first as her title.

Josephus reports that her proper name was Nikaulis or Nikaule (*Antiquities* VIII, 158), explained by some scholars to be a corruption of Nitokis, the equivalent of Neith-oker mentioned by Herodotus (II, 100). Samuel Krauss has sought to connect it with the name of a prince of the Jews of Ethiopia, Nikoli, reported in a version of the story of Eldad the Danite, a ninth-century traveller who brought a report of the Jews of Ethiopia to the communities of North Africa, Babylon and Spain. Krauss mentions as well the identification of the Queen of Sheba with the Sibyl Sabbe in several Byzantine chronicles and suggests that the statement in Genesis 10:7: 'the sons of Kush [i.e. Ethiopia] were Seba', etc. was the source of this identification. This, however, does not appear in Jewish sources.

A fascinating variant, not only of the queen's name but of her country, is to be found in a *targum* to Job 1:15. The text we now possess is late, but there are references in early rabbinic writings to such an Aramaic translation. (Unfortunately the recently published *targum* to Job from Qumran, Cave XI, does not contain the text under consideration.) The biblical text beginning with the previous verse reads: 'The oxen were ploughing and the asses grazing beside them, when the Sabaeans attacked and took them.' The Aramaic version reads, however, 'Suddenly Lilith queen of Smaragd fell upon and carried them off.' We have here a variant of *smaragdos*, the Greek word for emerald, used to 'translate' the Hebrew text-word *shb'* that could be as easily read *shebo*, the name of one of the precious stones in the breast-plate of the high priest noted in Exodus 28:15–20. One may assume that the translator understood the word in just this fashion, for whatever reason we cannot now ascertain, although the stories of the wealth of Sheba noted above may have given rise to this reading.

Before returning to the visit it is as well to consider the suggestion that the queen, despite the clear statement in the Bible, did not exist. In the Babylonian Talmud (Baba Bathra 15b) Rabbi Samuel b. Nahmani (a Palestinian teacher of the third century AD) reports in the name of Rabbi Jonathan (a Palestinian teacher of the mid-second century): 'Whoever says that the *malkath* of Sheba was a woman is in error; the word *mlkth* is to be read *malkuth*—the realm—of Sheba.' (It is not clear whether the entire quotation is Rabbi Jonathan's or whether the last part is an attempt by the redactor to explain his position.) The literal translation of the second clause is: 'What is *mlkth*? *malkuth* (kingdom) of Sheba.' Since there is no mention of a *mlkth* of Sheba in Job 1:15, it has often been assumed by those who read this passage that the reference is to I Kings 10:1. (This is the case even in the Soncino Press's English translation.)

If we for a moment accept the view that Rabbi Jonathan is referring to the passage in I Kings we must ask why he dismisses a biblical personage with a word. Krauss, in his essay on the names of the Queen of Sheba, refers to several scholars who argue that Rabbi Jonathan's position is part of a process of refurbishing the putative ancestor of Rabbi Judah the Patriarch, King Solomon. There were (and this much of their discussion is certainly correct) contemporaries of the Patriarch who dominated the Palestinian Jewish community at the end of the second and the beginning of the third centuries AD, who used the story of the queen's visit and the supposed liaison between herself and Solomon to discredit the king and thus to reflect unfavourably on Rabbi Judah's own often imperious claims. (Schechter, too, in his essay on the riddles propounded to the king, follows a similar line of thought.) Krauss rejects the argument on the grounds that the Bible itself contains enough compromising material about Solomon to make this legendary affair of little value for the Patriarch's opponents. (He forgot, however, that there is a difference between scriptural stories and nasty gossip about the ancestor of the most important scholar and communal leader of the period.) His own solution is entirely speculative and does not hold together. He suggests that Rabbi Jonathan's statement is directed against the claim of Ethiopia to be the true Israel, for if there was no Queen of Sheba there is no royal line descending from Solomon as the Ethiopians assert (see Chapter 5). Of course, he concedes that Rabbi Jonathan could obviously not have known the *Kebra Nagast* and acknowledges that Ethiopia had not yet been Christianized in the rabbi's days, but he vaguely connects all of this with the church's claim to be the true Israel and pursues that matter no further.

There is yet another passage found in the *Midrash ha-Gadol* to Genesis—stemming from Yemen and, though a medieval compilation, containing much early material—that builds upon the assumption that Rabbi Jonathan is discussing I Kings 10 when he transforms 'queen' into 'kingdom'. The midrash begins by referring to Genesis 25:6: 'But to Abraham's sons by concubines Abraham gave gifts while he was still living, and he sent them away . . .' Among those thus sent away was Jokshan, father of Sheba (Genesis 25:3). They were, the story continues, to remain apart from Isaac and his descendants until the Messiah had come. Now in the days of Solomon, the situation was so favourable, as I Kings 4:25 reports, that it seemed as though the Messiah had come. Therefore the scattered descendants of the concubines came to do homage to Solomon. It is this visit, says the midrash, that is referred to in II Chronicles 9:1 (the parallel to I Kings 10:1), and it quotes Rabbi Jonathan to support its interpretation. Actually the midrash only quotes the first clause: 'Whoever says that *mlkth* Sheba was a woman errs'. It follows this not with the rest of the talmudic citation but its own interpretation, using a familiar hermeneutical device: 'Do not read queen of Sheba but realm of Sheba'. It continues: 'The whole realm of Sheba came to serve Israel in the days of Solomon'. However, when it was recognized that Solomon was not the Messiah, the concubines' descendants returned home to await his coming. The passage concludes: 'And they are destined to return in the days of the Messiah, may it come quickly and in our days, for it is said in Scripture, "all of them will come from Sheba"' (Isaiah 60:6). It is evident that the passage offers no independent confirmation for Rabbi Jonathan's claim but is entirely dependent upon it and does not help us to solve the problem.

What then is Rabbi Jonathan's opinion? To understand that one must look—as Louis Ginzberg indicated and Yeshayahu Aviad, picking up the suggestion, emphasizes—at the entire context with which the rabbi is concerned. This reveals that the whole discussion deals with Job, who he was and when and where he lived. There is no need to recount the various opinions held; the one that concerns us first is that of Rabbi Nathan who said that 'Job lived in the time of the kingdom of Sheba since it says "the Sabaeans fell on them and took them away"' (Job 1:15). The sixteenth-century talmudic commentator Samuel Edels points out that this is not entirely helpful for, as he wrote, 'Sheba . . . often occurs in Scripture without reference to a specific period.' However, he argues that the use of the feminine verb in the verse in Job corresponds to the similar usage in I Kings 10 and thus suggests that the mention of Sheba in Job refers to Sheba in the days of Solomon. A few lines further on Rabbi Jonathan's interpretation is mentioned. Again Edels explains:

Apparently there is a problem, for the entire narrative in I Kings concerning the *malkath* Sheba uses the feminine gender throughout, concluding with the clause 'and she returned to her country, she and her servants'. The implication is that a woman is being referred to, for if it was intended otherwise why was not the noun read *malkuth*, 'kingdom', rather than *malkath*, 'queen'? Rabbi Jonathan's statement does not really intend to dismiss the queen, rather is it to be understood in this fashion—whoever understands the words *malkath* Sheba to mean that she was not a reigning monarch but merely the wife [=woman] of a king and was, therefore, called *malkath* Sheba, wife of the ruler as in the case of other kingdoms, errs. *Malkath* Sheba in I Kings means that she was herself queen of Sheba, ruling in her own right. Such is the case today; there are kingdoms ruled by women.

This explanation certainly escapes the problem of doing violence to the scriptural passage but one wonders if a simpler approach is possible. What is being discussed is not the passage in I Kings but the verse in Job. The translator, perhaps influenced by the feminine verbs, understood the passage to refer to the Queen of Sheba, in keeping with the tradition that Job lived in the days of Solomon. Rabbi Jonathan rejects the *targum's* translation and declares that whoever assumes that the reference in Job 1:15 is to the Queen of Sheba, as did the targumist, and not merely to the people of Sheba, is in error.

After these digressions we return to the *Targum Sheni's* story of the queen's visit. We had left the cock-of-the-woods placating Solomon with the report of his journey to the land of incense. Concerned to save his life, he was emboldened to exclaim: 'Now, if it please my lord the king, I shall gird my loins like a mighty man, and shall rise and go to the city of Kitor, in the land of Saba, and shall bind its king and governor in chains of iron, and shall bring them to my lord the king.' Of course Solomon was delighted with the prospect and dispatched a letter of demand together with an armada of birds so great as to obscure the sun and cause the queen such consternation that she 'took hold of her clothes and tore them in pieces'.

Solomon's letter we shall not quote, for though it was ferocious, the queen's counsellors were unimpressed: 'We do not know Solomon nor do we esteem his kingdom.' Womanly intuition, however, overbore their advice. She gathered a great fleet, loaded it with 'presents of pearls and of precious stones' and sent as well 'six thousand boys and girls who were born in the same year, month, day and hour, and who were of the same stature and of the same proportion; and they were all dressed in purple' (see Chapter IV, p. 97). That the queen was in haste to visit Solomon is evident from her letter of reply: 'Although the journey from Kitor to the land of Israel is of seven years, yet owing to the question I have to ask thee, I shall come in three.'

The story continues with an account of the queen's encounter with Benayahu son of Yehoyada, Solomon's courtier, sent to meet her, and of her mistaking him for his royal master. When at length she is conducted into his presence she finds him seated in an apartment of glass.

Thus far we have depended upon the narrative found in the *Targum Sheni*; now we turn to another account, *Ma'ase Malkath Sheba*, 'The Tale of the Queen of Sheba', written by Saadya ben Yosef, a Yemenite scholar, in 1702 and published from the manuscript by Yeshayahu Aviad. The third chapter of this version relates the visit of the queen to the court of Solomon, adding some details and omitting others. The most important of the additions is the description of the royal apartment. It was 200 cubits square (one cubit equals about 18 inches) and paved with marble. At one side was a garden from which flowed a stream of water on to the marble so that the entire floor seemed to be water. The *Targum Sheni* merely reports that the queen thought that Solomon was sitting in the midst of water and so, in approaching him, raised the hem of her garments, and disclosed that her feet were hairy. The *targum* has the king remark: 'Thy beauty is the beauty of women, and thy hair is the hair of men; hair is becoming to men, but to a woman it is a shame.' The queen ignores his unseemly remark and turns at once to her 'hard questions'. The very brief mention of the visit in *Alphabetum Siracidis* (*Alphabeta d'ben Sira*) (see below, p. 76) reports that the queen was hairy all over and that Solomon, quite intent on possessing her but apparently somewhat finicky, sent her various depilatories that proved effective. 'The Tale of the Queen of Sheba' has a somewhat different focus, for it alone reports that the queen is a 'demon'— a matter to which we shall return at length.

The visit to the royal apartment in this version follows the asking of the riddles, whereas in the *targum* it precedes it. In the latter, the disclosure of the hairy feet is by chance and is incidental; in 'The Tale of the Queen of Sheba' it is part of a plan on Solomon's part, for he wishes 'to lie with her'—he knows, of course, that her husband is dead (see below, p. 82)—but is repelled by her hairiness which was considered a demonic characteristic. Why it is necessary for the queen to reveal her hairy feet, the matter already being known to Solomon, is not explained. Indeed what seems to have happened is that the author wove together two strands, the disclosure and Solomon's previous knowledge, without much concern for the contradiction. He wanted both in his story, so he put both in. The same device— a depilatory—as in the *Alphabetum* is offered with the same results. Solomon and the queen sleep together and from the child of that union there descended Nebuchadnezzar (or possibly the child himself was Nebuchadnezzar—see below, p. 77). The queen sought to perplex Solomon with her questions and failing, praised him as scripture reports. The *Agadath Shir ha-Shirim* (a tenth-century haggadic midrash collection on the Song of Songs) says (lines 599–601), emphasizing the concluding words of I Kings 10:9, 'she did not praise him for aught but his righteousness', gave him gifts and 'he gave her what she desired'. The *Targum Sheni* makes no mention of her departure but the 'Tale' concludes, virtually repeating the words of I Kings 10:13 and II Chronicles 9:12: 'After this he sent her on her way and she returned unto her place. King Solomon gave to her all that she had asked for together with all that he gave her of his own and she turned to go unto her own land, she and her servants.'

The Riddles

We turn again to our main source, the *Targum Sheni*. The queen had ignored Solomon's ungallant reference to her hairy feet and had, instead, declared her intention to propound three riddles. Were he to answer them, she was ready to acknowledge him to be a wise man. Were he to fail, she would know him to be 'a man like all the rest'.

The first riddle put by the queen was:

> A cistern of wood: buckets of iron:
> they draw up stones: they cause water to flow.

Solomon's prompt answer was: 'A tube of kohl.'

Cassel, who read the first word incorrectly and thus translated it 'berries' instead of 'cistern' (both Aramaic words have the same consonants), quotes an explanation from *Metzah Aaron* (a commentary on the *Targum Sheni* published in 1768 in Fürth): 'It is a reed made of wood, in which is put dye for colouring the eye [lid]; and this dye is very hard, like stone; and when one wants to take out the stone, he must use an iron spoon to extract the colour, and when the eye [lid] is smeared over, then water comes out.' Although the commentator comes rather close, it is evident that he did not base his explanation on any exact knowledge. The tube of kohl is an item of feminine cosmetics going far back into antiquity. The material used is stibnite or antimony trisulphite, a hard substance ground into a fine powder and kept in a reed or other receptacle. To remove it, a small rod of wood, ivory or, as in the riddle, metal, is first moistened with water and then dipped into the powder. The paste thus formed on the rod is drawn around the eyes to make them appear larger; the outer corner is extended and the eyebrows are also shaped and lengthened.

The use of such cosmetics was severely criticized in the Hebrew Bible. Jezebel bedecks herself before she is killed by Jehu: '. . . and she painted her eyes . . .' (II Kings 9:30); Jeremiah, warning Jerusalem of impending woe, asks:

> And you, O desolate one,
> what do you mean that you dress in scarlet,
> that you deck yourself with ornaments of gold,
> that you enlarge your eyes with paint? (4:30)

The Babylonian Talmud reports that at the ordination of Rabbi Zira the scholars sang a verse from a wedding song in his honour that reflects their attitude:

> Neither eye-paint nor rouge nor [hair-] dye, yet
> radiating charm.

Wünsche in his *Rätselweisheit* (p. 22) quotes the fourth riddle in the thirty-fifth *maqamah* of the Arabic poet Hariri that has the same solution, although the riddle itself speaks of the slender servant (i.e. the metal applicator) who serves two identical maidens (i.e. eyes) making them appear more sprightly and youthful, and is called upon for greater effort as they grow older.

29. Detail from a parchment amulet showing the female demon Lilith. Above her are Sanoi, Sansanoi and Samnaghof (Sir Isaac and Lady Wolfson Museum, Jerusalem)

זה שלמה המלך העושה משפט משתי נשים "

30. The Judgment of King Solomon. Late thirteenth-century Hebrew manuscript bible
and prayerbook (British Museum)

31. The opening of the Song of Songs, with representations of King Solomon and a ▶
minstrel. From the Rothschild Siddur, Florence, 1492 (Jewish Theological Seminary of
America, New York)

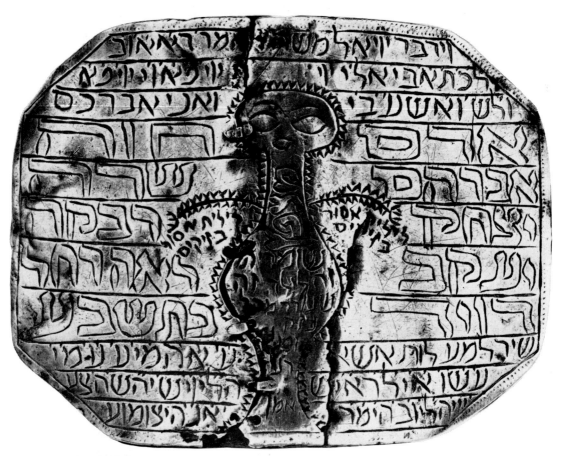

32. Amulet for protection of a new-born child against Lilith. Persian, eighteenth century (Israel Museum, Jerusalem)

The second riddle propounded by the queen is:

> [Like] dust it comes forth from the earth:
> It is nourished from the dust of earth:
> It is poured out like water:
> It illumines the house.

The king's immediate answer is: 'Naphtha'.

The *Bi'ur* (commentary) to the *Targum Sheni* in Netter's edition explains the riddle as follows: 'The explanation is that it flows from a hole in the ground and pours like water because it is a sort of liquid like quicksilver and it illuminates the house as is indicated in the Talmud in Chapter Two of the tractate Sabbath. It is called naphtha because it is volatile. Rashi [Rabbi Solomon Isaaci, the eleventh-century Rhineland commentator] explains that it sticks to the walls of the house.'

Cassel, apparently influenced by *Metzah Aaron*, which is dependent on Rashi, translates the last line 'sticks to a house', ignoring the evident meaning. Line two affords some difficulty and its explanation is omitted by the commentators. Perhaps the reference is to the clay lamp that contains the liquid, but the image is uncertain. Wünsche explains that the solution of the riddle depends upon the recognition that 'on the island of Naphtonia in the Caspian Sea and at Buku on the sea's west shore as well as in Karkuk in lower Kurdistan, flowing naphtha or mineral oil is a clear transparent material, used in the east for illumination' (p. 23).

The third riddle runs:

> A storm-wind rushes through their tops:
> It cries loudly and bitterly:
> 'Its head is like a rush.'
> It is praiseworthy for the free:
>> Shameworthy for the poor:
>> Honourable for the dead:
>> Disgraceful for the poor:
>> Joyous for the birds:
>> Grievous for the fish.

The answer: flax.

The first word of the riddle, ' 'arqalin', presents a problem. It has been translated 'storm-wind' following the lead of the author of the *Bi'ur* who notes: 'Meturgaman [an earlier commentator on whom he depends] says that not being as wise as Solomon he does not know what this means, but I have found its meaning to be "storm-wind".' Cassel emends the text to read 'procella' (Latin: 'violent storm'). Krauss (*Lehnwörter* II, 134) wishes to read it "askelin', bag-pipe player, and to interpret the text to mean 'the wind passes over a field of flax'. This is the meaning offered by Jastrow (p. 125b) whom he quotes. I. Löw in his note to Krauss remarks: 'Completely unclear in the context'. Levy in his *Chaldäisches Wörterbuch* translates it by the word 'orkan' (= tempest), while at the same time noting that the origin of that word is equally obscure. He offers as a second suggestion 'arcanum'. For this reason Sulzbach translates the first sentence 'this is more obscure than any other', and thus makes it refer to the quality of the riddle, excluding it from the riddle itself. Earlier scholars, with the same intent, suggested it be read as 'oraculum'. Grünbaum translates it 'Heerführer' = army commander, without indicating how he reads the text. Of Buxtorf's statement 'videtur esse Cannabis aut Linium, ut ex sequentibus colligi potest', Levy writes: 'The solution of the riddle is hemp or linen, but that cannot be mentioned in the riddle itself for then it would not be a riddle.'

The third line, 'Its head is like a rush', is a quotation from the *targum* to Isaiah 58:5, which reads 'bow down his head as a bulrush'.

Cassel's explanation of the riddle, while itself not entirely clear, is worth quoting:

> As a sail flaps violently in the storm, the linen made of flax (it) bows low its head like a rush. Linen is a cause of dignity to the rich and free who wear byssus (there is a play upon the word *horin* = free, with *hor* = white), a cause of shame to the poor who wear rags, an ornament for the dead in their shrouds—which are white as angels, and a mockery to the living (the rope of flax), a joy to the birds, who pick up the seed of flax, and a vexation to the fish on account of the nets.

What he means by his explanation of 'a mockery to the living (the rope of flax)' is obscure. The German text reads 'am leinenen Strick' and seems to have a pejorative sense but I have not been able to find note of such a usage. Possibly this refers to death by hanging. The *Bi'ur* explains: 'Because rope with which men are bound is made from flax.' Perhaps that is all Cassel intends. The *Bi'ur* seems to say that linen garments, i.e., princely garments, are a mockery when worn by the poor. The meaning may be what Cassel suggests by rags: the worn-out cast-off clothing of the rich shames the poor.

These then are the three riddles contained in the *Targum Sheni*. There are, however, several other versions of the riddles to which we now turn. In *Midrash Mishle*, the midrash to the Book of Proverbs, the following report of the queen's riddles is found.

> Said she to him: 'You are very wise, but if I ask you one question, will you answer me?' He replied: 'For the Lord gives wisdom, out of his mouth comes knowledge and discernment' (Proverbs 2:6). She said to him: 'What are these?
> Seven cease: nine begin:
> Two offer drink: one drinks.'
> He replied: 'In truth, when the seven days of menstruation cease, the nine months of pregnancy begin. The two breasts offer drink; the one child drinks.'
> Her second riddle is:
> A woman says to her son, your father is my father; your grandfather is my father; you are my son and I am your sister.

Solomon's reply: 'Surely these are the two daughters of Lot' (Genesis 19:30–38).

Her third and fourth riddles were not verbal. She had brought before him 'young children of like stature and dressed alike' (compare the account of her visit in the *Targum Sheni*, p. 70 above), and challenged him to distinguish between the males and females. He did so by having nuts and roasted grain spread before them. The different behaviour of each in picking up the goodies revealed their sex. Then she had some circumcised and uncircumcised youths brought into his presence and asked him to distinguish among them. This problem he solved by having the high priest open the Ark of the Covenant. The circumcised bowed down, their faces shining with the radiance of the Divine Presence. The uncircumcised fell prostrate on their faces. To the queen's question how he knew which group was which, Solomon replied by reference to a complicated bit of exegesis dealing with Balaam and a second explanation from Job's comforters, the point of which was that 'those who are not sons of the covenant of Abraham cannot bear the Divine Presence' (Ginzberg, VI, 290, note 43).

Here there are four riddles, and the same is the case with the *Ma'ase Malkath Sheba*, 'The Tale of the Queen of Sheba'. In that work the first three riddles correspond to the first three in *Midrash Mishle*, while the fourth corresponds to the first riddle of the *Targum Sheni* with a slight alteration of the first and third items: 'a receptacle of copper' rather than 'a cistern of wood'; 'lifts up dust' rather than 'they draw up stones'.

There is, however, a text, published by Schechter in *Folklore* at the turn of the century, that contains nineteen riddles, the first four of which correspond to those in *Midrash Mishle*. The sixteenth, Schechter writes, 'reminds us very much of the second riddle in the version of the Second Targum . . . this fact may, perhaps, suggest that our version once contained all the riddles of the Second Targum'. The riddle runs thus: 'What is that which is produced from the ground, yet man produced it, while its food is of the fruit of the ground?' The answer is 'a wick'. The mention of 'its food is of the fruit of the ground' may be a reference to the naphtha of the *Targum Sheni* but too much cannot be built upon such a foundation. Schechter cites an Arabic gloss to the manuscript explaining 'yet man produces it': 'Men plait the wick and then light it, for if it had not been plaited it would not burn evenly.' All of the riddles are cited in Ginzberg's *Legends* (IV, 145–9; VI, 230–1, notes 43–7) and Schechter provides references to the wide-ranging discussion of the occurrence of these in non-Jewish as well as Jewish literature.

What seems evident is that the author of the text published by Schechter, Yahya ben Suleiman, who flourished before 1430, brought together a simple version of the Sheba legend containing many more riddles than are found in the earlier stories. Schechter argues that the Jews of Yemen have presented many 'very ancient Rabbinic sources' so that 'the late age of the compiler would not prove very much against the antiquity of his version of the legend'. However, as we have seen, 'The Tale of the Queen of Sheba', another Yemenite version of an even later date, says nothing of this longer collection but is content with three of the riddles from *Midrash Mishle* and one from the *Targum Sheni*. There is then no reason to accept Schechter's text as anything more than a compilation of materials most of which were unrelated to the visit of the Queen of Sheba. Ginzberg writes: 'It is noteworthy that the fifth and eighth riddles are introduced by the words, "and furthermore she asked him", from which it may be inferred that three different sources have been made use of by the compiler of this Midrash . . .' At any rate, the queen's riddles seem to have played no significant role in a field in which the medieval Jewish community took great pleasure, namely the compilation of riddles. Abrahams in his volume on Jewish life in the Middle Ages and Löw in his work on the life-cycle of the Jews make reference to the widespread development of riddles but offer little indication that any literature in this connection grew up around the story of the visit of the queen to Solomon.

'Your Devastators and Destroyers Will Come Forth From You'

The *Alphabetum Siracidis*, that strange little book, of which Abraham Epstein wrote, 'There is not limit to the frivolity found in this booklet', is a medieval collection of proverbs, twenty-two in Aramaic and twenty-two in Hebrew, alphabetically arranged. It is attributed to Jesus ben Sira, author of *Ecclesiasticus* included in the Apocrypha of the Old Testament. In it there is a report of an anachronistic meeting between Ben Sira and the Babylonian king, Nebuchadnezzar. The latter, at the instigation of his wise men, invited the former to his court to test him, for the courtiers were dismayed at the reports of Ben Sira's wisdom and were plotting his downfall. At the beginning of the encounter Ben Sira sent the king a rabbit with its head shaved as smooth as parchment and the latter was anxious to find out how this had been accomplished for he was sure that neither a razor nor any other instrument had been used. Ben Sira triumphed over his hidden foes and the king offered him the crown of Israel which he refused on the ground that he was not of the line of David. Then, the king asked, would he remain at court and answer a series of questions about matters that puzzled him? The first of the twenty-two put—and the only one with which we are concerned—dealt with the shaven animal: how was it done? With a depilatory that had been invented by Solomon 'at the time when your mother the Queen of Sheba came to him bringing gifts so that she might see his wisdom'. She was 'pleasing in his eyes and he sought to lie with her'. As we have mentioned, the king was dismayed when he saw that 'she was hairy all over' and in order to correct this deficiency he, according to Ben Sira, invented the depilatory the result of which was entirely effective, so that he came to her at once.

We have already noted the hairiness of the queen and shall again return to it. What is noteworthy here is the mention that the queen is the mother or ancestress of Nebuchadnezzar with the implication (or is it?) that Solomon is the father or ancestor. Schechter (*Riddles*, p. 350) assumed that the latter is indeed the case. He sought to explain the talmudic passage that was understood to deny the existence of the queen by relating it to this story. 'The legend that scandalized the Rabbis was probably that which is to be found first in the *Pseudo-Sirach*, according to which the relation between Solomon and the Queen ended in a love affair of which Nebuchadnezzar was the result. This legend, again, is based on the scriptural words: "And the King Solomon gave unto the Queen [Malkath] of Sheba all her desire" (I Kings 10:13; II Chron. 9:2 . . .).' But it must be noted the *Alphabetum* does not cite this text. In a comment of Rabbi Joseph Kara (end of the eleventh and beginning of the twelfth centuries) on I Kings 10:1, this passage is referred to: 'In the Book of Ben Sira [the *Alphabetum*] it is written that the Queen of Sheba was the mother of Nebuchadnezzar and was a descendant of Abraham's concubines.' The conclusion of this comment recalls the statement in the *Midrash ha-Gadol* to Genesis referred to above that the entire kingdom of Sheba descended from Sheba, son of Jokshan, the son of one of the concubines of Abraham.

In the 'Tale of the Queen of Sheba', published by Aviad, it is explicitly stated: 'She came unto him and he lay with her and from her went forth Nebuchadnezzar.' But the basis for this is not the verse from I Kings. Indeed, the intention of the author was not, wrote Aviad, 'to relate the tale of the Queen of Sheba and King Solomon as a mere story; the proper name for it is rather "this is the genealogy of Nebuchadnezzar"'. This is made quite clear by the verse with which the author brought his story to an end. It is that quoted above as a heading, Isaiah 49:17, but with a midrashic twist. The word *mimmekh*, 'from you', can be ambiguous. As it stands within its context, it is part of the divine promise of restoration—Zion's enemies will depart and the city will be restored. Yet taken from the context it is possible to understand it to mean 'out of you', so that the verse may mean 'you will be the source, i.e. the progenitor of your own foe'. Such, of course, was Nebuchadnezzar.

This midrashic conceit is by no means original here. In the *Midrash Tanhuma*, Habakkuk 1:7 is interpreted in a similar fashion. The midrash reported that there were a number of persons whose punishment was self-derived. For example the words from Habakkuk, *mimmenu mishpato use'eto yetze*, regularly translated 'their law and their majesty proceed from themselves', are applied to Adam, and understood to refer to Eve who proceeded (*mimmenu*) from Adam and was the instrument of his judgement. In this same passage Nebuchadnezzar too is noted as one of those who generated the source of his own downfall, his son and successor Evil-Merodach. Indeed, the *pesher* (interpretation) to Habakkuk among the Qumran materials seems to interpret the verse in a similar fashion, indicating that the nations attacked by the Kittim (i.e. the Romans) are responsible for their own fate; their defeat derives from their own wrong-doing (Silberman, 'Unriddling the Riddle', p. 338).

A nineteenth-century editor of and commentator on the *Targum Sheni*, L. Munk, suggested that the reference to Solomon's rulership over the realm of spirits and beasts and the visit of the Queen of Sheba, occurring so unexpectedly in this work, is to be explained 'only on the assumption . . . that the author was of the opinion that Nebuchadnezzar was the descendant of a son of Solomon and the Queen of Sheba. The mention of Nebuchadnezzar provided the opportunity for mentioning the Queen of Sheba and further, Solomon's rule over the realm of spirits and beasts' (notes, page 23). He mentions in connection with this the work of the Italian cabbalist, Isaac Menahem Azariah da Fano, *Asarah Maamarot* (II, 23). Indeed, Aviad notes that this episode is frequently referred to by the disciples of the great sixteenth-century Palestinian cabbalist, Isaac Luria, among whom was da Fano. The passage to which Munk refers reads as follows:

> Nebuchadnezzar was worthy to be called 'lion' [Jeremiah 4:7] because he was of the house of David, of the seed of Solomon from the Queen of Sheba, after she had become a proselyte. Yet since she was not sincere, her evil nature was disclosed and she reverted to her original nature. When he obtained dominion, they gave him the gold of Jerusalem, for much of it had been given to King Solomon by his grandmother . . .

In a citation of this work by a later writer, the verse from I Kings 10, 'he gave her all her desire' is quoted and explained as meaning that she desired him to have sexual relations with her. Aviad has brought together in a long note many of these sources as well as those relating to the parallel story that traces the Ethiopian royal family to this same liaison. One of the most fascinating of these fancies is that which holds that Tamar, Malkath Sheba and Rahab are one transmigrating soul, this indicated by the name Tamar composed of the initial letter of each name. Here the queen is said to have borne 'children' to Solomon.

It is interesting to note that the bluntness of the *Alphabetum* is mitigated in the later works. The queen becomes a proselyte and is then married to Solomon. Ginzberg writes that out of delicacy he has omitted the details and says that 'Solomon married the Queen of Sheba', although he makes no mention of her conversion. The article in the Jewish Encyclopaedia (XI, 235–6) ignores the whole matter.

Queen of the Demons

What seems to lie behind much of the material thus far examined is the hardly spoken yet very real belief that the Queen of Sheba was a demon. The most explicit statement—and it, too, is no more than a hint—is that in the *Targum* to Job which calls her Lilith. No more explicit yet certainly not opaque are the passages in the

Targum Sheni and *Alphabetum Siracidis* that make reference to her hairiness. Ginzberg (VI, 192, note 58) notes the belief that demons 'have their bodies and faces covered with hair . . .' in his discussion of this whispered background, but does not pursue the matter in any great detail. None the less it is everywhere present, emerging into explicitness in the cabbalistic schools of the early Middle Ages and in folklore, particularly of the German Jewish communities, in the late Middle Ages and on into the seventeenth and eighteenth centuries.

While it is possible to see this development as late and entirely separate from either the biblical story or the riddle tradition, there may well be an ancient connection between the two. Chastel in his long and detailed essay, 'La legende de la Reine de Saba', indicates that there is an intimate relation between them. He points to the two themes, the description of the queen as a hairy-footed creature and the posing of riddles, and suggests a parallel, *mutatis mutandis*, with the meeting of Oedipus and the sphinx.

The biblical text does not, of course, deal with what may thus be understood to be both sides of the queen's demonic nature—only that of the riddler, and then without the riddles. The later texts hint at the other side by reference to the queen's hairiness, without suggesting any connection between the two. Yet the two are, Chastel writes, to be understood together and the second supplies the clue to the first in which the power of the demons expresses itself.

As indicated above, the role of the queen as poser of riddles is not widely developed in later Jewish thought. However, as we shall see, her more clearly identifiable demonic nature is the subject of considerable discussion.

This matter is examined in great detail by Gershom Scholem in his Hebrew essay 'New Chapters Concerning Ashmodai [legendary king of the demons] and Lilith', particularly in the section 'Lilith and the Queen of Sheba'. (See too his entry 'Lilith' in *Encyclopaedia Judaica*.) It is pertinent to note that in midrashic and talmudic literature Lilith is a figure borrowed from Assyro-Babylonian mythology. There she is a storm demon. In Jewish legend she becomes, because of the assonance of her name with a Hebrew word for night, *layil*, a night demon, a succubus. Scholem suggests that this figure was merged with another species of demon, the *lilin* or *lilioth*, killers of infants, mentioned in incantation bowls coming from Babylon in the eighth and ninth centuries and in *Alphabetum Siracidis* (although not in connection with the Queen of Sheba). In the Middle Ages, particularly in the writings of the cabbalists, this composite figure was identified with the Queen of Sheba, because of her demonic qualities noted above.

Scholem mentions first the quotation found in *Sefer Pardes Rimmonim* of Rabbi Moses Cordovero (mid-sixteenth century) that, he argues, comes from Rabbi Moses de Leon, the author of the basic portions of the *Zohar* (a cabbalistic commentary on select books of the Bible composed of an intertwined series of mystical sermons and haggadoth which, during the later Middle Ages and even today among some groups, stands third in sanctity to the Bible and the Talmud). This is an elaborate interpretation of the words 'gold of Sheba' (Psalm 72:15), in which Lilith, Queen of Sheba, is identified with Lilith the Evil One, understood to be both diphtheria and the demon causing it. She is, in this role, to stalk the streets of Rome at the end of days, devastating the city; while the King Messiah, provided with an amulet of 'the gold of Sheba', will rebuild Jerusalem, bringing new life to it. This is the secret of 'the gold of Sheba'. In the *Zohar* itself (III, 19a), the destruction of Rome by Lilith at the command of God is noted but these enlarged details including the identification of Lilith and Sheba are lacking. Thus the passage is to be interpreted, argues Scholem, in the light of the commentary by Rabbi Moses Cordovero.

There are two direct references to the Queen of Sheba in the *Zohar* itself. In the first, found in *Parashat Balak*, III, 194b (the English translation of this, published by Soncino Press, is truncated so that its full import is not entirely clear) she appears as a witch of the filthiest sort, questioning Solomon about the rules of witchcraft in order to discover how to use the serpents that sprang forth from the bones of the heathen seer Balaam:

> And then he did kill him; for such is the way of that side, he who follows it is killed by it and it is with his soul when it departs from him, and he is punished in the other world and never finds burial, and his bones rot and become noxious serpents, and even the worms that eat his body become serpents. We have found in the Book of Ashmodai which he gave to King Solomon that anyone who desires to make powerful enchantments, if he knows the rock where Balaam fell, will find there snakes formed from the bones of that wicked one, and if he kills one he can make certain enchantments with its head and others with its body, and others again with its tail, there being three kinds in each one. One of the questions the Queen of Sheba asked Solomon was how to take hold of the bones of the serpent of three enchantments.

The continuation of the passage gives the details of the enchantment by which the serpents may be taken hold of. The person who possesses such a serpent becomes impervious to all weapons for all are subservient to him.

The second mention of the queen in the *Zohar* reveals her as a demon. This passage is found in a section called *Hashmatot ha-Zohar*, according to Scholem a collection of zoharic materials dealing with the commandments. In it the author sought to explain the meaning of the ceremony of *halitzah*, the drawing off of the sandal of him who refuses to marry the childless widow of a brother in levirate marriage, and in particular the meaning of the sandal itself. The author took as his starting point the widespread belief that the feet of demons are unlike those of humans. Thus, for example, in the Babylonian Talmud, the tracks of demon feet are said to be 'like those of a rooster'. This being the case, demons do not need sandals. With this supposition in mind, the verse from I Kings 10, 'she came to test him with riddles', is interpreted. One of the 'riddles' was that Solomon make shoes for her. Solomon was, however, not deceived. This is what is implied, writes the author, in the biblical text, for it reads 'and the king told her what was on her mind' and not, 'he made or did for her [what she asked]'. (The text is not quoted exactly but is paraphrased.) Solomon disclosed the queen's secret that she was a demon so that there was no need for him to make shoes for her. Scholem notes at this point that the detail that the queen's feet were like those of an ass is lacking in Jewish sources, being found only in the Arabic legends. As we have seen above, our other sources merely refer to the hairiness of her feet, not their form. However, it is altogether possible that what we have is a conflation of two motifs, brought about by a similarity of words, *sa'ir/sa'irah*, meaning hairy, and *sa'ir*, a goat-demon. Chastel points to the latter when he writes: 'The Queen of Sheba is presented as a creature with hairy feet . . .' and explains: 'The "hairy-one" (*se'ir*) is the name given by the Hebrews to certain demons who, in particular, inhabit the desert.'

To return, however, to the Spanish cabbalists: Scholem suggests that it is the *Zohar* and its author, Rabbi Moses de Leon, that is the source of this identification of the Queen of Sheba and Lilith. Such an identification depends, however, upon an earlier recognition of the demonic nature of the queen; it is unfortunate that, as noted above, the first columns of the *targum* of Job from Qumran have not been preserved, for from them we could know for sure whether the identification of Lilith and the Queen of Sheba found in the current *targum* was early, or represents a late and apparently cabbalistic addition.

Before turning to the folkloristic materials found in seventeenth- and eighteenth-century German Jewish sources, note should be made of the chapter in 'The Tale of the Queen of Sheba' that not only suggests the demonic nature of the queen, but indeed explicitly affirms it. Aviad argues, in his introduction, that although the author lived in the Muslim world, it should not be assumed that he took his material from the Qur'an, the *Thousand and One Nights* (possibly *c.* eighth century AD) and other Arabic sources. He drew, writes Aviad, not from books but from story-tellers, from the oral tradition of the Jewish Arabic world. It is, of course, entirely possible that such is the case, but one cannot conclude that such stories are 'uncontaminated' by their environment. It seems certain that Jewish sources regard the queen as demonic; her origins, however, are not made clear. Nonetheless a brief résumé of the 'Tale' is in order, for it has no parallel in Jewish sources. (See below, Chapter IV, p. 96, for what is clearly the Arabic source of this version of the legend.)

Ben Yosef, the author, begins by noting that profound scholars have said that the mother of the Queen of Sheba was a demon and that the daughter had married the King of Sheba and upon his death had reigned in his stead. The queen's father was a vassal of the King of Sheba who had almost fallen victim to the king's game of propounding riddles to the great men of his court and, after a fixed period, seizing their wealth when they were unable to answer. The vassal had been one of those impoverished and when he was unable to answer the latest riddle put to him was given a test which if performed would bring clemency and, if not, death. In the course of the trial—to make a journey of three months in thirty days—the courtier had spied two serpents, one black, the other white, in mortal combat. He succoured the white serpent and continued on his journey, coming in due time to his goal. On his return journey he was met by a princely figure who invited him to his palace and revealed that he was the white serpent—a demon (perhaps djinni is what is meant, since in this story these creatures are not malignant) who now was desirous of repaying him for his help. Part of the repayment was the hand of the djinni's sister in marriage. Upon his return to Sheba, he was received with honour by the king and, with the assistance of his wife—as wise as she was beautiful —saved his fellow courtiers by answering all the king's riddles. His wife gave birth to a daughter even more beautiful and wise than her mother and, when she was twelve, the king asked for her hand, married her and made her his consort, 'placing the crown of the kingdom upon her head and declaring her sovereign while he yet lived'. When her mother died, she became sovereign of the djinn as well, and, following the death of the king, reigned in his place.

A second chapter then deals with the wars of Solomon and a concluding chapter tells of the queen's visit to Solomon and of the 'begetting of Nebuchadnezzar'. The story certainly reflects its Arabic ambience. Whether it preserves any indigenous Jewish material is not at all certain, given the present fragmentary state of knowledge concerning the folktales of the Jews in Arabic lands.

It does seem evident, however, that there was a penetration of Arabic concepts into Jewish material. Scholem reports that in the *Tzefune Tzioni* of Rabbi Mena-hem Tzioni who lived in Cologne in the fourteenth century there is a catalogue of the rulers of the demons drawn from Arabic sources, among whom is noted 'Balkis the Queen for whom Solomon sent and who came in the twinkling of an eye'. Her identification with Lilith, however, is not found in this source, one that had considerable influence on practical (i.e. magical) cabbala in Germany. Another strange appearance is, according to Scholem, found in a unique manu-script, the *Magen David* of Rabbi David Messer Leon (beginning of the sixteenth century). Here there is a reference to two similar demons, Queen Shebiliya' and Ogret daughter of Mahlat. The former, he writes, is a singular occurrence. The latter is most frequently coupled with Lilith in cabbalistic writings. Perhaps Sebiliya' is a fusion of Sheba and Lilith by Rabbi David or his source.

However she arrived, the Queen of Sheba is a standard personage in German Jewish folklore and in the books on magical healing of that community. Grunwald quotes a story found in *Maase nissim*, entitled 'Maase von der malke Schebho' in den haus zu der sonnen, fruher zu der teufelskopf'—'A story of the queen Sheba in the house "At the sign of the sun" formerly "At the sign of the devil's head"'. It recounts the tale of a handsome but poor man in the city of Worms to whom there came one day a woman more beautiful than any he had ever seen. Her golden hair was so long that it had to be carried in a golden bowl by two noble maidens. This was Queen Sheba (*not* the Queen of Sheba) who promised him gold and silver if he would meet her each day at that very spot at the stroke of twelve. He was to tell no one of his secret lest he pay for his indiscretion with his life. His wife, despite the gifts he showered upon her, plagued him to reveal the source of his wealth, but he disclosed nothing. Observing that each day at noon he withdrew to take his nap, she followed him and discovered him together with the queen. When the latter became aware that her secret was discovered, she threatened him. He insisted that he had revealed nothing so she spared his life but took from him all his wealth and warned him that she would strangle his two children. Three days later as he crossed the Rhine bridge he saw a bier floating below. On pulling it to the bank, he found the corpses of his children inside.

Scholem, commenting on the story, notes that the version published by Grunwald blurs any mention of sexual relations between the queen and her 'victim'. He suggests as well that the description of the queen's hair may well be reminiscent of the Lilith legends, although he concedes that such a characteristic is found among the legends of many nations. He does not, however, relate it to the Rhine legend of Lorelei with her golden hair, that, given the locality, naturally comes to mind, nor to the Venus of the Venusberg. The death by strangulation of the two children does, of course, point towards Lilith as the demon who brings diphtheria. Thus, it would seem, we have several motifs, some of Jewish and others of German origin, united in this story. Sulzbach in the notes to his translation of *Targum Sheni* suggests the equation of the queen (although he makes no mention of this story) with Luna Lucifera 'who as Venus or Astarte leads men on their demonic night-rides', and offers the somewhat extravagant conjecture that the talmudic passage discussed above that seems to say 'the Queen of Sheba is not a woman' really has reference to her non-human nature and that indeed the text of the *Targum* to Job originally referred to *malkat shamayim*, the Queen of Heaven mentioned in Jeremiah 7:18, and cited in an abbreviation that was incorrectly resolved. While this is far-fetched, none the less it underscores the validity of relating the demonic motif to the queen.

Grunwald quotes a formula for summoning the queen from a collection of German-Jewish charms:

Will man die Königin von Saba sehen, so besorge man ½ lot gold (?) in der apothek; ferner ein wenig Weinessig und ein wenig Rotwein und knete alles zusammen. Als dann šmir es im un' sag: Du, Königin von Saba, komme in . . . in ½ Stunde, ohne Schaden oder irgend einen Verlust zuzufügen. Ich beschwore euch, dich und Malki'el, im Namen Taftefil. Amen. Selah.

('If one wishes to see the Queen of Sheba, let him procure ½ lot of gold(?) from the apothecary; also a little wine vinegar and a little red wine; let him knead these together, smear himself with it and say "You, Queen of Sheba, enter in . . . in half an hour, without inflicting harm or injury. I conjure you, you and Malki'el, in the name Taftefil. Amen. Selah".') It is followed by the notation: 'Tested and proved'!

Scholem quotes a much more elaborate conjuration from a confused and abridged eighteenth-century manuscript now in the Jewish National Library in Jerusalem. The main outline of the procedure provides for a table at which twelve men are seated, corresponding to the twelve guests at the queen's table. In addition a young boy with a pitcher of wine and a glass is placed at the right of the 'queen's chair' in the place of her cupbearer; to the left, her 'chief baker' with two loaves in his hand; behind the chair, the 'chief cook' and at his side a young girl. The name of each of the guests is mentioned and finally the queen herself is called. The conclusion of the text is, as Scholem indicates, fragmentary and so corrupt as not to be understood. However, it seems evident that such conjurations were indulged in during the seventeenth century.

The apostate Friedrich Brenz in his polemic *Jüdischer abgestreiffter Schlangebalg* reports in 1614 that some German Jews summoned by sorcery 'a woman splendidly clothed whom they called the Queen of Sheba' who came with her companions, and they 'danced and frolicked and then came to them'. The behaviour of the demons corresponds to that described in the *Targum Sheni*, where they dance before Solomon. The conclusion seems to be a veiled reference to sexual activity—a motif that belongs to the tradition of Lilith as a succubus. Although Rabbi Zalman Zebi Aufhausen, the apologist who responded to Brenz in his *Der Jüdische Theriak* (1615), wrote: 'Ich es nicht kann. Hab's auch nicht gesehen', he admitted that there were those who indulged in such practices which he unhesitatingly called witchcraft. There are other reports about such practices, all of which suggest either sexual fantasies or are 'cover stories' for activities condemned by the religious authorities of the community.

In all of these we see the latest traces of the ancient motif that the Queen of Sheba, either as propounder of riddles or as hairy or goat-footed, is in some way a threatening figure who seeks to harm in one way or another and has, as mother of Nebuchadnezzar, been an unending source of sorrow for the people of Israel.

IV

The Queen of Sheba in Islamic Tradition

W. Montgomery Watt

IT is generally agreed that there was considerable Jewish influence in Arabia at the beginning of the seventh century AD, when the Islamic religion was founded. Not merely are there many stories in the Qur'an about personages from the Old Testament, but they are told in an allusive fashion which suggests that the first hearers of the Qur'an were already to some extent familiar with the tales. It is also noteworthy that in many cases the form of the story is not exactly that of the Old Testament, but resembles more closely what is found in the elaborations of the biblical stories current among the Jews and known to us as apocryphal works on Old Testament themes and as rabbinic haggadot. This last point makes it all the more likely that knowledge of these stories had reached Mecca by oral channels and was then incorporated into the Qur'an. It is just conceivable that someone in Mecca learned to read books in Syriac and had read a Syriac translation of the Old Testament (it is almost certain that there was no Arabic translation in existence at this time); but the extra-canonical forms of the stories would not have spread in this way. They could only have been passed to Arabs by word of mouth. It thus becomes important to consider in what places there were possibilities of contact between Jews and Arabs.

Traders from pre-Islamic Mecca went by caravan to points in the Byzantine and Persian empires, and in the course of their travels they could have met and conversed with Jews. One thinks, for example, of the Jews who had been settled in Iraq for many centuries. On the whole, however, it is unlikely that much Jewish oral tradition was dispersed to Mecca in this way. It is also unlikely that any Christian monks and scholars with whom the traders came into contact would have communicated the rabbinic form of the stories. It is virtually certain, then, that it was from groups of Jews resident in Arabia that the Arabs gained their knowledge of the stories. Who were these groups of Jews?

One place where there was a number of Jews was the Yemen, for in the early sixth century we hear of a Jewish king there called Dhu-Nuwas. This may be a title meaning 'Lord of Nuwas', a place, for it seems to have been applied to more than one person. The most important of these had as personal names Yusuf (or Joseph) Ash'ar. It is not clear whether he had a Jewish mother and was brought up as a Jew or whether he was converted to Judaism later in his life. His existence is vouched for by inscriptions; but, while these solve some problems, they lead on to others. Thus, while Arab-Islamic tradition speaks of a reign of thirty-eight years, most of the inscriptions are concerned with events from 523 to 525. Dhu-Nuwas was responsible for a great persecution of Christians which led to the establishment of Ethiopian rule over the Yemen in 525 and the end of his own reign. This Jewish kingdom seems to have been too short-lived to have had much cultural influence, but it gives additional grounds for supposing that there were other Jewish communities in the Yemen at this period. These might have had some influence on the Arabs to the north, especially in view of the contacts between the civilization of South Arabia and the nomadic Arabs.

Whether there were Jews in Mecca itself in any numbers is not clear. There was no Jewish settlement there, but from time to time, perhaps sometimes for fairly long periods, there may well have been foreign Jewish traders. These would be attached to Meccan individuals or clans as 'protected neighbours', and there would be opportunities for friendly conversation.

The main channel, however, through which Jewish stories reached the Arabs was almost certainly the Jewish settlements in various oases of the Hejaz (the western region of Arabia; capital Mecca), notably Medina (the chief religious centre), Khaybar, Wadi-l-Qura, Fadak and Taima. These Jewish communities were probably descended from refugees who had fled Palestine after the quelling of the Jewish revolts by the Romans in AD 70 and 135. They spoke Arabic and, except in respect of religion, had become thoroughly Arabized. It has been suggested that their numbers had grown through the adoption of Judaism by Arab groups, but this is not certain. It is known, however, that they intermarried with Arabs. One of the poets who attacked Muhammad after his victory at Badr in 624 was reckoned a Jew because his mother belonged to one of the Jewish clans of Medina, although his father was from a nomadic Arab tribe. There is no way of knowing exactly the standard of religious practice among these Jewish communities, but there were undoubtedly a few 'scholars' among them, and these may have possessed copies of the Hebrew Bible and been able to read it. They could also have been transmitters of other Jewish religious lore.

Of these Jewish communities, that in Medina is best known to us. It was divided into three clans and several other smaller groups, the clans sometimes being on different sides in the quarrels which split the oasis. Two of the main clans were agriculturists, whereas the other consisted of goldsmiths and armourers and engaged, at least to a slight extent, in trade. Throughout Arabia the Jews appear to have been agricultural pioneers. In Medina they had the best lands, and the pre-Jewish Arab settlers were in a position of subordination to them. The main Arab clans of Medina, however, had arrived after the Jews and, when Muhammad migrated there in 622, were the dominant partners in a complex series of alliances.

The presence of these Jews in Medina contributed to the preparation of the Arabs of Medina for the acceptance of Muhammad as prophet, by familiarizing them with such conceptions as prophethood and revelation and perhaps also with the idea of a Messiah. Finally it must be emphasized that, though the Jewish communities in Medina and elsewhere were largely Arabized, the view adopted here implies that there was still widespread among them a knowledge of canonical and extra-canonical Jewish stories.

Though most of the Jewish material first appears in Arabic in the Qur'an, some of it was certainly known to the Arabs before Muhammad, as may be seen from fragments of pre-Islamic poetry. Western scholars at the turn of the century were inclined to question the authenticity of this poetry, since it was not written down until at least a century after Muhammad, but most of it, it is now generally agreed, is genuinely pre-Islamic and can be used as evidence for pre-Islamic times.

In this poetry, then, though no reference to the Queen of Sheba has been found, there is a number of references to David and Solomon. David, curiously enough, since there is no trace of this in the Jewish material, appears as the inventor and maker of armour. One verse, speaking of the transience of all earthly things, says that even David despite his power (i.e. his armour) was destroyed by the passing of time. It has been suggested that perhaps at some later period there was an armourer called David, and that he came to be confused with the famous king. There can be no certainty about this suggestion; but, even if it is true, it would still show some knowledge of David as a great king, and this would ultimately derive from Hebrew tradition.

Solomon also appears as a maker of armour, but he is much more besides. He is a great king with a kingdom which seems to be universal. Not only are men subject to him but also the djinn (or genies) and the winds. Nine angels are said to stand before him ready to perform his commands. He has further a reputation as a builder, in particular of the castle of al-Ablaq near Taima, the home of the supposedly Jewish poet as-Samaw'al ibn-'Adiya'. Of as-Samaw'al's father the poet al-A'sha wrote: 'Neither was 'Adiya' preserved from death by his possessions and the unique castle of Ablaq in Jewish Taima, which Solomon son of David had built in time past, which had a high pillared hall . . .' It is interesting that Solomon should thus be connected with Arabia, even though Taima is considerably to the north of Medina.

These references in the poets show that certain Old Testament personages were known to the Arabs before Islam, and that this knowledge was widespread. It is to be attributed primarily to the presence of Jewish communities in Arabia, but Christians may also have contributed to the diffusion of the material.

South Arabian Influences

The great civilization of South Arabia, as it has been revealed by archaeology, was little known to the Arabs of Muhammad's time. Travellers had been impressed by some of the architectural remains; and certain Arab tribes retained the memory of a time when their ancestors had been settled in the south and then, because of some worsening of conditions, had moved away and taken to a nomadic life. This adoption of nomadism is traditionally connected with 'the breaking of the dam of Marib'. Inscriptions have been found which speak of a bursting and restoration of the dam about AD 450 and again about 542. Popular imagination seems to have seized upon the bursting of the dam as a symbol of the breakdown of the old civilization, though the process of breakdown was apparently a slow one and was due to various economic and political factors. It seems probable that the bursting of the dam was not an accidental event or series of events which caused the failure of the civilization, but rather a result of the declining vitality of the civilization, due to economic and other causes, which made it impossible to keep the irrigation system in a proper state of repair.

The former prosperity of South Arabia and its decline are briefly referred to in the Qur'an (34:15–19):

A sign there was to Sheba in their dwellings,
two gardens on right and left—
'Eat of the provision of your Lord and thank him—
a goodly land, a forgiving Lord.'
They turned away, and we sent on them the torrent of the dam;
in place of their two gardens we gave them
two with bitter fruit, tamarisk, lote-trees a few.
That was our recompensing them for ingratitude;
do we punish any save the ungrateful?
Between them and the towns we blessed we set towns manifest,
and allotted among them [stages of] the journey;
'Journey night and day, secure.'
They said, 'Our Lord, lengthen our travels.'
They wronged themselves, and we made them legends
and tore them in little pieces.
Signs in that for the patient and grateful!

Some of the phrases in this passage are obscure, but the general sense is clear. The people of Sheba had once enjoyed great prosperity. Horticulture and agriculture had flourished, and they had a profitable trade with 'the towns we blessed', that is, probably those of Syria and Palestine. They were not grateful for the prosperity, however, but tried to become even wealthier. The phrase translated 'lengthen our travels' is sometimes taken to mean 'set a greater distance between halts for

33, 34. The Queen of Sheba (left) and King Solomon (right), from a Persian version of the Sindbadnama, c. 1375 (India Office Library)

35. Solomon with
animals and djinns,
and Sheba sur-
rounded by angels,
page from the col-
lected works of
Sa'di, Shiraz style,
1566 (British Lib-
rary Board)

36. Page from the Subdat al Tawarikh, a manuscript by Luqman-i Ashuri (Chester Beatty Library, Dublin)

37. The Queen of Sheba visiting Solomon. From *Majalis al-ushshaq*, a sixteenth-century Persian collection of anecdotes, Shiraz style (British Library Board)

38. The Queen of Sheba with the hoopoe. Persian manuscript, Qazvin style, *c.* 1590 (British Museum)

water'. This is far from convincing, but it is difficult to suggest anything better. Whatever the precise interpretation of the phrase, it implies that the men of Sheba were dissatisfied with conditions which were really satisfactory, that they embarked on an ambitious scheme to extend their trade, and that in so doing they somehow overreached themselves and ended in disaster. The disaster is described as 'the torrent of the dam', where 'torrent' is mostly used of the flood of water and debris which rushes down a dry wadi after heavy rain. Perhaps heavy rain led to the bursting of the dam, but it is more likely that the word 'torrent' was applied to the rush of water after the dam gave way. The words rendered 'tore them in little pieces' (literally, 'rent them a full rending') may describe the disruption of the community of Sheba and the adoption of nomadic life by small scattered bands. Many of the Arab tribes of Muhammad's day had a tradition that they had lived in South Arabia before taking to the desert when the old civilization declined.

The factual material underlying this passage is presumably part of the common stock of memories held by the Meccans. The facts, however, have been used to illustrate a common moral lesson of the Qur'an, namely, the destruction of sinners as a punishment from God. Among those punished for their sins the Qur'an also mentions twice (44:37; 50:13), but without any detail, the people of Tubba'; and, since Tubba' is the name given to the Himyarite kings of South Arabia, this may also refer to the men of Sheba. In all this the Qur'an is not presenting new facts, but is using known facts to point a moral.

Besides actual memories of South Arabia found in the Arabia of Muhammad's time, modern scholars have thought they could detect specific features which were due to the influence of the civilization of the south. In view of the great achievements of South Arabian civilization it would be surprising if it had not affected the rest of Arabia in many ways; but in the case of any particular feature it is difficult to prove that it could have come from nowhere but the Yemen. The clearest examples are linguistic. Thus it is now mostly agreed that the name of God, 'the Merciful', *ar-Rahman*, came from South Arabia, though there are obscurities about its earlier history. Similarly the word *sarh*, which occurs in the Qur'anic passage about the Queen of Sheba, seems to come into Arabic from South Arabian, since in the inscriptions (where only consonants are written) the form *srht* occurs, meaning 'high building'. It is generally held that this in turn comes from the Ethiopic *serehe*, meaning 'room, temple, palace', but with the connotation of high and conspicuous. A somewhat similar Aramaic word is occasionally used of a 'fortified place', but mostly has a quite different meaning and is unlikely to be the source of the Arabic word. The high buildings which are still a feature of south-west Arabia have a long history, and it is appropriate that they should be described in Arabic by a word derived from South Arabian.

The Queen of Sheba in the Qur'an

The Queen of Sheba enters Arabic literature and Islamic culture through a passage of the Qur'an which will be quoted presently. The nature of the Qur'an, however, has often been misunderstood by occidental writers, and the character of Muhammad's achievement distorted; a brief explanation is therefore relevant at this point.

Muhammad was born about the year 570 AD in Mecca, a commercial centre, which had recently come to control most of the trade between the Indian Ocean and the Mediterranean. Commercial prosperity had led to social tensions, and Muhammad, as he meditated on these, had two visions which convinced him that he was called to be a prophet or messenger from God to his people. On the basis of messages or 'revelations' of which he somehow became conscious (and which were later collected and written down to form the Qur'an, as we have it) he called on his fellow Meccans to believe in the power and goodness of God, to worship him and, among other things, to act responsibly with their wealth. Many accepted this new religion, but opposition also grew, and in 622 Muhammad and about seventy followers made the Hegira or migration from Mecca to Medina, where most of the inhabitants had professed themselves Muslims (followers of the new religion of Islam). Muhammad and his Meccan followers were regarded as one clan in a federation of nine Arab clans, and thus he had little power initially. Nevertheless through the spread of the religion among the Arabs and by his own gifts as a statesman Muhammad, by the time of his death in 632, had created a political unit embracing something like half of Arabia.

After the death of Muhammad his political unit expanded at a phenomenal rate to become an empire stretching from the Pyrenees and the Atlantic to Central Asia and north-west India. In the present context two points are to be emphasized. The first is that the expansion beyond Arabia was primarily a political expansion, and that the conquered peoples were not in any way compelled to become Muslims. Religious expansion was secondary and gradual, due partly to the inherent attractiveness of Islam as a religion and partly to the fact that non-Muslims, being 'second-class citizens' in an Islamic state, felt a kind of social pressure to conform. Muslims, whatever their origin, came to have a strong sense of brotherhood, and the social and institutional fabric of the Islamic community was such that it continued to flourish after the break-up of the empire (there are now some 500 million Muslims in the world). The second and more important point is that in association with Islam there developed a culture which came to incorporate all the wisdom and experience of Middle Eastern man as stored up from the great civilizations of the past—from the Sumerians and the Egyptians, the Greeks and the Persians, the Jews and the Christians. Medieval Muslim scholars were less conscious of history than modern occidentals, at least to the extent that they had no concept of development, and no interest in tracing ideas or practices back to their origins where these were extraneous. Most of the features of Islamic culture were therefore regarded as indigenous. The treatment of the story of the Queen of Sheba is a good example of this process of cultural assimilation.

The occidental misunderstanding of the nature of the Qur'an lies in regarding it as the product of Muhammad's conscious mind. Such a view does violence to the most reliable sources, and is linked up with the distorted image of Muhammad as a scheming impostor, which was part of the Christian war propaganda of the Crusading period and has not yet entirely disappeared. Historical scholarship demands that we should regard Muhammad as a religious leader of complete integrity who sincerely believed that he could distinguish between his own thinking and the messages or 'revelations' which came to him from beyond himself. The standard Muslim view is that the revelations were messages from God—indeed, God's own speech—conveyed from God to Muhammad by the angel Gabriel and intended for transmission to his followers. This is usually interpreted to mean that the Qur'an may truly record historical facts for which there is no normal historical evidence; but this interpretation does not seem to be an essential of the standard Muslim view. The Qur'an speaks of itself as 'an Arabic Qur'an'—the word itself means 'recitation'—and this implies that it is not merely in the Arabic language but is also adapted to the thought-forms of the Arabs and their level of factual information. The stories in the Qur'an seem to presuppose that the hearers already have some acquaintance with the details; and pre-Islamic poetry confirms that in many cases this must have been so. The originality of the Qur'an thus consists in the religious lesson of which the stories are the vehicle.

A non-Muslim occidental scholar could not accept the Muslim view as it stands. He would be inclined to say that the Qur'an must have emerged somehow from Muhammad's unconscious, or even from the collective unconscious functioning through Muhammad. Such a view makes it possible to maintain that Muhammad was sincere in asserting that the Qur'an came from beyond himself, that is, from beyond his conscious mind, and also to maintain that the Qur'an shows Jewish, Christian and other extraneous influences; these influences operated through the factual material already present in the mind of Muhammad and his contemporaries before the emergence of the unconscious contents with their fresh and original religious lesson. This occidental view, moreover, implies neither the truth nor falsity of the Qur'an, but leaves open the question of truth and validity, to be settled by other criteria. The relation of this occidental view to the standard Muslim view is ultimately a matter for theology and must be left aside in the present study.

When what has just been said is applied to the passage about Solomon and the Queen of Sheba, it will be seen that we may expect to find in it both factual material and an original religious message. The factual material consists in the stories and legends which had reached Mecca by oral channels. For the religious lesson, on the other hand, no immediate sources are to be sought, though there may be parallels with other parts of the Qur'an and with biblical teaching. Indeed the religious lesson is not something which can be precisely formulated, for a passage of scripture, whether Bible or Qur'an, has many different layers or depths of meaning.

The whole passage (27:15–44) may be rendered as follows:

15 To David and Solomon we gave knowledge;
   they said, 'Praise is God's
   who has preferred us over many of his servants, the believers.

16 Solomon was heir to David;
   he said, 'O people, we have been taught the speech of birds;
   and we have been given [something] of everything;
   this is indeed preference clear.'

17 There were gathered to Solomon his hosts,
   of djinn, men and birds marshalled in order.

18 At length they came to the valley of the ants.
   An ant said, 'O ants, go into your dwellings;
   then Solomon and his hosts unawares will not crush you.'

19 [Solomon] smiled, amused at her speech;
   he said, 'O Lord, marshal me so that I may be thankful
   for the favour you have shown to me and to my parents,
   and so that I may act uprightly, as you approve;
   and by your mercy set me among your upright servants.'

20 He reviewed the birds, and said,
   'Why do I not see the hoopoe? [Has he some extenuating
   reason] or is he one of the absentees?

21 I will punish him severely or kill him;
   or else he will bring me clear authority [for his absence].'

22 [The hoopoe] remained a little longer [before appearing]
   and said, 'I have comprehended what you have not comprehended;
   I have brought you a sure message from Sheba.'

23 I found a woman ruling them
   who had been given [something] of everything,
   and who had a great throne.

24 I found her and her people
   worshipping the sun instead of God.
   The Devil had made their works seem fair to them,
   and had barred the way to them,
   so that they are not proceeding aright—

25 that they are not worshipping God
   who brings out the hidden [things] in the heavens and the earth
   and knows what you conceal and what you publish.

26 God, there is no god save him,
   the Lord of the Great Throne.'

27 [Solomon] said, 'We shall in time see
   whether you have spoken truly or are one of the liars.

28 Take this writing of mine and deliver it to them;
   then withdraw, and see what they return [as answer].'

29 [The queen] said, 'O peers,
   there has been delivered to me a noble writing.

30 It is from Solomon; it runs,
   "In the name of God, the Merciful, the Compassionate;

31 do not act proudly against me,
   but come to me in humble submission [? to God]".'

32 She said, 'O peers, advise me in my affair;
   I do not decide an affair until you are present with me.'

33 They said, 'We have strength, we have fierce spirit,
   but it is for you to command;
   consider what you will command.'

34 She said, 'Kings, when they enter a town, destroy it,
   and make its highest people the most abject;
   thus will they do [with us].

35 I will send him a gift and will see
   with what [answer] the messengers return.'

36 When [the messenger] came to Solomon, [the latter] said:
   'Will you [further] enrich me with goods?
   What God has given me is better than what he has given you.
   It is you [not I] who have joy in your gift.

37 Return to them; and we shall certainly come at them
   with hosts against which they have no resource,
   and we shall certainly drive them out from [their town]
   in abjection and defeat.'

38 [Solomon] said, 'O peers, which of you will bring me her throne
   before they come to me in humble submission [to God]?'

39 An efreet of the djinn said,
   'I will bring it to you before you rise from your place;
   I have strength for that and am trustworthy.'

40 The one with knowledge of the writing said,
   'I will bring it to you in less than the twinkling of an eye.'
   When [Solomon] saw the throne resting beside him, he said,
   'This is of God's bounty to test me,
   whether I am grateful or ungrateful;
   he who is grateful is grateful for his own [advantage];
   he who is ungrateful [does not affect God]—
   my Lord is rich and noble [needing neither recognition nor thanks].'

41 He said, 'Disguise her throne for her, and we shall see
   whether she proceeds rightly
   or is one who does not proceed rightly.'

42 When she came, one said, 'Is this your throne?'
   She said, 'It is like it.'
   We have been given knowledge before her
   and we were in humble submission [to God].

43 What she worshipped apart from God
   had barred [the way] to her;
   she was of an unbelieving people.
44 One said to her, 'Enter the palace.'
   She thought it a pool and uncovered her legs.
   [Solomon] said, 'It is a palace paved with glass.'
   She said, 'I have wronged myself;
   to God, the Lord of the worlds, with Solomon I make submission.'

There is much in this account which is mysterious. Even when allowance is made for the abruptness of Qur'anic style, where much is left unstated (as in the transition from Solomon's command about the letter in 27, 28 to the queen's reaction in 29), yet several points are obscure. Thus verses 39 and 40 appear to give parallel accounts, and it is not stated by whom 43 and the latter part of 42 are spoken, whether by Solomon, or the queen's followers, or some other persons. Other matters—motivations, for example—are only hinted at. Nevertheless the general point of the story is clear. It is the summoning of sun-worshippers to a belief in the true God and their eventual positive response to the summons. In this the Qur'an is markedly different from the very similar story in the *Targum Sheni* where the queen is required to come and do homage to Solomon in order to enhance his glory.

In the Qur'an Solomon is regarded not merely as a great and wealthy king, with power over birds, beasts and djinn and with knowledge of their speech, but also as a prophet of God. Like all prophets he summons men to believe in God, the only divine being, and to submit themselves to him as his servants and worshippers. This submission to God is 'Islam', and in the Qur'an the great biblical figures such as Noah, Abraham, Moses and Jesus, are spoken of as prophets and Muslims, that is, men who have submitted themselves or surrendered to God. In verses 31, 38 and 42 the words 'in humble submission' are used to render the participial form *muslimin*, 'submitting'. In verse 31 the word could conceivably mean 'in submission to me, Solomon', and this would be in accordance with the Aramaic form of the story; but it is more likely that the correct interpretation is submission to God, as is certainly to be understood in the other verses, while in verse 44 (where the indicative of the verb is used) God is explicitly mentioned. (The word *islam* is simply the corresponding verbal noun.)

It may also be noted that there is a parallel between the wealth of Solomon and that of the queen, since the same phrase is used of both (verses 16, 23). This points the contrast between Solomon's gratitude to God for all his favours, together with his acknowledgement of him as God, and the queen's failure to acknowledge God. When Solomon threatens the queen with war, she tries to buy him off with her wealth, but this is of no avail since he is wealthier than she is. The incident of the throne is perhaps intended to show the queen that Solomon equalled her even in respect of this, her most cherished possession. No motive is stated for the queen's visit to Solomon; she may have intended either to submit or to try to persuade him to relent. In either case she is completely convinced by the sight of the throne and by the wonderful floor and decides to become a Muslim.

The Literary Elaboration of the Story

As will be seen from the passage about the Queen of Sheba, there is much in the Qur'an which is not immediately comprehensibile. Other stories are told more fully, notably that of Joseph in *sura* 12; but even in this last there is some brevity and abruptness, and some things are told allusively instead of in straightforward narrative. It is therefore not surprising that during the first century of Islam there appeared a class of men who retold the Qur'anic stories at much greater length. The details might be filled out from the Bible or from Jewish and Christian extra-canonical works or from Arab legends or even from the story-teller's imagination. A wide public accepted such tales gladly. The more exuberant flights of imagination were pruned away by later Muslim scholars, but much had become part of the intellectual world of Islam and was generally accepted. There are countless brief allusions to this material in literary works; much of it is repeated in the commentaries on the Qur'an; and it has been collected and systematically arranged in two books which have survived, both known as *Stories of the Prophets*, and written in the first half of the eleventh century by al-Kisa'i and ath-Tha'labi respectively. There are also less important works of the same kind. The following paragraphs give some idea of the way in which the story of the Queen of Sheba was elaborated.

The relevant part of the story of Solomon commences with a visit by him to Mecca. Although there is nothing in the Bible to suggest such a visit, it is not surprising to find it spoken of in an Islamic context. It is well known that the Qur'an (2:125–8) associates Abraham with Mecca and gives him an important part in building the Ka'ba and instituting the practice of making circumambulations round it. (The Ka'ba is a small cube-shaped building in the centre of the Haram or sanctuary area of Mecca. Built into one corner is the Black Stone, perhaps regarded as a seat of divinity in pre-Islamic times; but any such suggestion was removed by Islam, and the pious Muslim circumambulates the Ka'ba and kisses the Black Stone merely because these actions are prescribed in the revealed law of Islam.) Solomon as a good Muslim (according to Islamic ideas) was presumably thought of as taking part in these activities. With him at Mecca Solomon had an army consisting of men, djinn, demons, birds and beasts. The djinn (singular *djinni*, 'genie'), familiar to us as the 'genies' of the *Thousand and One Nights*, are spirits with superhuman powers which may be either good or bad; the Qur'an recounts (72:1–19) how some djinn heard Muhammad preaching and became Muslims. A demon (Arabic *shaytan*, 'Satan') is malevolent and leads men astray by 'whispering' in their hearts.

At Mecca Solomon had the idea of going to the Yemen, and set out with this vast cavalcade. The journey would normally have taken a month, but by the aid of the winds which he commanded he and his army accomplished it in the time between the rising and setting of Canopus. When Solomon wanted water for his ablutions before prayer and for his evening meal, it was discovered that the hoopoe had disappeared, an absence of considerable consequence, for the hoopoe had the faculty of 'seeing' water under the ground and showing Solomon where to dig for it. Meanwhile Solomon's hoopoe, which was called Ya'fur, had seen the garden of the Queen of Sheba and in it the hoopoe of the Yemen called 'Afir; and the latter had persuaded Ya'fur to go with him on a tour of the queen's domains. From this tour Ya'fur returned to Solomon with much information about the queen. In true Arab fashion there was much about her genealogy, but the chief point was perhaps that her mother was a female genie, or, as another informant put it, one of her male ancestors was a genie.

Then there was an alarming story about how she came to rule the people of Sheba. Her father had been king and she was his only child, but, when he died, only some of the people supported her, whereas many supported a male claimant to the throne. At this point ath-Tha'labi cannot resist inserting a remark ascribed to Muhammad on being asked about the queen of Sheba: 'No people prospers which entrusts its affairs to a woman'. This saying is not found in the collections of 'sound' anecdotes about Muhammad and is not really in accordance with the Qur'an, so that it rather reflects the tendency to male dominance in Islamic thought and practice. The rival claimant gained power, but he acted harshly and pursued the wives of his subjects. They would have liked to depose him, but were unable to do so. The princess realized that here was a situation which she could turn to her advantage. She gave a hint to the usurper that she was prepared to marry him. He then approached her male relatives with a proposal of marriage. They expressed the view that she would refuse, but he made them take the proposal to her. To their surprise she accepted, saying that she wanted to have a child. Then on the wedding night she made the usurper drunk and cut off his head; and on the following day the whole people acknowledged her as queen.

The report of the hoopoe also contained an account of the castle or palace she had built for herself near the town of San'a' and of her surpassingly beautiful throne. He also said that it was she who had instituted the worship of the sun, following an interpretation she placed on some words of her ministers.

Solomon had been furious when the absence of the hoopoe was discovered and threatened to 'punish him severely or kill him'. The early story-tellers seem to have allowed their imaginations rein in describing the details of the punishment intended. Solomon was mollified, however, by the hoopoe's bearing and the character of his report, though he was not altogether convinced of its truth. His letter to the queen thus became in part a test of the credibility of the hoopoe. When the hoopoe, bearing the letter, reached the queen at Marib, three days' journey from San'a', she had locked the doors of her palace and placed the keys under her pillow. There are various accounts of what happened next. The most colourful is that there was a small window in the queen's chamber through which the sun shone as it rose, at which the queen got up and worshipped. This window the hoopoe covered with its wings so that the queen missed the sunrise. When she later sprang up in dismay on seeing the sunshine, the hoopoe flung the letter in her face.

Some interesting facts from Islamic East Africa seem to be evidence for the great influence of Qur'anic stories such as this. In that region a more romantic version of the story is popular, according to which the hoopoe gave Solomon such a rapturous account of the queen's personal beauty that he at once wanted to marry her. Now in East Africa it is common practice when one visits a house, instead of knocking, to stand at an open door or window and say *hodi*, which the dictionaries say means 'may I come in?'. A leading authority on Swahili culture, however, maintains that the proper phrase is *hodi-hodi*, and that this is derived from *hudhud*, the Arabic name of the hoopoe. In effect, then, one is saying, 'I want to come in, but I do not want to intrude like the *hudhud*.'

The queen next calls her council, and an exaggerated account is given of this. It is said to have consisted of 12,000 lords or earls—the South Arabian term *qayl* is used—each of whom had 100,000 fighting men. There is the interesting Islamic touch that the queen addressed them from behind a veil. Perhaps it was felt that for a queen to show her face even to noblemen was undignified as well as immodest. There is another Islamic touch in the statement that she decides to send a present to Solomon to discover whether he is a king or a prophet, taking the view that, if he is a king, he will accept the present, whereas, if he is a prophet, he will not. The underlying thought is perhaps that it is open to a king to compromise, since he is considering his own interests, whereas a prophet is following the commands of God and has no scope for bargaining. Certainly Muhammad's own practice had been to accept no presents from non-Muslims.

A discussion of the nature of the presents sent gave great opportunities to the story-tellers. Sometimes there was a puzzling character about them to test Solomon's wisdom; sometimes they were an indication of the great wealth of the queen. In the first category came a present of pages and maidens all dressed alike; reports of the number of each sex varied from ten to five hundred (cf. Chapter III, p. 70). Solomon distinguished the two sexes by asking them to wash hands and face; the girls poured water from one hand into the other, whereas the boys held the water in both hands at once. Another present was a small closed casket; Solomon was asked to guess what it contained and did so correctly. The contents posed further problems, for there was a valuable pearl with no hole bored through it, and an onyx stone with a crooked hole through it. Neither men nor djinn could advise Solomon on how to pierce the pearl and thread the onyx, but a djinni showed where to go for help. He first summoned a woodworm and it bored through the pearl, and then he summoned a maggot and it went through the onyx with a thread in its mouth. Thus Solomon demonstrated his wisdom.

In the second category of gifts, those intended to display the queen's wealth, came blocks of gold, a crown set with jewels, and quantities of musk and amber. Solomon was told beforehand of the gifts by the hoopoe, and set vast numbers of djinn to work making bricks of gold and silver. These were placed on a huge parade ground, several leagues in extent, and on them were set strange and wonderful sea-creatures. Round the whole was a high wall of gold and silver, while in the centre sat Solomon with rank upon rank of djinn, men and beasts round him. Having thus demonstrated not only his wisdom but also his superior wealth, Solomon returned the presents to the queen's envoys, with a criticism of their undue concern for worldly possessions and honour, and a threat to march against Sheba.

On the return of the envoys the queen realized that she was dealing with someone greatly superior to herself, and sent a message to say that she was coming to visit Solomon and to learn about the religion to which he summoned her. Before leaving she made her throne secure in the innermost room of one of her palaces or castles behind seven locked doors, set guards over it, and ordered her deputy to take special care of it. Two reasons are suggested for Solomon's commanding the throne to be brought to him. One is that he wanted to possess the throne, but realized that it would be unlawful for him to seize it after the queen became a Muslim. This reason is inconsistent with the criticism of worldly wealth put into Solomon's mouth, and presumably belongs to a different version. The other reason is that Solomon wanted to demonstrate the extent of God's power. Neither of these reasons, of course, is necessarily the interpretation given to the passage by the first Muslims; the first is materialistic, while the second seems to presuppose later theological developments.

The difficulty of the apparently parallel character of verses 39 and 40 of the Qur'anic version is interpreted by supposing that after the offer of the efreet Solomon said that this, namely, 'before you rise from your place', was not fast enough. 'The one with knowledge of the writing' is sometimes said to be an angel, but more commonly it is taken to be Solomon's vizier or chief minister who had knowledge of 'the greatest name of God'. When God is addressed by this name and asked to do something, he immediately fulfils the request. In this particular case he is said to have sent angels to bring the throne under the earth from Marib to Syria. (Not all versions speak of Solomon as having made the journey to Mecca and the Yemen.) The reason for the bringing of the throne is said to be that the demons were afraid that Solomon would marry the queen and that she, being partly descended from the race of the djinn, would betray their secrets to him with the result that the djinn and demons would be perpetually subservient to Solomon and his descendants. To obviate this they spread tales about her which came to Solomon's ears. In particular they said that she was somewhat weak in intellect and that her legs were like a donkey's because her mother was of the djinn. Solomon's question about the throne was to test her intellect, and her answer satisfied him that there was no defect there.

In the final scene it has been suggested that the words 'enter the palace' mean rather 'enter the court', but on the whole linguistic evidence favours the meaning 'palace' or 'castle', and one should doubtless think of the lofty buildings still characteristic of South Arabia. In entering the palace the queen presumably enters a reception hall. The story-tellers add verisimilitude to her deception by describing how there was running water with fish swimming about in it under the clear glass. When she uncovered her feet and legs, Solomon saw that they were very shapely and entirely human, but that they were rather hairy. This set his mind at rest, but he consulted the djinn and demons about depilatories. Meanwhile on entering the palace and sitting down beside him the queen had asked him a riddle: 'Where is there flowing water that is neither on earth nor in the sky?' With the aid of his superhuman counsellors he was able to answer, 'The sweat of a horse'.

After the conversion of the queen to Islam, the most usual version of the story is that Solomon married her—though not before she had used depilatories and hot baths! He then ordered the djinn to build three great palaces for her in the Yemen, and it was his custom to visit her for three days each month in one of these, commuting from Syria, as it were, with his superhuman means of transport. There is also a variant, however, according to which he married her to the Tubba' or ruler of Hamdan.

All that has been presented so far as the literary elaboration of the Qur'anic story may be regarded as the standard account in Arabic. It appears in the collections of *Stories of the Prophets* and in commentaries on the Qur'an, besides being alluded to in countless other works. Within this standard account there are variants, as has been noted at several points. There are also further elaborations, however, not only in Arabic, but even more so in Persian and Turkish, and these bring in various motifs from folklore. The historical writer al-Mas'udi (d. 956) mentions briefly the story of the birth of Bilqis (as the Queen of Sheba became known in Islamic writings). The following slightly different and much fuller account is from a later Turkish source, and is given as an example of this type of material.

Once a king of Sheba called Yeshrah (elsewhere Anishurah), as he travelled across a great plain, came upon two huge serpents or dragons, one black and the other white, locked in mortal combat (cf. Chapter III, p. 82). The white one was seriously wounded and would have been destroyed had not Yeshrah killed the black serpent with a diamond-pointed arrow. Some time later a handsome youth called on the king and said he was the white serpent, and that he belonged to the djinn. When the king declined his offers of service, the youth suggested that he should marry his sister.

The king was captivated by her beauty and in marrying her agreed not to question any of her acts, good or bad. In due course she bore him a son, but, when a dog approached her, threw the baby to him and allowed him to run off with it. Then she had a girl, but flung her into a blazing fire. A second daughter was as beautiful as the houris of Paradise, and the king asked his wife not to treat her like the others; for this she rebuked him. When the vizier sided with an enemy and poisoned the provisions for the army, the queen destroyed them, and the king angrily demanded a reason. She explained and demonstrated how a dog which ate a piece of bread died, and then told her husband that, since he had broken his agreement, their marriage was at an end. She also informed him that the two older children were alive, but that the third would succeed him and be a great queen (Bilqis). With the aid of a troop of djinn which she sent, the king put down the rebellion, and looked after his beautiful daughter until his death.

Links with the History of South Arabia

The intellectual world of a great culture is not created solely by its story-tellers, important as these are in giving memorable form to the myths which feed its imagination. There must also be scholars and scientists, theologians and philosophers; and such men Islamic culture had in abundance. In particular there were historians who presented a picture of world history and showed the place of the Islamic empire in this vast canvas. A central position was given to Old Testament history, especially in so far as this was referred to in the Qur'an. Into the biblical framework were fitted numerous details from Persian legend and history, and rather fewer from Graeco-Roman. One historian, though he has a fairly accurate list of Roman emperors, actually gives less space to the Roman empire than to the story of Joseph (which is told in some detail in the Qur'an). The Islamic historians, however, were interested in South Arabia, as being part of the Arab homeland, but they had no written documents and were unable to decipher the inscriptions. Nevertheless they assiduously collected material from oral tradition, and pieced this together as best they could. Since the Queen of Sheba was mentioned in the Qur'an she naturally received a due share of attention.

First of all the queen receives a name. Usually she is called Bilqis, but a few exact scholars mention Balqama as an alternative. Neither name occurs in the Qur'an. The derivation of Bilqis has puzzled modern scholars. The most usual view is that the name comes from the Greek *pallakis*, 'concubine', through a Hebraized form *pilegesh* or *pilgesh*. It is just conceivable that Bilqis might be a misreading of Josephus's name Nikaulis. The queen is also given a genealogy. Her father is said to have had the bye-name of al-Hadhad or al-Hadhhadh (which is reminiscent of the *hudhud* or hoopoe, but this may be accidental); but his actual name and that of his father are given in so many forms that it would be pointless to discuss them here. Bilqis is then given a place after her father in the list of kings. The difficulties of the Arab historians in reconciling all the various items are illustrated by the fact that at one point al-Mas'udi (d. 956) says that Bilqis reigned for a hundred and twenty years, and then a few pages later quotes another source which says she reigned for seven years. Solomon is then said to have reigned over the Yemen for twenty-three years, after which it reverted to a South Arabian king.

Solomon is further said to have built three great palaces for Bilqis, namely, Salhin, Ghumdan and Baynun, all in the Yemen, and to have built that of Baalbek as her dowry. The building was carried out by demons—a way of saying that later generations had lost the art of constructing such buildings. A variant is that Solomon built Salhin for Tubba', the ruler of Hamdan, when he arranged for the latter's marriage to Bilqis. The ruins of these buildings still existed in the early Islamic centuries; but in Syria and the Yemen there was also a tendency to link any antique building materials with Bilqis and Solomon. Thus two variegated columns in Damascus were said to have come from the throne of Bilqis (presumably that transported at the desire of Solomon), and similar materials in the cathedral or Qillis built by Abraha at San'a' in the sixth century were said to have been taken from the palace of Bilqis.

Certain other ruins in the Yemen are called 'the throne of Bilqis' by the geographer Yaqut (d. 1229). They included a number of columns, and may well be identical with the site near Marib still known as the Mahram or sanctuary of Bilqis, which has been visited by modern travellers and found to be the temple of a pre-Islamic moon god Ilumquh. It seems pointless to ask, as has been done, whether the queen has been divinized or whether either the moon god or some old sun goddess has been transformed into a queen. The truth is rather that once Bilqis had caught the imagination of Muslims many features of the old forgotten culture of South Arabia came to be associated with her.

The Mystical Treatment of the Story

At the heart of Islamic culture was the religion of Islam. Religious fervour was maintained throughout the centuries by the piety and devotion of countless Muslims, expecially those called the sufis or mystics; and this piety and devotion was nourished above all by meditation on the ideas and stories of the Qur'an. The earlier mystical writers often took phrases in isolation from their context. Thus, commenting on the words of the queen in verse 34, 'kings, when they enter a town, destroy it', one such writer said, 'when mystical knowledge enters the heart, it drives out all vain desires and all self-will, so that there is no room in the heart for anything but God'.

Later writers paid more attention to the story as a whole. As an example of this type of writing we may here describe the treatment of Bilqis by Jalal-ad-Din ar-Rumi (d. 1273) in his *Mathnawi*. The references are mainly found in Book IV between couplets 563 and 1112, but it is the author's practice to interrupt the story with digressions of varying degrees of relevance. His reflections on points of the story, too, merge into general reflections in such a way that it is impossible to summarize what he says. All that is attempted here is to mention the points in the story and show how he interprets each. His general position is to take Solomon as a type of the Perfect Man and Bilqis as the soul at first firmly attached to the material world and then leaving behind the material world in the search for God.

The first matter mentioned in Book IV is the gift of Bilqis to Solomon, forty mules laden with gold bricks. For the last forty stages of the journey to Solomon, however, the envoy is riding on gold and realizes that his gift is worthless to Solomon. The poet then says to his hearer: 'O thou who hast brought intelligence to God as a gift, there intelligence is less [in value] than the dust of the road' (568). Addressing the envoy Solomon says: 'I do not bid you bestow gifts on me; nay, I bid you be worthy of the gifts [which I bestow]' (574). A little later Solomon bids the envoys return with the gold, and instead to bring him the pure heart (614). He emphasizes the worthlessness of material gold and also of earthly kingdoms. When you come to God in worship, 'the [inward] savour of a single prostration before God will be more sweet to thee than two hundred empires' (665). Solomon then summons the army of Bilqis and tells them to bid her come quickly since the time is opportune (718–25). He then threatens her with the revolt of her army; that is to say, the parts of the body, such as an eye and a tooth, will rise against the soul in obedience to God and will cause aches and pains. He appeals to Bilqis to relinquish her kingdom—'when thou gainest me, all the kingdom is thine' (799).

When 'an orient light' from Solomon reaches Bilqis, there is a revival among the people of Sheba (839–44). She sets out from Sheba, gladly relinquishing her kingdom and her wealth; but she still grudges her throne, and Solomon is aware of this. He also realizes that the throne is both heavy and has much delicate filigree work, so that it is almost impossible to transport it; but he wants her to have it so that she will not feel grieved when she comes to him, and at the same time he knows that she will eventually reject it and then it will become a reminder to her of her undue attachment to material things (859–88). The throne was brought not by the malevolent efreet, but by the vizier Asaf pronouncing the greatest name of God (903–7). The Divine Mercy then summons Bilqis to join her sisters in heaven and leave her worthless possessions on earth—'Come and behold the Kingdom!

Gather pearls on the shore of God's sea!' (1041). The summons to Bilqis is repeated (1095, 1101), but it is no longer addressed to the personage in the story but to every questing soul.

It is amazing how through the centuries the figures of Solomon and Bilqis have attracted to themselves the hopes, fears and aspirations of countless ordinary men and women. The stories are not mere entertainment, but the imaginative form in which men try to express and communicate their understanding of the world in which they live. Solomon's control over the djinn and demons, for example, makes conscious man's longing to triumph over space and time; and such ideas have doubtless contributed to the motivation of the development of science and man's conquest of nature. After all, Solomon's monthly journeys from Syria to the Yemen to visit Bilqis with the aid of djinn or winds could now be accomplished by jet plane and helicopter.

It is easy to see how Solomon, who among the Jews was renowned above all for his wisdom, came to be also a magician and so, being able to control aspects of the material world, a kind of scientist. The figure of Bilqis is more complex. The hairy legs mark a connection with the underworld and the demonic. This can also be magic, and her encounter with Solomon can be seen as the encounter of two rival magics. The connection with the god or goddess Ilumquh could indicate something similar. This aspect is more important than that of being a woman and a symbol of the feminine. Romantic interpretations indeed exist, but they are less prominent than the others. Mystically it is appropriate that a woman should represent the soul, but it is her wealth not her femininity that is emphasized.

The elaborations and interpretations of the story of Bilqis and her meeting with Solomon are an interesting example of the function of what may be called 'imaginative forms' in man's intellectual life. Because the story was mentioned in the Qur'an it had *droit de cité* in Islam. It had already been developed somewhat in extra-biblical Jewish literature; and now in an Islamic context and with various specifically Islamic features it gathered to itself many themes from popular imaginative thinking.

V

The Queen of Sheba in Ethiopian Tradition

Edward Ullendorff

NOWHERE else in the world are the story of the Queen of Sheba and the Solomon–Sheba notion of kingship as important, as vital, and as pregnant with practical significance as in Ethiopia. True, the legend of Solomon and the Queen of Sheba has enjoyed a great vogue in many parts of the ancient East, but only in Ethiopia has it been woven into the very fabric of society and into the country's constitutional framework. Details of the tale may vary, especially the narrative of the king's seduction of the queen, but most of the principal post-biblical ingredients can already be found in the *Targum Sheni* to Esther or the *Alphabetum Siracidis*, the Qur'an (Sura 27:15–45), and many other sources. In fact, the main features of the story must have had a long period of gestation in Ethiopia and have possessed all the elements of a gigantic conflation of cycles of legends and tales. When it was committed to writing, early in the fourteenth century, its purpose was no doubt to lend support to the claims and aspirations of the recently established Solomonic dynasty. Its author, the *nebura ed* (i.e. prior and governor) Yeshaq of Aksum, was thus mainly redactor and interpreter of material which had long been known but had not until then found a co-ordinating hand, an expository mind, and a great national need.

Thus the Ethiopic *Kebra Nagast* ('Glory of the Kings'), with its centre-piece of the Queen of Sheba's visit to Solomon, their union, the birth of a son, and the subsequent removal of the Ark of the Covenant from Jerusalem to Aksum (followed by the transference of the Divine Presence from Israel to Ethiopia), is not merely a literary work, but—as the Old Testament to the Hebrews or the Qur'an to the Arabs—it is the repository of Ethiopian national and religious feelings, perhaps the truest and most genuinely indigenous expression of Abyssinian Christianity.

The idea of kingship, with its special Ethiopian connotation, may be encountered in a number of early sources. Conti Rossini and Caquot derive the sacral kingship in Ethiopia from the Semitic civilizations of the ancient orient, while Haberland appears to detect here an aspect of the general African 'Königskultur', though not denying the importance of its Christian and Old Testament roots.

The royal and imperial style of *negusa nagast*, 'King of Kings', in use to the present day, makes its first appearance already in the fourth-century Aksum inscriptions where it is attested in a Greek, South Arabian, and Ethiopic form. There is no

39. Abyssinian painting depicting the king and queen, from *Chronique du règne de Menelik II* by Guebre Sellassie, Paris 1930 (School of Oriental and African Studies, London)

40. The story of Solomon and Sheba. From *Ethiopia and the Bible* (photo BBC)

41. Detail of a traditional Ethiopian representation of the Sheba story. Top, left to right: Sheba sets out to visit Solomon; they meet. Bottom, left to right: Solomon seizes her; they then sleep together (picture by courtesy of Ethiopian Airlines)

valid reason to connect these royal styles with the Iranian *shahanshah* nor, in all probability, even with the Akkadian *shar sharrani*. The superlative form 'King of Kings' (Ezekiel 26:7, though here applied to the King of Babylon), 'song of songs' is, of course, known in the Old Testament. And in Rabbinic literature we even encounter *melekh malkhe hammelakhim*, 'King of the Kings of the Kings'.

The medieval Amharic royal songs also exhibit modes of address and forms of veneration peculiar to Ethiopian kingship. Any future edition and translation of this important source of early Amharic will need to pay attention to these aspects as well. In these songs the emperor is likened to the lion, an image as old as Genesis 49:9 where the lion of Judah makes its first appearance. And verse 5 in Chapter 5 of Revelation has attained great prominence in Ethiopia: 'Weep not: behold, the Lion of the tribe of Judah, the Root of David, hath prevailed to open the book and to loose the seven seals thereof.' The application of the phrase 'the Lion of the tribe of Judah hath prevailed' to the royal house of Ethiopia, as part of the imperial styles, is of no great antiquity, but at the present time it is firmly established in constitutional usage.

While the lion is probably derived from Ethiopia's Semitic past, there is another animal, though of much less importance, which affirms the Abyssinian connection with its African setting, i.e. the elephant. *Janhoy* signifies 'majesty' and is probably composed of the exclamatory particle *hoy* and the Cushitic *jan* (= Amh. *zohon*) 'elephant'. *Jan* is likely to be the element from which 'Prester John' is derived.

Two literary sources possess particular significance for the notion of Ethiopian kingship, the *ser'ata mangest*, i.e. 'statute of kingship', and the *fetha nagast*, i.e. 'legislation of the kings'. The former describes the institution of the monarchy and its detailed ceremonial, beginning with 'the royal statutes which came from Jerusalem together with Menelik, the son of Solomon and the Queen of Sheba'. The latter, the foremost traditional law-code of Ethiopia, devotes one section (No. 44) to the duties of the kings.

In Ethiopian historical, religious, and legal documents there clearly emerges the national dogma of a dynastic continuity, stretching from David to Haile Sellassie. The king's throne is the 'throne of David' and he himself is the son of David, the son of Solomon, King of Zion. Article 2 of the revised (1955) constitution of Ethiopia states:

> The Imperial dignity shall remain perpetually attached to the line of Haile Sellassie I, descendant of King Sahle Sellassie, whose line descends without interruption from the dynasty of Menelik I, son of the Queen of Ethiopia, the Queen of Sheba, and King Solomon of Jerusalem.

The 'oil of kingship' mentioned in article 4 of the constitution should be compared with the anointing in I Samuel 10:1 and 16:13. The English version of this article speaks of the person of the emperor as 'sacred', while the Amharic text (presumably, though not necessarily, the original) has a phrase which suggests that his honour must not be diminished. Yet, many indications point to a quasi-sacred separateness of the person of the emperor: he is shielded by a screen from the gaze of the populace; he used not to eat in public; at times his face was veiled and he spoke through an intermediary, the *afa negus*, 'mouth of the King'. Ethiopian Christianity is rich in its Old Testament heritage, and the notion of Abyssinian kingship derives support from the ideas of Israelite kingship. Ethiopia, as the second Zion, embodies the continued existence of the royal house of Judah.

The principal source of this notion of Ethiopian kingship and its roots in the Old Testament and Hebraic ambience is the *Kebra Nagast*, the Ethiopian national saga. This great medieval storehouse of traditions and legends represents, above all, the supreme flowering of the Solomon–Sheba cycle.

The story of the Queen of Sheba, based on the biblical account of the queen's visit to King Solomon, has undergone extensive Arabian, Jewish, Ethiopian, and other elaborations, some of which have already been considered, and has become the subject of one of the most ubiquitous and fertile cycles of legends in the Middle East. Its mythopoeic power persists up to the present time and remains in some areas a favourite formula for literary and artistic inventiveness. Its fascination is not, however, confined to the East: in European music, painting, and literature the Queen of Sheba's fame continues unabated (see Chapter VI). On one hand, she is Lilith the seductress and, on the other, the virtuous ancestress of the Ethiopian nation. Several places of origin and many different names are ascribed to her; yet from this vast and confused skein of traditions and tales it is possible to disentangle some basic features which are common to all the stories about that famous encounter between the Queen of the South and the greatest of the Kings of Israel.

The earliest extant form of the Queen of Sheba narrative is the version preserved in I Kings 10:1–13 and II Chronicles 9:1–12. There are some small, but not insignificant, differences between these two Old Testament accounts which are of little relevance to the development of the Solomon–Sheba legend but of considerable interest to the methods of text-transmission. The Old Testament story represents the briefest and most concise version; and it is, perhaps, this very terseness which has encouraged later elaborations and embellishments. There are two Hebrew expressions in particular which appear to have invited the widespread tale of the union of king and queen in either marriage or concubinage: the queen '*came* to Solomon . . .' (I Kings 10:2). The Hebrew verb *bw'*, 'to come, to enter', is also used as the technical term for coitus. And in verse 13 we are told that 'Solomon gave unto the Queen of Sheba *all her desire*. . . .' In the wake of certain Talmudic interpretations, medieval Jewish commentators show an awareness of less innocent embellishments to this verse.

The salient features of the Old Testament narrative, on which this vast network of traditions and legends is based, are as follows: the Queen of Sheba had heard of Solomon's fame and decided to come to Jerusalem to test the King's wisdom. She brought with her spices, gold, and precious stones. Solomon answered all her questions, while the queen inspected the house he had built and all the manifold details of the administration of Solomon's realm. Finally, the queen was convinced that reality exceeded by far the reports which had reached her. She blessed Solomon and his God, rejoiced in the good fortune of the King's subjects, and delivered the rich presents which she had brought. She then returned to her own country together with her retinue.

This narrative appears to be interrupted, in both its versions in I Kings and II Chronicles, by two verses relating to the Ophir fleet which fetched gold, precious stones, and wood which was particularly suitable for the manufacture of musical instruments. This might be either a glossator's interpolation *à propos* of the queen's gifts, which reminded him of similar imports by Solomon assisted by Hiram's sailors, or it might well be part of the story referring to additional gifts which the queen had delivered by the Red Sea fleet. In any event, the mention of these commercial and seafaring activities in the area of the southern Red Sea appears to corroborate the historicity of the Queen of Sheba's visit to King Solomon—shorn, of course, of its more extravagant features. It scarcely matters very greatly whether we have to seek the queen's home in South-west Arabia or in the horn of Africa (the reference to rich forests [verses 11 and 12] might possibly favour the latter assumption), for the connections between the two shores of the southern Red Sea have at all times been close.

The Queen of Sheba appears in the New Testament as the 'Queen of the South' (Matthew 12:42; Luke 11:31). Ethiopian tradition as embodied in the *Kebra Nagast* has come to identify 'Candace queen of the Ethiopians' (Acts 8:27) with the Queen of the South and has fused the two queens, belonging to such different periods, into one person. While there can scarcely be any doubt that the eunuch who was baptized by St Philip must have been the servant of one of the Meroitic queens who bore the name Candace, Ethiopians have, from a very early period, applied this episode to themselves as an essential step in the Christianization of Ethiopia's past.

It is likely that some versions of the Old Testament story about the Queen of Sheba had already reached Ethiopia in pre-Christian times. They were no doubt brought into the country by some of the South Arabian immigrants and were subsequently adapted in such a manner as to contribute in the most effective way to the ennoblement of the Ethiopian nation. With the introduction of Christianity into Ethiopia, in the fourth century, a Christian layer was superimposed on the Hebraic-Semitic traditions prevalent at the time. It was thus natural, and even essential, that the national ancestress of the nation, the Queen of Sheba, should be identified with 'Candace queen of the Ethiopians', the only express mention of Ethiopia in the New Testament.

Additional colour was lent to the story of Ethiopia as the first Christian nation by the narrative, in the seventh book of the Apocryphal Acts of the Apostles, according to which Matthew baptized the King of Ethiopia. Matthew had arrived at Naddaver, the capital of Ethiopia, where King Aeglippus reigned. Magicians and charmed serpents held sway over the people. Matthew was welcomed by a eunuch named Candacis, whom Philip had baptized, and succeeded in breaking the spell of magicians and serpents. He baptized king, court, and country, and the people built a large church in thirty days. Aeglippus was succeeded as king by his brother Hyrtacus who killed Matthew because he had refused to sanction Hyrtacus' marriage to Ephigenia, the daughter of Aeglippus.

The evolution of the Sheba cycle in Josephus, in Talmudic and Midrashic literature, as well as in the Qur'an and Muslim sources, has been described elsewhere in this volume. Most of the motifs and elements that make up this conglomeration of stories can be detected, in one form or another, in the huge network of conflations which is embodied in the Ethiopic *Kebra Nagast*. How this medieval romance in Abyssinia came to admit, to appropriate, and to weld all those disparate strands, is a matter of some complexity which goes beyond the limited aims of this survey. One has to recall, however, Ethiopia's position at a crossroad of civilizations and a meeting point of many cultural influences. In the syncretistic patterns of Aksum, and its medieval successors, Jerusalem and Mecca and Alexandria have all left their profound marks.

We must now have a closer look at the *Kebra Nagast* and its centre-piece, the Solomon–Sheba story. If I am not mistaken, Alvares was the first European to refer to this work, but it was not until James Bruce brought home two copies of the *Kebra Nagast* (which eventually found their way into the Bodleian Library where in 1848 they were catalogued, with magisterial thoroughness, by the great August Dillmann, that this important book could be properly studied. In 1870 F. Praetorius published, for the first time, the Ethiopic text and a Latin translation of Chapters 19–32 dealing with the Sheba story. And in 1905 there appeared the first complete edition and translation of the entire *Kebra Nagast* at the hands of C. Bezold.

The object of the *Kebra Nagast* was to prove that Ethiopia was the lawful successor and heir of Israel as the chosen people of God; that this purpose was achieved by the transference from Jerusalem to Aksum of the Ark of the Covenant; and that the instrument of God's will was Menelik, son of King Solomon and the Queen of Sheba. Since Christ himself was also descended from David and Solomon, it follows that the King of Ethiopia is a kinsman of Christ.

Of the 117 chapters of the *Kebra Nagast*, Chapters 21–63, 84–94, 113–117 are concerned with the Sheba–Solomon cycle. To these one might well add Chapters 1–20, for they serve as an introduction to the principal theme offering a 'history' from Adam to Solomon and dealing with the construction and significance of the Tabernacle.

The head of the queen's trading caravans was a man called Tamrin who supplied King Solomon with materials for the building of the Temple. When he returned from Jerusalem he told the queen of Solomon's wisdom, power, and riches. At length the queen decided to see for herself and departed for Jerusalem with caravans of rich presents. When she reached her destination she found Tamrin's reports fully confirmed and marvelled at Solomon's wisdom and justice. She conversed with him daily and learnt about his God until she decided to abandon the worship of the sun, stars, and trees and to worship instead their creator, the God of Israel.

When the time came for the queen to leave Jerusalem and to return to her own country, Solomon was so impressed with her beauty and intelligence that he determined to beget a son by her. He invited Sheba to a magnificent banquet consisting of ten highly seasoned courses. When the other guests had left he suggested to the queen that she sleep in his tent. She agreed on condition that he would not take her by force. Solomon complied with this request, provided Sheba promised on her part not to take anything in the king's house. Solomon then mounted the bed on one side of the chamber and had the queen's bed prepared at the other end. Sheba soon awoke, for the seasoned food had made her very thirsty. She rose and drank from a bowl of water that had been placed in the chamber. Solomon seized her hand and accused her of having broken her oath. He then worked his will with her.

That night Solomon had a dream in which the sun departed from Israel and shone brilliantly over Ethiopia for ever. Soon after this the queen returned to her own country laden with the king's gifts. He had also given her a ring as a token of remembrance. Nine months and five days later Sheba gave birth to a son whom she called Ibn al-Hakim, 'son of the wise man', i.e. Menelik. (It has generally been thought that Menelik is a corruption of the Arabic name—cf. Bezold, *op. cit.* pp. v–vi.) When the boy had grown up he showed great curiosity as to the identity of his father, and as soon as his mother revealed the truth he determined to go to Jerusalem to visit Solomon. Sheba gave him the king's ring as proof of his identity together with a letter in which she begged Solomon to send her part of the cover of the Ark of the Covenant, so that it might be venerated in her country.

On arrival at Solomon's court Menelik was received with splendour and joy, and everyone was astonished at Menelik's resemblance to his father. While at Jerusalem he studied the laws and institutions of the Hebrews, but at length he decided to return to his mother's realm. Thereupon Solomon summoned the elders of Israel and commanded them to send their first-born sons with Menelik, in order to found a kind of Israelite colony in Ethiopia. And Zadok the priest anointed Menelik King of Ethiopia. Before the young men departed from Jerusalem, they abducted the Ark of the Covenant and carried it with them to Ethiopia. The divine presence had now left Jerusalem and settled over Aksum, the capital of Ethiopia.

When Menelik and his retinue reached his mother's country, the queen was waiting to receive him and the Ark. There was great rejoicing and the queen abdicated in favour of her son. From this time onwards the people abandoned their idols and accepted the God of the Hebrews, and Menelik sat upon the throne of David, King of Israel.

The basic features of the Queen of Sheba story have been embodied in the traditional pictorial representation of this legend. This generally appears, as on the illustration (Ill. 40), in forty-four squares arranged in four rows of eleven each. The following is a rough translation of the accompanying Amharic legend:

(1) They worshipped the serpent
(2) They planned to kill the serpent
(3) They mixed poison
(4) And fed it to the goat
(5) They went with the goat
(6) And gave the goat to the serpent
(7) Having killed the serpent
(8) They informed the King that they had killed the serpent
(9) They informed Makeda [the Ethiopian name of the queen]
(10) Makeda's father died
(11) Makeda reigned
(12) With the merchants of Jerusalem
(13) She sent spices
(14) With the spices they departed
(15) The spices they presented
(16) Makeda goes to Solomon
(17) Makeda in the boat
(18) Makeda at Solomon's gate
(19) Makeda and Solomon
(20) Solomon gives a banquet
(21) Makeda's dinner
(22) He confronts Makeda
(23) How he takes her maid
(24) He sleeps with her maid
(25) How he seizes Makeda
(26) He sleeps with Makeda
(27) He gives her a signet ring
(28) Makeda returns home
(29) Menelik and the maid's child are born

(30) Menelik and his companions play Gänna [hockey]
(31) 'Tell me about my father'
(32) Makeda shows him [in the mirror]
{ (33) Menelik and his retinue set
{ (34) out for Jerusalem
(35) Menelik with his father
(36) Menelik understands
(37) Menelik and companions at school
(38) He gives them the Ark
(39) They go off with the Ark
(40) He shows the Ark
(41) She enthrones (her son/the Ark) according to the light
(42) The seal prevails
(43) Makeda's (deathbed) confession
(44) He erects the obelisk.

The fundamental change of atmosphere that can be discerned in the Ethiopian version—as compared with the Jewish and Muslim legends—is obvious even in this crude pictorial representation: the queen is always shown *en face* (i.e. good), while Solomon is pictured in profile (i.e. evil). The emphasis here is not on Solomon and his wisdom but on the Queen of Sheba and her purity and nobility. No longer is Solomon exposed to the wiles of the seductress, Lilith, the earthy demon, but he himself assumes the role of seducer and, by a ruse, takes the virgin queen who— and this is the culmination and purpose of the entire Ethiopian saga—gives birth to a son, Menelik, the founder of the Ethiopian dynasty. From him are said to be descended all the kings of Ethiopia down to the present day—as, indeed, is embodied in the current constitution of the Ethiopian Empire. Here, in the cold terms of legal phraseology, we find the continued insistence on the *mystique* of a direct descent from King Solomon and the Queen of Sheba, a powerful reminder of the enduring efficacy of the Old Testament story and its wide ramifications.

Apart from this totally different atmosphere, the Ethiopian *Kebra Nagast* exhibits other significant changes of detail (as compared with the versions included in the Qur'an or the *Targum Sheni* to Esther): nothing is said about the queen's hairy limbs, nothing about the glass floor, or Sheba's descent from demons. The tale of the hoopoe is replaced by the realistic story of Tamrin, the head of Sheba's caravans, who is engaged in large-scale trading operations with Solomon and is impressed with the king's wisdom and might. When the queen decides, on the basis of Tamrin's enthusiastic reports, to go to Jerusalem and see for herself, the *Kebra Nagast* version does not deviate substantially from the biblical account but simply supplies many details on which the concise story in the Old Testament is silent. One of the more important embellishments is the queen's decision to abandon the worship of the sun and to turn, instead, to the God of Israel.

The centre-piece and, at the same time, the original contribution of the Ethiopian version lie in the colourful description of events leading up to the birth of Menelik, i.e. Solomon's banquet, the bed-chamber scene, the removal of the *shekhina*, the 'Divine Presence', from Israel to Ethiopia, the abduction of the Ark of the Covenant, and the establishment of the throne of David in an African realm.

The veneration of the Queen of Sheba and her appropriation as the national ancestress of the Ethiopian people are of some antiquity, and certainly precede the medieval romance embodied in the *Kebra Nagast*. An interesting piece of evidence is furnished by the Ethiopic Bible translation (fourth to sixth century AD) which usually adheres fairly closely to the text of the Septuagint, but in I Kings 10:1, in the phrase 'she came to prove him with hard questions', the Ethiopic version interprets the Greek ἐν αἰνίγμασιν (with riddles) as 'with wisdom'. This deliberate alteration is, as far as I know, the earliest indication of the Ethiopian attitude towards the Queen of Sheba, for in this reading the quality of wisdom is related not to King Solomon but to the Queen.

We have already seen certain aspects of the vast network of conflation to which the Sheba story was exposed. The confusion, for example, of the Queen of Sheba legend with the New Testament account of Candace was not, however, a deliberate forgery on the part of Ethiopians but was an aspect of the ancient blending of Candace–Sheba and Solomon–Alexander stories. The Syriac and Ethiopic versions of the Alexander romance contain an account of the meeting of Alexander and Queen Candace which is, in some of its features, reminiscent of the encounter between King Solomon and the Queen of Sheba.

The various Ethiopic versions of the Alexander romance, i.e. in particular the translation of the Pseudo-Callisthenes and the (probably) original Ethiopic composition of the Christian Romance of Alexander, present a remarkable example of a literary anachronism. The entire atmosphere is Christian in colouring, and Greek gods appear in the guise of Enoch, Elijah, etc. The resemblances to the Solomon–Sheba cycle are at times quite striking.

Alexander asks to be presented to Queen Candace and, accompanied by her son, he sets out for her realm. He is graciously received by Candace who gives him rich presents. Alexander recognizes her beauty and noble stature and admires her palace and other possessions. He marvels at everything shown to him, for he had never before seen such royal splendour maintained by any king. It is, of course, clear that in this narrative Alexander plays the role which Sheba assumes in the biblical and Ethiopian story, while Candace has the part of Solomon.

Candace and Alexander have many conversations in the queen's private chambers and at length she recognizes him, by his portrait, as Alexander. This motif, it will be observed, also recurs in the Solomon–Sheba–Menelik story. When Alexander feels humiliated at having been vanquished by a woman, Candace consoles him with her love: 'Then Candace took Alexander's hand and made him sit by her side on the couch, and she embraced him, and she put on him her royal crown; and he lay with her that day and that night until daybreak'.

Candace marvelled at Alexander's knowledge and wisdom and gave him the royal crown and the glorious raiment in which she had slept with him. On his departure one thousand horsemen from among the nobles of the army set out with him, and Candace embraced him and reminded him of their past intimacy.

While the detailed structure of the Alexander–Candace romance varies a good deal from the Solomon–Sheba legend, there are many individual features and motifs which are clearly common to both cycles. It is unnecessary to labour this point at length.

There also exist a Christian Arabic and a Coptic version of our legend. The former is almost certainly dependent on the Ethiopian type of the story and thus constitutes a process of borrowing in a direction opposite to the usual flow. This Arabic legend is of a composite nature: it omits all mention of an intermediary (hoopoe or merchant) between king and queen, restores the tale of the polished floor, and, to heal the queen's affliction, it introduces a piece of wood which was later used for the Cross. The details of Sheba's seduction by Solomon tally very largely with the Ethiopic prototype. The Coptic version offers little of special interest, but it seems to have been current throughout the Christian Church in Africa.

A modern form of the legend, which yet embraces many archaic elements as well as comparatively recent folkloristic accretions, has been preserved among the Tigre in the north. A Tigre girl by the name of *Eteye Azeb* (i.e. 'Queen of the South') seeks a cure for her deformed foot which had turned into an ass's heel. When she hears of King Solomon's powers she departs for Jerusalem together with a companion. They appear disguised as men, but the king's suspicions are aroused. At night he has a skin with honey suspended in the room, and when the two girls believe him to be asleep they get up and start licking the honey. Solomon then finds his suspicions confirmed and he takes the two women by force. The remainder of the story follows the *Kebra Nagast* version fairly closely: the birth of the son, his visit to his father, and the removal of the Ark from Jerusalem to Aksum.

The ass's heel is, of course, the counterpart of the deformed or hairy foot, but it is remarkable that this feature, so carefully avoided in the classic account of the *Kebra Nagast*, was allowed to survive in this north Ethiopian tale. Otherwise there is—*mutatis mutandis*—broad agreement, and the bed-chamber scene reveals a close connection in all essential matters.

In modern Ethiopia the name of Sheba has a considerable vogue in trade names and advertising. Hertz, the world-wide car rental firm, state in their advertisement that 'the Queen of Sheba has passed ... but the mystique of her name still lends enchantment to the Ethiopian scene'. There is a Saba Bookshop in Addis Ababa, and Ethiopian Airlines offer jets over the land of Sheba. Ethiopia's national drink, *Tej*, is bottled by Saba Tej, and the finest traditional Ethiopian fabrics may be purchased at Saba Mode. For an intimate and relaxing atmosphere one is enjoined to frequent the Sheba Club.

Finally, a word about the Queen's names: in the Old Testament she is, of course, the 'Queen of Sheba', while in the New Testament she appears as the 'Queen of the South'. This latter idiom goes back to a Semitic *mlkt ymyn* or *mlkt tymn* (for south is on the right-hand side when you stand facing the rising sun). The Arabic name Bilqis is almost certainly related to Hebrew *pilegesh* and Greek παλλακίς. In the *Kebra Nagast* the queen's name is given as Makeda which has no obvious explanation: some have thought it might be connected with (Alexander) the 'Macedonian', while others would not exclude the possibility that Makeda might reveal a popular identification with Candace.

VI

The Queen of Sheba in Christian Tradition

Paul F. Watson

IN the quest for Sheba, Christian interpretations of the biblical story have been of little help. Throughout the Middle Ages and the Renaissance, the legend of the Queen of Sheba was treated chiefly as an instance of the truth of Christian doctrine. Rarely was interest shown in the problems raised by the story—the race of the queen, the location of her realm, the reasons for her quest. The true quest for Sheba did not begin until the nineteenth century. Nevertheless, the history of the Queen of Sheba in the Christian tradition is a fascinating chapter in itself. The story inspired learned biblical exegesis, pious fictions, charming legends, and several supreme works of art.

To understand the fate of the Sheba legend in the Middle Ages, it is necessary to consider the interests and prejudices of those who shaped Christian doctrine during the fourth and fifth centuries. For theologians like Ambrose or Augustine, the Queen of Sheba was significant only because Christ cited her. Matthew and Luke recorded an angry sermon that Jesus addressed to the Pharisees (Matthew 12:39–42; Luke 11:29–32—see p. 11). The Queen of Sheba in the New Testament was used as prophetic witness to the Last Judgment that was soon to come.

A Christian scholar of the fourth century would then have consulted the historical account in Kings and Chronicles with carefully selective attention. The Queen of Sheba came to Solomon to prove his wisdom with hard questions, she communed with him of all that was in her heart, and Solomon responded fully to all her questions. When the queen saw the glory of the house of the Lord 'there was no more spirit in her'. The Christian reader would have noted her apostrophe to Solomon (I Kings 10:8–9). After giving the king a great treasure of gold and spices, the queen returned to her own land. In the Old Testament the story was used to emphasize the glory and wisdom of Israel, and its king. It could be used equally well for Christian purposes.

The connection between the historic Queen of Sheba and the prophetic queen from the south was hinted at by the prophets of the Old Testament. The land of Sheba was often cited as a sign of the future submission of the Gentiles to Israel. Thus Isaiah:

All they from Sheba shall come: they shall bring forth gold and incense; and they shall show forth the praises of the Lord (Isaiah 60:6).

David the Psalmist wrote of the same vision,

> He shall have dominion from sea unto sea, and from the river unto the ends of the earth . . . the Kings of Tarshish and of the isles shall bring presents, and the kings of Sheba and Seba shall offer gifts (Psalms 72:8–10).

These references to Sheba could be easily related to the prophecies of Jesus in the Gospels.

Medieval interpretations of the Sheba legend were also shaped by methods of biblical exegesis established by the Fathers. According to Augustine, the Bible was to be read in a twofold way: as a literal record of events, and as a metaphorical disclosure of Christian truth. Thus stories and figures from the Old Testament were held to prefigure events and persons of the New. In proclaiming himself to be a greater than Solomon, Jesus established the Jewish king as a type of the Messiah.

A typological interpretation of the Sheba legend appeared around the year 400 in the *Lines to be Inscribed Under Scenes From History* by Prudentius. The poet describes an ideal programme of decoration for Christian basilicas based on the symbolical concordance of the Old and New Testaments. 'Wisdom builds a temple by Solomon's obedient hands, and the Queen from the South piles up a great weight of gold. The time is at hand when Christ shall build his temple in the heart of men, and Greece shall reverence it, and lands not Greek enrich it.' Prudentius weaves together Christ's words and David's psalm to define the Queen of Sheba as a type of the Gentiles who accept Christianity.

A more exacting system of typology was constructed in the Dark Ages after the fall of the Roman Empire. In the seventh century, Bishop Isidore of Seville succinctly defined the significance of the Queen of Sheba:

> Solomon prefigures the image of Christ who raised the house of God in the heavenly Jerusalem, not with stone and wood, but with all the saints. The queen from the south who came to hear the wisdom of Solomon is to be understood as the Church, which assembles from the utmost limits of the world to hear the voice of God (*Allegoriae quaedam Scripturae sanctae*, 91–92).

Isidore's interpretation is an important shift away from Patristic thought, where the Queen had stood only for the Gentiles. In elevating her as a type of the Church, the bishop placed her in the same mystic company as the Virgin Mary, Bride of Christ and image of the Christian community.

Isidore's allegories were repeated without dissent by theologians of the early Middle Ages. In his *Quaestiones super Regum Libros* Bede of England followed the Bishop of Seville almost word for word in explaining the historical account of the queen's visit. Her desire to prove Solomon with hard questions is like the eagerness of the Church to know Christ. The journey to Jerusalem is like a bride's journey to her spouse. Bede and Isidore also uncovered a hidden reference to the Queen of Sheba in Psalm 45: 'Upon thy right hand did sit the queen in gold of Ophir'. In the *Glossa Ordinaria* Wilifred Strabo squeezed every syllable of the Book of Kings dry for typological significance. For example, the queen's exclamation 'Happy are thy men' should be read as 'Blessed are the men whose King is Christ'. In 834 Hrabanus Maurus commented that the Queen of Sheba was named Nicaule, and that she was also sovereign of Ethiopia. This information, quoted from the *Jewish Antiquities* of Flavius Josephus, is used by Hrabanus to confirm the truth of Isidore's gloss.

The 'typological' Queen of Sheba soon found her way into the visual arts. An illuminating instance is from the *Hortus deliciarum* written between 1159 and 1175 by Herrad of Landsberg, prioress of an Alsatian convent (Ill. 42). A page of her manuscript represents Solomon and the queen enthroned side by side and accompanied by a courtier displaying a sword. She seems to listen attentively to the king. There is little in the scene to distinguish it from representations of twelfth-century courts, except for a battery of elucidating inscriptions supplied by Abbess Herrad. The first reads 'The queen from the south, that is the Church, comes to hear the wisdom of the true Solomon, Jesus Christ.' The Isidorean significance of the image is further enriched by its resemblance to the standard visual formula representing Christ and the Virgin enthroned together in the Court of Heaven. As we have seen, both Mary and the Queen of Sheba were types of the Church. Moreover, the Song of Solomon was commonly interpreted as alluding to the union of Christ and his Church. In its bloodless way Abbess Herrad's image brings to mind Ethiopian legends of the union of Solomon and the queen.

Stone effigies of the queen and Solomon appear on the north façade of the Baptistery of Parma. They were carved after 1196 by Benedetto Antelami as niche figures. Solomon, a bearded massive figure holding a scroll, turns slightly to address the Queen of Sheba. She clasps her long mantle in her left hand, and raises the other to secure the straps of the cloak. From her girdle hangs a delicate reticule. These simple touches endow the figure with slight movement and a charming femininity. Despite these secular overtones, however, the group is a counterpart in stone to the ideas of Herrad of Landsberg and Isidore of Seville. The couple is associated with other figures of prophets and is placed near an important representation of the Adoration of the Magi.

The statues at Parma are indebted in style to French art. Antelami's couple is close to columnar figures from the early Gothic cathedral of Chartres. Here they are found in the right portal of the north transept, erected during the first quarter of the thirteenth century. The left jamb is adorned with the figures of Balaam, the queen, and Solomon (Ill. 43). Opposite them stand Joseph, Judith and Jesus ben Sira. The Queen of Sheba at Chartres is a slender and charming version of

Antelami's figure. The French sculptor has created flowing patterns of drapery folds that enhance her grace. The queen also participates in a courtly tableau. While Balaam inclines deferentially to her, she is duly subservient to the robust King Solomon.

Katzenellenbogen has demonstrated that this group forms part of an elaborate sculptural programme. The north transept façade of Chartres is dedicated to the triumph of Mary and the Church. The Queen of Sheba's visit to Solomon is symbolized by the tiny servant crouching beneath her feet. She is next to Balaam, who predicted that a star would arise from Jacob, or as Bede put it, that the Church would arise from Christ. Moreover, the queen is placed opposite Judith, a traditional type of the Virgin. The typological system of Chartres is richer and much more intricate than earlier Romanesque programmes.

Solomon and Sheba frequently adorn other Gothic cathedrals of the thirteenth century. In the south portal of the main façade of Amiens, they are placed next to Herod and the three Magi. On the opposite jamb figures enact the Annunciation and the Presentation, while the Virgin herself adorns the *trumeau* between. The slender queen has doffed her crown to demonstrate her submission to Solomon. Her gesture is explained by a delightful relief in the embrasure beneath, where the king bests his visitor in the trial of hard questions. At the great coronation church of Rheims, the king and queen are placed on the buttresses that separate the central portal from the north and south entrances. Both figures have the robust beauty of their earlier counterparts at Chartres. Towards the end of the thirteenth century Rheims was enriched by groups of Solomonic statuary placed around the rose window of the west façade. In this new programme king and queen share the same narrow perch. Though the queen clutches her mantle in much the same way as her predecessors, the graceful rhythms of her figure, her sly glance, and the tender regard of Solomon endow the figures with a courteous, even coquettish air. We have moved from Solomon and Sheba as symbolic icons to the meeting of the couple as courtly narrative.

Romanesque and Gothic representations of the visit of the Queen of Sheba were rarely produced as isolated scenes. An instance is a beautiful stained-glass window from the north aisle of Canterbury cathedral, designed in the late twelfth century. The queen stands in the centre of the scene, and is framed by a door. As she looks towards Solomon seated on a handsome throne to the left, she gestures towards her suite, composed of two servants astride camels of a remarkably equine sort (Ill. 44). Close to this scene is another roundel where the Adoration of the Kings is represented. The reasons for this association are supplied by an inscription framing the first scene: 'The queen gives these presents to the house of Solomon; in such wise the Kings give to the threefold Lord three gifts.' A contemporary representation of the queen's visit is from the Klosterneuburg altar of 1181 by Nicolaus of Verdun, which is covered with scenes from the Old and New Testaments, arranged typologically. The Visit of the Queen of Sheba is associated with the meeting of Abraham and Melchizedek (Genesis 14:18–20), and the Epiphany. Nicolaus has underlined the theological sense of the scene by making two of the queen's servants kneel, as do the Magi nearby (Ill. 45).

If the Queen of Sheba was a type of the Church, her journey to Solomon was a prefiguration of the adoration of the Magi. The association can be traced back to the commentaries of Isidore and Bede, who point out that in both motifs the Gentiles come from afar to adore the true God. Scriptural warrant for this interpretation of the Old Testament story was easily found in the words of Isaiah, 'All they from Sheba shall come . . .', and from the Psalmist, 'the kings of Sheba and Seba shall offer gifts'.

What texts and commentaries do not fully explain is the interest of medieval artists in the nature of the Queen of Sheba and her realm. At Canterbury, the queen is accompanied by camels and negroid servants. Nicolaus of Verdun paints his queen black. At Chartres, a maid of Ethiopic hue crouches beneath the queen's feet. These details may have been suggested by the confusion of Ethiopia and Sheba in the prophetic texts, and in the summary of Josephus provided by Hrabanus Maurus. Yet it seems equally plausible to suppose that these exotic details may be derived from Eastern and Arabic traditions circulating during the period of the Crusades.

The ethnographic interests of medieval artists were suppressed in such monkish compilations as the *Speculum Humanae Salvationis* of the early fourteenth century. This was a selection of events from the life of the Virgin paired with appropriate Old Testament types. The method of exposition is demonstrated by an illustrated manuscript produced in Alsace around 1330 (Ill. 46). The drawings are in a spare style which is entirely subservient to the Latin text below. On the left folio are the Adoration of the Kings, and the kings adoring the Star of Bethlehem. Opposite are David receiving aid from three biblical worthies (2 Samuel 17:27–29), and the Queen of Sheba adoring Solomon. Here the scene parallels that of the kings worshipping the star. The queen kneels and holds a chalice at the bottom step of Solomon's throne, an elaborate pyramid of six steps with paired lions and a Gothic chair on top. The furnishings follow the account given in Kings. The interpretation is purely medieval. The poem below says that Solomon enthroned is an image of Christ seated in the Virgin's lap: 'the Throne of the true Solomon is the most Blessed Virgin Mary, in which sits Jesus, the True Wisdom'. Hence the child-like Jewish king, the two disembodied arms that support him (alluding also to the Trinity), and the purely devotional role of the Queen of Sheba.

The typological structure of the *Speculum Humanae Salvationis* served as a model for painters of the later Middle Ages, as an altarpiece of 1444 indicates. A panel from the 'Heilspiegelaltar' by Konrad Witz represents the Queen of Sheba presenting gifts to Solomon. The king is shown as a youth clad in a satin robe sewn with pearls. Though Witz created solid three-dimensional figures placed firmly in space, his intentions were as didactic as those of the *Speculum*'s creators. The scene is stripped to essentials. The queen kneels and presents a chalice, like those used in the Mass. The theme of eucharistic adoration was made explicit by the adjacent panels, which represented Melchizedek greeting Abraham, and David succoured by Shobi, Barzillai and Machir, as in the manuscripts of the *Speculum Humanae Salvationis*.

Another typological handbook, the *Biblia Pauperum*, was of great importance for the development of the Sheba theme in the late Middle Ages. This was not really a Bible, nor was it intended for the poor. It was a carefully selected series of events from the life of Christ, paired with their types from the Old Testament, and accompanied by brief citations from Scripture. The *Biblia Pauperum* was an aid to preachers. The earliest manuscripts appear in the early fourteenth century in Bavaria, Austria and Bohemia.

A manuscript painted around 1330 illustrates the scheme of the *Biblia Pauperum* (Ill. 47). The Adoration of the Kings is placed in a roundel and separated from its types, the visit of the Queen of Sheba at the right and Abner's submission to David at the left (II Samuel 3:19–22). Grouped around the Epiphany are four prophets—Isaiah, Balaam, Micah and the Psalmist. The arrangement of images is made even more explicit by additional inscriptions. The prototype for this manuscript is a slightly earlier *Biblia Pauperum* now in St Florian, Austria.

The Austrian provenance of our manuscript is further demonstrated by stylistic similarities between the visit of the queen and the Klosterneuburg altar. The fourteenth-century painter has emulated Nicolaus in his pattern of composition, and in painting the Shebans black, or at least a deep blue. The figure types, however, have become youthful, slender, and courtly. Solomon perches daintily on his throne, while a servant tucks the wealth of Sheba into a fold of her cloak. The typological scene is also a Gothic pantomime.

The *Biblia Pauperum* was widely diffused in the form of manuscripts and printed books during the fifteenth century. Two blockbooks will demonstrate its popularity. The first was printed in Germany around 1440. Here the images of Gothic tradition are set forth with the directness of contemporary playing cards. The queen's visit is reduced to two figures. The queen points upwards to a star overhead, in what is perhaps an uncanonical reference to the star of Bethlehem, or even a reference to the Greek tradition that the Queen of Sheba was a sibyl. In either case, the craftsman was concerned chiefly with establishing a visual concordance with the Epiphany. Less abrupt in presentation is a blockbook produced in the Netherlands late in the fifteenth century. The scenes are arranged in a coherent architectural frame, like

42. Page from the anonymous Alsatian *Hortus deliciarum*, 1159–75; destroyed 1870 (British Museum)

REX SALOM · REGINA S BA

44. Stained-glass window in the north aisle of Canterbury Cathedral, late twelfth century
(Victoria and Albert Museum photo)

43. Figures from the left jamb of the right portal, north transept façade, Cathedral of
Chartres. First quarter of thirteenth century (Photo Marburg)

45. Enamel plaque by Nicolaus of Verdun on the Klosterneuburg Altar, Klosterneuburg, Austria; after 1181

47. Page from the *Biblia pauperum*, South German, *c.* 1330 (Österreichische Nationalbibliothek, Vienna) ▶

46. Page from the *Speculum Humanae Salvationis*, Alsatian, *c.* 1330 (Staatsbibliothek, Munich)

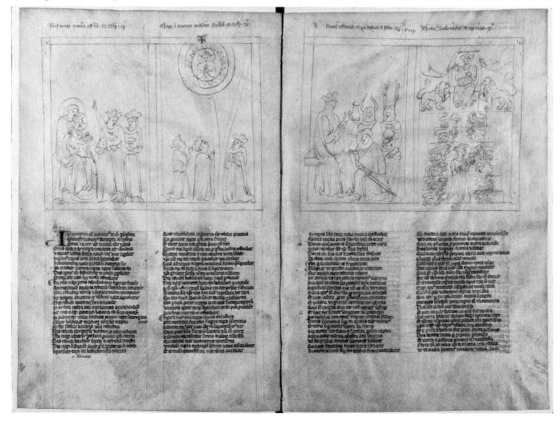

Egitur in secdo libro Regum qd abner princeps milicie
Saulis. venit ad dauid in urin et ad eum reducerent
prim totum isrl qui adhuc sequebatur domu saulis quod
un psigurabat aduenem magor ad xpm uenientem qui eu
mysticis munib; honorabant

Egitur in tercio libro Regum quod regina saba uenit
ad salomem in urin cu magnis muneribz cu honoratone
Hec quidem regina erat que significabat bn
gntes que dnm de longinquo cum munib; uenerent
adorare dnm nrm ihu xpm.

Plebs uocat hic gentes xpo uenit cupientes. Ecce ad
dauid

deatur unxit eius mirra libar. Hoc typice gentes notat ad xpm
uenientem

Abn · dauid · Anna de sisila uenient · Salo · Regina sab

Sophonias

Micheas · Balaam

Recept eni legis erat quod nisi primogeni
geniti prin reduise debetur oue pauper au que dinem
hire non possunt duos turtures ul columbas offerre debe
bant p pio. hoc ipsum purificacone q glosa dicit ad iplout
quatus purificari non indiget

Egitur in uno libro Regum q quidem Anna mater
samuelis ipm samuele ablactauit tunc obtulit
eum sacerdoti. hely in ipso intali faciendo que oblato
un psigurabat oblatione dnm in templo factam sanen
in sacerdotis

Senue fecundis unes fue bona mundis Cui nil debetur

legis agelur. Templo te rex pins natus notat iste
nis Malachias

Purificatio

Ysaias · Sophonias

48. Left panel of *The Adoration of the Magi*, an early sixteenth-century Flemish triptych, showing Solomon and Sheba (Prado, Madrid)

49. Early fifteenth-century *Bible moralisée*, by the Boucicaut Master and assistants (Bibliothèque nationale, Paris)

50. Agnolo Gaddi: choir fresco in S. Croce, right wall

51. Piero della Francesca: choir fresco in S. Francesco, Arezzo, middle register, right wall

the panels of a triptych. Once more, however, the desire for typological imagery remains strong. Abner, the Queen of Sheba, and the oldest king all kneel, and all three are clad in green. The queen's gifts are presented in receptacles like those of the Epiphany. Solomon places his hand on the chalice held by the Queen, even as the Child touches the gift of the oldest king.

This didactic image served as a model for painters during the late Middle Ages. The three scenes of the *Biblia Pauperum* are the themes of a triptych in Madrid painted by an unknown Netherlandish master early in the sixteenth century. At the centre is the Adoration of the Kings, while the Queen of Sheba is in the left wing. As in the blockbooks, her kneeling pose repeats that of the senior king. But the painter seems to have been as interested in telling a story as in illustrating a dogma. He lingers over the elaborate setting of Flamboyant Gothic windows, and delicate Renaissance columns. He revels in the rich costumes of Solomon's court. His king is no longer the bearded worthy of the blockbooks but a young and handsome man not unsusceptible to the queen's charms. Medieval traditions of symbolic narrative are beginning to fade away (Ill. 48).

Illustrated bibles of the Middle Ages sometimes present aspects of the visit of the queen not explored by the sculptors of the cathedrals or the illustrators of devotional manuals. In French translations of the Bible illuminated by the Boucicaut Master and his shop in Paris around 1400, Solomonic scenes are placed as frontispieces to Proverbs. One version shows Solomon receiving the queen. The illuminator was captivated by the queen's long trailing gown, and by the exquisite courtesy of Solomon as he bids her rise. Another manuscript shows how the queen proved Solomon with hard questions. Graceful doll-like personages debate on a tiny stage as their seconds look on. In both cases the Boucicaut Master has thought of the Sheba legend as an elegant episode (Ill. 49).

The most important representations of the Queen of Sheba in late medieval art illustrate a legend with barely a shred of biblical evidence for it. This is, of course, the legend of the True Cross, where the queen has a brief but important role. The most familiar version of the tale is in the *Legenda Aurea* compiled by the Dominican bishop Jacobus de Voragine in the late thirteenth century. He tells us that when Adam lay dying, his son Seth travelled to the Garden of Eden to buy a few drops of oil from the Tree of Mercy. The Archangel Michael gave Seth instead a branch of the Tree of the Knowledge of Good and Evil, telling him that on the day when this tree would bear fruit, Adam would be made whole.

Seth returned to find that Adam had died. He planted the branch of the Tree over his father's grave. In time it grew into a mighty tree. Centuries later Solomon cut down the tree to use it in the building of the Temple. His workmen, however, discovered that it absolutely refused to meet construction specifications, being at times too short, at others too long.

Thereupon they became impatient and threw it across a pond to serve as a bridge. And when the Queen of Sheba came to test Solomon with hard questions, she had occasion to cross the pond, and she saw in spirit that the Saviour of the world would one day hang upon this tree. She therefore refused to put her foot on it, but knelt instead to adore it . . . Solomon had the tree taken away and ordered it to be buried in the earth.

In due time the wood was exhumed, to be fashioned into the Cross. It was rediscovered by Helen, the mother of Constantine, and rescued from the Persians by the Emperor Heraclius.

The legend of the True Cross reflects the era of the Crusades and the cult of relics. The sources of the story, as Jacobus de Voragine admits, were Byzantine Greek legends, such as that recorded in the *Brief Chronicle* of Georgios Hamartolos, a monk of the ninth century. He identified the queen as a sibyl, and told how she disguised her maidservants as men, and vice versa, as a test of Solomon's wisdom. Another eastern legend was that of the *reine pédauque* (goose-footed queen), whose deformity is cured when she wades across the brook. These and other tales seemed to have circulated freely in the west during the Crusading period. In fact, the *Legenda Aurea* presented only the most sober account of the legend of the True Cross.

The *Geschiedenis van het heylighe Cruys*, a blockbook published in the Netherlands in 1483, demonstrates the popular appeal of the True Cross legend. The book consists of sixty-four woodcuts accompanied by quatrains in Dutch. In addition to the *Legenda Aurea*, the compilers relied on French manuscript sources, and on the traditions of folklore. Much emphasis is placed on Solomon's comic misadventures with the wood, and Harmatolos' 'Sibyl' makes a brief appearance. Three woodcuts

Fig. 13. Pages from the *Geschiedenis van het heylighe Cruys*, Dutch block-book, 1483 (British Museum)

are devoted to the Queen of Sheba (Fig. 13). In the first she humbly wades through the brook:

> Here too may be fully seen
> The river passing, Sheba's queen;
> But off her sandals taketh she
> To ford the river through, you see.
>
> The Queen of Sheba see again
> Reproving Solomon, quite plain
> For that he did so boldly dare
> The holy wood to lay down there.

In the third episode, Solomon's men reverently take up the wood, under the Queen's watchful eye. The spirit of these illustrations is direct, anecdotal, and often broadly comic. Poor Solomon is lectured at by his visitor, in an image not unlike Dutch domestic life.

The scene of the queen wading the ford was often represented in northern Europe, sometimes as an independent print, but more often as part of cycles of the True Cross legend which adorned churches. An instance is a fresco from the Chapel of the Holy Trinity in Stratford-on-Avon, painted after 1497. The artist seems to have combined the traditional encounter of Solomon and the queen with the Dutch woodcut type. At either side of the fresco stand the queen and Solomon, dressed in the finest early Tudor fashion. In between is an amorphous patch of blue, where the wood floats. To judge from the copies of this lost cycle, the painting must have been executed in a naïve and primitive style, like that of playing cards.

The most extensive fresco cycles based on the legend of the True Cross are found, not in northern Europe, but in Italy in churches which possessed relics of the Cross. Adorning the choir of S. Croce in Florence is a series of frescoes painted around 1390 by Agnolo Gaddi. The cycle begins on the right wall with the death of Adam, painted in a lunette. The Queen of Sheba appears in the register beneath (Ill. 50). Agnolo sets the scene amid dark forests, toy-like mountains, and a winding river which bisects the fresco. The queen kneels to adore the wood, a bridge thrown across the stream. At the right, Solomon has the wood buried. Our attention wavers between the devotions of the queen, and the attractions of her suite. Behind her regal figure crowd four maids extravagantly dressed, a nobleman stroking his falcon, several lugubrious courtiers, three inquisitive and playful horses, and a negro groom. Like the northern artists, Agnolo was unable to resist the exotic appeal of eastern legend.

The fresco in S. Croce became the accepted version of the queen's adoration of the wood in Tuscan art. Agnolo's scheme was repeated almost line for line by Cenni di Francesco in S. Francesco, Volterra, in 1413, and slightly modified by Masolino in 1424 for S. Stefano in Empoli. Of this cycle, only Masolino's concise and elegant sinopia underdrawings survive.

In 1452, the Bacci family of Arezzo commissioned Piero della Francesca to paint a cycle of the True Cross legend for the choir of S. Francesco. The frescoes were completed by 1464. The right wall shows Adam's death in the lunette, the queen's visit below, and Constantine's victory over Maxentius in the lowest tier. The second scene shows the queen's worship of the wood, and then her reception by Solomon. The burial of the wood has been relegated to the window wall, and placed out of sequence. Piero's fresco revises earlier formulas of the legend both in content and form.

The fresco is equally divided between landscape and architecture (Ill. 51). The perspective system is focused upon the holy wood, placed over the stream in the centre. At the far left in a simple hilly landscape are two grooms attending to the queen's horses. They stand quietly in conversation, unaware of the miracle nearby. The Queen of Sheba, plainly dressed and simply painted in profile, kneels to adore the wood. In a frieze-like group behind stand her ladies, one of whom looks out to the viewer inviting him to contemplate the scene as another gestures towards her mistress. The beauty of the fresco lies in the simplicity of Piero's art. The repeated gestures of the servants and the artful treatment of landscape serve to underscore the narrative. Nothing could be more unlike the crowded tapestry of Agnolo Gaddi's scene. Yet Piero never confuses economy with barrenness. An early morning light that steals in from the left brings out cool and delightful colours. The moment is enlivened by a few touches of anecdote—a horse whinnies in the chill morning, a negro maid stands apart in quiet wonder. These grace-notes enhance our sense of solemn, even majestic reverence.

Equally noble is the second half of Piero's fresco. Solomon and his masculine court gather to greet the queen amidst the Corinthian columns of the Temple of Jerusalem. As Solomon grasps the queen by the hand, she bends gravely to reverence him. Once more the queen is shown in profile, while another maidservant looks out towards the spectator. In repeating these figures, Piero has re-emphasized the traditional significance of the queen's journey to Israel. Moreover, the queen is made visually subordinate to Solomon, a grave and noble figure splendid in a robe of brilliant brocade. Like his successors in the fresco cycle, Constantine and Heraclius, Solomon is a man of moving dignity. It has been suggested that Solomon's rehabilitation was inspired by contemporary events in the East, including the fall of Constantinople in 1453. Another factor in Piero's interpretation may well have been the example of Lorenzo Ghiberti's Gates of Paradise, installed at the Baptistery of Florence in 1452.

A meeting of Solomon and the Queen of Sheba is one of ten bronze panels of the Gates of Paradise. Documentary evidence indicates that the doors were commissioned in 1425, and that the panels were designed and cast by 1437. The programme is a cycle of the Old Testament beginning with the fall of Adam, and culminating with Solomon. This last relief was described by Ghiberti himself in his *Commentaries* as 'how the Queen of Sheba comes to visit Solomon, with a great company. She is adorned, with many people about' (Ill. 52).

Ghiberti might have added that his scene is dominated by architecture. The queen's company and Solomon's retinue fill a piazza in the foreground. Behind is a platform, approached by steps, where the sovereigns meet. On a raised podium behind soars the Temple of Jerusalem, a late Gothic basilica with a high nave, square crossing, and a tall choir. The building is not unlike the nearby Cathedral of Florence. The Temple looms over the crowd, and gives special emphasis to Solomon and the Queen of Sheba, who are framed by the perspective of the nave.

The traditional motif of the queen's visit is treated in an equally novel way. The king is not enthroned, nor does the queen kneel. Their meeting is gracious and ceremonial. The aged Solomon grasps the queen's hand while she prettily responds to his welcome. The couple are almost like bride and groom come to church to take vows of marriage.

The matrimonial metaphor is not unwarranted. Professor Krautheimer has convincingly argued that Ghiberti's relief alluded to preparations made during the 1430s in Florence for a council that would unite the Greek and Latin Churches. Such a council did occur in 1438 and 1439 in Ferrara and Florence, attended by the Pope, the Greek Patriarch, Emperor Sigismund of Germany, and the Emperor of Constantinople. In Ghiberti's scene, the queen's travelling hat held by a servant to the left is Greek in style. Her company has a vaguely eastern cast to it, for several servants are Negroes, while others wear turbans and Tatar head-dress. An incident at the far left, where a man bursts in brandishing a hawk, may be derived from the *Second Targum* to the Book of Esther, which records the Jewish legend of the bird sent out by Solomon to discover the coming of the queen. All these details, which go beyond the usual oriental incidents of pictorial tradition, suggest that Ghiberti and his learned advisers were pre-occupied with eastern images. The meeting of the Queen of Sheba and Solomon, therefore, may allude to the proposed union of the Churches. Furthermore, Abyssinian delegates to the Council of Florence used the biblical account as a metaphor for current affairs, treating Solomon as a figure of the Latin church, and the Queen of Sheba as a type of the Greek.

Ghiberti also described his queen as 'adorned, with many people about'. In contrast to Piero della Francesca's simple and monumental fresco, this small panel contains nearly seventy attendants, of all ages and shapes. Little children jostle grave adults. Orientals mingle with westerners clad in togas or Roman armour. Horses collide, rear up, turn away. A dog sniffs inquisitively. A small orchestra provides music. Some of this rich detail illustrates the central theme, as where the Shebans in the lower left seem to recoil with awe from the splendour of Solomon's establishment. The overall effect, however, is of happy tumult, where Ghiberti's chief concern was to display his inventiveness. The solemn union between Solomon and the queen from the south is also a secular festival.

Ghiberti's relief was immensely important for Florentine secular art. His sovereigns reappear in the pages of a 'Picture Chronicle' made in Florence around 1460 and sometimes attributed to Maso Finiguerra. The pair clasp hands, like dignitaries on a state visit. By giving Solomon a crown suspiciously like the papal tiara, the draughtsman has made the topical allusions of Ghiberti's scene explicit.

Drawings of this sort must have been used as models by painters of *cassoni* like Apollonio di Giovanni, the proprietor of a large workshop active around 1460. The meeting of Solomon and the queen appears on at least eight panels ascribed to him. His indebtedness to Ghiberti is seen on a panel now in New Haven. The king greets the queen in front of a temple full of Renaissance architectural details, ncluding putti bearing swags. The royal figures are refugees from the Gates of Paradise. The queen, however, wears the regalia of a Byzantine potentate, including a crown like that made famous by the last Greek Emperors. In another *cassone* of the same subject (Ill. 53), Solomon's crown is like a travelling hat favoured by the emperor Sigismund of Germany. Apollonio has further embroidered on Ghiberti's ideas by stressing the wealth of Israel, and the exotic company of Shebans. In the New Haven *cassone* the queen is accompanied by gentle maidens, aged councillors, young dandies, a bearded dwarf, and a lonely white mastiff. The meeting is in danger of being swamped by spectators.

The pendant to the meeting scene in *cassone* painting is the queen's journey, which is shown in a panel in Alabama. In the background lies a glittering city, perhaps Jerusalem, perhaps even the capital of Sheba itself, but in any case a Gothic painter's version of Rome. At the left the queen interrupts her quest to adore the wood. The procession resumes to fill up the long panel with charming incidents. Its dominant feature is the queen's gilded travelling throne. Apollonio wove a new subject out of several disparate sources, including suggestions from Ghiberti's relief, the familiar episode from the True Cross legend, and late Gothic versions of the Journey of the Magi, as exemplified by a famous altarpiece of 1423 by Gentile da Fabriano. It is unlikely that Apollonio's borrowings from the Epiphany were motivated by typology. His interest in the Bible is in illustrating how 'she came to Jerusalem with a very great train, with camels that bear spices, and very much gold, and precious stones' (I Kings 10:2).

Cassoni of this sort were chests commissioned for the weddings of wealthy young women. They were part of the bride's dowry, contained her trousseau, and were often prominently displayed in wedding ceremonies. The usual themes of *cassone* painting were amatory subjects derived from Virgil, Ovid, and Petrarch. André Chastel has surmised that the content of the Sheba theme in *cassone* decoration was marital. The queen's journey could be likened to a bridal procession, and her meeting with Solomon to an ideal marriage, coupling wisdom and wealth. Apollonio di Giovanni's references to the Union of the Churches support this interpretation. In a version of the visit in London, Apollonio has even depicted the queen's portable throne as a bed-like object. Four winged Cupids support its canopy, as others ride postillion on the queen's horses. We are in a situation not to be confused with the *Biblia Pauperum*.

To stress the amatory implications of the Sheba legend requires a rather loose interpretation of the Book of Kings. Textual confusion has produced its masterpiece in two charming panels by Sano di Pietro, a Sienese contemporary of Apollonio di Giovanni. In the first panel Sano shows preparations for the queen's journey. While porters load camels in the piazza of a fortified Italian town, the queen's chariot passes through the gates. It is drawn by white horses, and crammed with ladies and trumpeters. The quest ends at Jerusalem, where the queen's car is about to collide with an even larger chariot filled with Solomon's harem. Sano seems to have confused Solomon's wisdom with his sexual prowess (Ill. 55).

Another marital image appears on the obverse of a marriage salver painted around 1475 by an unknown Umbrian master (Ill. 56). Here the royal pair meet in front of an ornately fantastic basilica, carefully labelled as Solomon's temple. The couple are enclosed and emphasized by an arcade that also separates them from their suites. The couple join hands in a gesture denoting marriage which was current in the fifteenth century, and which goes back to Roman usage. This union is further emphasized by the reverse of the salver, where a nude Cupid displays two cornucopias, traditional symbols of wealth. It is as if the meeting of Solomon and the

Queen of Sheba were an augury of love, riches, and wisdom for the Italian couple who commissioned it.

Anecdotal incidents and decorative profusion were expunged from the Sheba theme during the High Renaissance of the early sixteenth century. Around 1519 Raphael and his studio decorated the vaults of the Vatican loggie with frescoes illustrating biblical history. In the twelfth bay, Solomon's judgment was placed opposite his visit from the queen, as in medieval illustrations, in order to emphasize the king's wisdom. Raphael and his team of assistants also reverted to the simplicity of Romanesque narrative in portraying the queen's visit. The proverbial temple has shrunk to a mere container for a small number of noble figures. A courtier seen from the back points dramatically to Solomon, who rises to greet the queen from the south. She in turn indicates tribute offered by athletic servants as she pays homage to Solomon. The mood of the scene is one of heroic activity. There was also a new attempt to be archaeologically correct. Solomon is dressed as a Hebrew high priest, not an oriental Pope. The Queen of Sheba is black.

An equally severe treatment of the theme is an engraving attributed to Marcantonio Raimondi (Ill. 57). It is usually dated a year or so before the loggia frescoes, and is probably based on drawings by Raphael himself. The meeting takes place on a marble platform set in front of a massive temple to the right, and a curiously fragmented townscape at the left. Solomon's throne is emphasized by three great columns. The figures are arranged in this setting in a frieze-like fashion, the Jews to the left and Shebans at the right. Between them is the Queen of Sheba, who once more indicates her tribute. Marcantonio's interests seem to be confined to the formal possibilities of classical figures, graceful expressions, and telling gestures. The emotional tone of this High Renaissance engraving is chillingly abstract.

The Sienese architect and painter Baldassare Peruzzi contributed two variations to these Raphaelesque themes. The first is a frescoed lunette in the Palazzo della Cancelleria, Rome, executed around 1519. The general programme of the 'Volta dorata' is an Old Testament cycle, like Ghiberti's Gates of Paradise. Peruzzi's fresco was derived from Marcantonio's engraving. Here the painter has made a cogent revision of the townscape, by giving Solomon a proper habitat instead of the building lot he occupies in the engraving. In consequence the stage is clearly set, Solomon performs with greater energy, and the queen is given new importance by her isolation against the sky. Peruzzi's fresco is as secular in intent as the images of his Tuscan predecessors. According to Vasari, the 'Volta dorata' was commissioned by Cardinal Raffaelle Riario, Bishop of Ostia and chamberlain to the Pope. The visitation lunette is near a representation of Solomon's judgement in the vault. The juxtaposition suggests that these scenes allude to the worldly virtues of the chief legal and administrative officer of the papal state. Equally flattering to an unknown worldly patron is Peruzzi's second version of the visit, a ceiling fresco in the garden loggia of the Casina Vagnuzzi in Rome, dated around 1521. The scene is a pretty variant on the Cancelleria fresco, set in a vault organized like an antique Roman decoration. The queen is accompanied by delicious grotesques, charming figures of the pagan gods, and personifications of Fame, Chastity, Peace, Liberality and Victory. The Sheba theme is a wonderfully sugared compliment to the proprietor of the Casina Vagnuzzi.

A Venetian version of these Roman images is a vast canvas painted by Paolo Veronese shortly before his death in 1588 (Ill. 58). The composition is that of Marcantonio's engraving, but smothered. The painting is dominated by the bristling, glistening architecture of the background. Solomon sits enthroned at the left, as in the Roman examples. Surprisingly youthful, he seems about to be swamped by Sheba's splendours. Far below him kneels the young and beautiful queen, clad in the best Elizabethan fashions, and attended by maids bearing vessels of treasure, a charming black girl with two doves, a dwarf restraining a mastiff, and a delightful lapdog. Sweating servants manhandle strongboxes, while more courtiers fill up the courtyard, leaving only enough room for two camels. As in Raphael's fresco, several details indicate attempts at biblical correctness. Stone lions guard the king's throne, as they do also in the Bible and the *Speculum Humanae Salvationis*. Yet the final impression is of the visit as a wonderfully opulent pageant, closer in feeling to Apollonio di Giovanni than to High Renaissance Rome.

Jacopo Tintoretto, Veronese's great rival in Venice, seems to have been fascinated by the legend of the Queen of Sheba, for no fewer than seven paintings of the visit survive. These demonstrate Tintoretto's deep feeling, energetic style, and restless inventiveness. The earliest version is a *cassone* panel of around 1545 (Ill. 54), part of a group of six Old Testament scenes probably intended as secular decoration.

More variations are found in works at South Carolina and Chenonceaux. In the American canvas Tintoretto merely varies the Marcantonio scheme, reversing its direction and raising the point of sight. The viewer now looks down on a piazza littered with the queen's wealth which a Jewish scribe records. Prominently displayed are tusks of ivory. Another biblical touch is the architecture of Solomon's throne: the twisted columns are copied from antique columns in Rome then thought to be those of Solomon's temple. The painting in France is far less mannered and static. We are now placed behind Solomon's throne to witness the debate between king and queen. She also indicates her homage to Solomon, as a husky Negro servant opens cases of gold. The composition is as dramatic as the content, as Tintoretto plays off masses of figures in the foreground against deep spaces to the rear.

The most influential of Tintoretto's explorations of the Sheba theme is a ceiling painting executed around 1555. The viewer looks upwards into the painting. As the buildings of Jerusalem recede dramatically on either side, the queen's maids

Fig. 14. South German woodcut illustration to G. Boccaccio, *De Claris Mulieribus*, Mathi as Apiarius, Berne, 1539

look down and point to the debate. The Queen of Sheba is dramatically etched against the sky, so that her gesture of expostulation is clearly read. No reference to the wealth of Sheba is made, except for the actors' finery. The painting, now in Madrid, was undoubtedly made to adorn a Venetian palace. Other pictures in the series illustrate the deeds of virtuous women of the Old Testament. The companion to our painting, for example, was Queen Esther being accepted by Ahasuerus. As in Roman fresco decoration of the High Renaissance, the biblical story is made to serve secular purposes.

Tintoretto's interpretation of the queen's visit as a debate is preceded in time by a German woodcut published in Basle in 1539 as an illustration to Boccaccio's *De Claris Mulieribus* (Fig. 14). Solomon, attended by a burly majordomo, leans forward to argue with the queen, a middle-aged bluestocking. At her feet is a pile of books. Another burns vigorously in the background. The visit has become a sixteenth-century disputation. The German illustrator has admirably caught the spirit of Boccaccio's fourteenth-century treatise on famous women. Following Josephus, Boccaccio calls the queen Nikaula, and makes her Queen of Ethiopia. 'She did not give herself up to rest and womanly softness among the delights of wealth', but pursued a career of study. The illustrator also alludes to the world of 1539. The pile of burning books was a familiar image during the dispute between Catholics and Protestants in the North. Perhaps Tintoretto's paintings were equally topical in Venice.

The illustrator of the 1539 *De Claris Mulieribus* was influenced stylistically by his compatriot, Hans Holbein the Younger, to whom we owe one of the most unusual representations of the Sheba theme. Holbein's contribution is a drawing on vellum, touched in with azure and gold (Ill. 59). In an elaborate Renaissance hall is Solomon's throne, set in a panelled wall hung with cloths of honour sprinkled with golden stars. Here sits Solomon staring at the spectator. Before him pirouettes the Queen of Sheba and her suite. As her ladies promenade to the left, the slender queen directs Solomon's attention to servants proffering vessels of gold, wheat, and spices. All the company move with the grace of Marcantonio and Raphael.

Despite its Italianate composition, the drawing is as encrusted with inscriptions as a page from the *Biblia Pauperum*. On either side of the throne is inscribed the queen's apostrophe to Solomon as recorded in the Vulgate text of Kings. Above the throne is a paraphrase of I Kings 10:9: 'Blessed be the Lord thy God, which delighted in thee, to set thee upon the throne of Israel'. On the steps of the throne is a little-cited passage from Chronicles, 'You have surpassed with your own virtues the reports that I heard' (II Chronicles 9:6). Perhaps the Latin *fama* can be taken in its Renaissance sense as well, because the battery of inscriptions is not intended to be an aid to the pious.

The key to Holbein's drawing is Solomon, who is neither the gentle patriarch of medieval tradition, nor the pretty youth of the Italian Renaissance. Holbein's Solomon is squat, stocky, sprawling, and scowling. He is, in fact, a thinly disguised portrait of Henry VIII of England. The biblical inscriptions thus make perfect sense as allusions to the political state of England, and the supremacy of the monarch. The traditional interpretation of the Queen of Sheba as the Church would not be an inappropriate reference to Henry's ecclesiastical policy. Finally, the image of a wisely subservient woman would have been welcome at Henry's court. The drawing is usually interpreted as a demonstration of Holbein's qualifications for the position of court painter. The tactic succeeded.

The Italianate ideas so suavely handled by Holbein are less happily adapted in a painting attributed to Jan van Scorel and dated around 1540. This is a Flemish version of the Marcantonio formula, where the visit of the queen is arranged in frieze-like fashion. Other Italian touches are the ostentatious architecture *all'antica* and the Roman armour of Solomon's soldiers. Porters present gifts in gratuitously difficult poses which indicate the influence of Italian Mannerism. Yet the painting retains a pleasant Flemish feeling in such homely touches as the sleeping dog, the precisely rendered costumes, and the sharp observation of light.

The treatment of the Sheba theme in northern Europe during the sixteenth century is remarkably slight after the richness and quantity of fifteenth-century examples. The Reformation is to blame. In Protestant countries there was little need for biblical images in general. In the Catholic territories the Church pruned away spurious and apocryphal materials. Consequently, such charming fictions as the legend of the True Cross were bound to wither away.

During the seventeenth and eighteenth centuries, however, the story of the queen's visit to Solomon became almost as popular as it had been in the Middle Ages. In his monumental compilation of Baroque subjects, Anton Pigler cites at least two score examples. Most of these were produced in Catholic countries. In part the revival of the theme is due to a renewed interest of the Church in the devotional uses of religious painting. The ecclesiastical image had to compete, however, with the secular versions of the subject established during the Renaissance. These conflicting tendencies in Baroque art are demonstrated by the contributions of Peter Paul Rubens and Pietro da Cortona.

In 1620 Rubens painted a series of ceiling paintings for the new Jesuit Church of Antwerp. Though the building was destroyed by fire in 1718, its decoration can be reconstructed from engravings, drawings, and the painter's preliminary oil sketches. The north gallery of the Church was decorated with scenes from the Old and New Testaments; the Adoration of the Kings was paired with the visit of the Queen of Sheba. This revival of medieval typological schemes was typical of much Catholic church decoration during the Baroque period.

Rubens' painting is in the colourful traditions of Tintoretto and Veronese. The queen is a mature woman of dusky hue. Further exotic colour is offered by a mischievous black page in the foreground, encumbered with monkey and hawk. Solomon's throne, guarded by carved lions, gleams with gold. This profusion of detail is never allowed to smother the scene. The composition and the perspective focus attention upon the eloquent gestures of greeting and submission. The exuberance of Rubens is an expression of religious purpose.

Contemporary with these decorations for Antwerp is a ceiling fresco in Rome by Pietro da Cortona. The gallery of the Palazzo Mattei di Giove is adorned with ceiling scenes from the life of Solomon. In the centre of the vault, the queen's visit is paired with the king's idolatry, as if to demonstrate the wisdom and frailty of the monarch. Pietro da Cortona's scene is a revival of the Marcantonio formula of a century before. As in the art of Rubens, a Renaissance model is simplified, condensed, and re-edited, so that visual weight is now given to the commanding figure of the queen, who gestures in a sweeping diagonal to her Raphaelesque servants. In programme, the fresco decorations are in the secular traditions of Peruzzi's paintings of the High Renaissance. The wisdom of Solomon, and the ministrations of a wealthy woman, must have been a comfort to the aged marchese Asdrubale Mattei, whose palace this was.

In Italian painting of the seventeenth century, the theme of the Queen of Sheba became a series of variations on the ideas of Rubens and Cortona. In a painting by Francesco Maffei, the event is seen from close up, as a swirl of youthful and graceful figures, gold, clouds, armour, gesticulating limbs, and patches of light and shadow. Mattia Preti treated the motif as a quieter affair, in the Venetian taste. The queen sits in the centre displaying her wealth to an appropriately astounded king, while a pert lapdog looks out at the observer. Luca Giordano wove together ideas from Rubens, Cortona and the High Renaissance in a canvas where the queen stands quietly in converse with Solomon, while servants and courtiers prowl restlessly about in a patchy light. These examples, and others, indicate that the ancient theme was highly suitable to the Baroque taste for movement, colour and opulence.

Since many Baroque images of the Sheba legend were not commissioned for churches, it is reasonable to assume that the subject connoted secular wisdom, as in the early and High Renaissance. Confirmation of this point is provided by a delightful engraving of the eighteenth century, an illustration of the *Historiae et Allegoriae* compiled by Johann Georg Hertel between 1758 and 1760. Hertel's volumes were an adaptation of Cesare Ripa's *Iconologia*, an immensely important handbook of attributes and allegories. In the illustration designed by Gottfried Eichler the Younger, Sapientia is personified as a vigorous young woman, plainly dressed, who grinds a crown, gold, and silver underfoot as she looks up into a stream of light. Ripa explains that Wisdom scorns the things of this world. In the background Hertel and Eichler have introduced the familiar scene of the Queen of Sheba, here enthroned in a rococo confection, as an exemplification. The Latin tag above explains the addition: 'The Queen of Araby goes to Solomon, for she has heard that he is a man of great wisdom. On arriving, she cannot admire his wisdom, and riches, enough.' Herter and Eichler do not explain how we are to reconcile the wealth of Araby and Israel with the unworldly love of wisdom enacted by Sapientia.

A few years before the publication of the *Historiae et Allegoriae* in Augsburg, Sebastiano Conca completed a ceiling fresco for the nave of S. Chiara in Naples. This work of 1755 is one of the last appearances of the Queen of Sheba in a Christian context. Conca composed the scene as Marcantonio had suggested, but treated it in less severe fashion. The young king clad in armour rises courteously from his throne to greet the queen, who is silhouetted against a large and enthusiastically classical building. A breeze stirs her cloak into great swirling folds which sweep into an agitated crowd of servants, porters, ladies-in-waiting, and a gentle maid who shades her mistress with a parasol. This sunny pageant, like Eichler's engraving, belongs to the world of the opera and oratorio, not the church or the study.

On 17 March 1749, Handel's oratorio *Solomon* was performed at Covent Garden in London. Its principal themes are the building of the Temple, and Solomon's dalliance with his Egyptian wife. A secondary motif is the arrival of Nicaula, Queen of Sheba, the music for which has become enormously popular. 'From Arabia's spicy shores, bounded by the hoary main, Sheba's queen these seats explores.' Her quest is for wisdom:

> But to hear fair truth distilling
> In expression choice and thrilling
> From that tongue so soft and killing
> That my soul does most delight.

Handel and his librettist demonstrate Solomon's wisdom, not through proverbial utterances, but by a display of the power of music, stolen from St. Cecilia and Dryden.

> Thy harmony's divine, great king!
> All, all obey the artist's string,
> And now, illustrious prince, receive
> Such tribute as my realm can give.

As one student has aptly observed, the religious side plays a rather modest part in Handel's *Solomon*. His music is a fitting counterpart to the airy palaces, the glare of gems and gold, and the comings and goings of the Queen of Sheba in Baroque art.

Paradoxically, the most famous and most significant Baroque version of the Sheba theme bears no resemblance to the scenes of Conca and Cortona. Claude Lorrain's *Embarkation of the Queen of Sheba* (Ill. 60) was painted in Rome during 1648 together with a *Wedding Feast of Isaac and Rebecca*. Both were commissioned by the Duc de Bouillon, then general of the papal armies; both now hang in the National Gallery in London.

There are slender connections between Claude's painting and traditional Renaissance and Baroque treatments of the theme. The pairing of Rebecca and Sheba, for example, echoes humanistic concerns with famous women of the Old Testament, as in Tintoretto's ceiling series in Madrid. The pairing of the queen's journey with a wedding may even refer to the amatory aspects of the story stressed by *cassone* painters. Indeed, Claude's theme of embarkation has its only precedent in the gaily decorated furniture panels of two centuries before.

And yet Claude's *Embarkation* is like no other representation of the Queen of Sheba. Arabia's spicy shores are represented as a magnificent harbour opening upon the sea. The queen steps delicately down to the quay from her palace, the architecture of which evokes both Palladian Venice and antique Rome. The building is balanced by a magnificent temple on the other side. At the quay in the foreground, porters carry trunks to the gondola-like ships of the queen's fleet. People and buildings, however, are made subordinate to the vast expanse of sea and to the sun in the far distance.

As an illustration of events from the Book of Kings, Claude's painting is fanciful. Since the Bible stresses camels and caravans, the queen's journey to Jerusalem must have been by land. Such an expedition even the painters of *cassoni* faithfully represented. But the point is that Claude was not even pretending to illustrate Scripture. The queen's journey has become a voyage simply because Claude wished to paint an ideal seascape framed by noble buildings, agreeably contrasting with the pastoral scenery of the pendant *Wedding Feast of Isaac and Rebecca*. In both paintings the true subject is nature transfigured by light. What matters in the *Embarkation* is not the hubbub of transportation, but the wonderful golden light which steals across the harbour, reflected by the waves, to dissolve the airy palaces of Sheba's realm. The ancient legend of the Queen of Sheba has now become poetry.

Claude's stately pillars would have made an appropriate setting for the plays of his contemporary, the Spanish dramatist Pedro Calderón de la Barca. Calderón wrote two versions of the Sheba legend: the first, *El árbol del mejor fruto* of 1661, is a religious passion play; the second, *La sibylla del oriente y gran Reina de Sabá*, was probably performed somewhat later for the royal court of Spain. Both are based on the medieval legend of the True Cross and both exalt the Eucharist, the central sacrament of the Catholic faith. In their sources and religious aims the plays are analogous to such pictorial programmes as Rubens' canvases for the Jesuit Church of Antwerp. Equally Baroque is Calderón's lavish treatment of his theme. *El árbol del mejor fruto* reads like an oratorio where all the personages declaim long set speeches in florid language. Personifications such as Music and Idolatry are added to elevate the narrative. *La sibylla del oriente* is even more splendidly ornamented with tableaux and musical choruses, like a courtly masque. Biblical figures grow larger than life: Solomon in all his glory is assisted by willing vassals, Hiram, King of Tyre, and the King of Egypt; the queen has become sovereign sibyl of great India to the East, Empress of Ethiopia, and invincible Queen of Sheba. The meeting of the royal pair is grandiose:

> Sheba and Solomon
> seem to be as one;
> of genius and beauty
> she's a divine prodigy,
> and he a human miracle
> of glory and wisdom,
> so that in upholding
> glory and prudence
> the twain seem as one.
> She in the lands of the East
> holds the sun in sway,
> as he in the climes of the South
> keeps a more extensive realm,
> so that in offering
> honour with honour,
> the twain seem as one.

Calderón's plays are magnificent finales to a Christian tradition and yet are symptomatic of its decline. Calderón seems to have ferreted out every available scrap of information, Christian, Jewish, and Islamic, on the land of Sheba and its queen. He repeats, for example, the legend of the crystal floor and transforms the queen's attendants into Negroes. The dramatist's curiosity is almost archaeological. The plays end with the queen's veneration of the True Cross, ignominiously disguised as a bridge. Calderón's stress on the insight of the queen, and consequent diminution of Solomon's glory, is novel and anticipates post-Christian concerns of the nineteenth century.

The plays of Calderón, the music of Handel, and the paintings of Claude are the last significant representations of the legend of the Queen of Sheba within a Christian tradition that refers to the account given in the Old Testament and conventional interpretations in ecclesiastical and humanistic thought. Yet this tradition by no means exhausts the fascination that the queen has exerted on artists, writers and scholars in the West. She is not only an *exemplum virtutis* but also a figure of folklore and a heroine of romance. These last manifestations can be classified as 'sub-Christian' and 'post-Christian' respectively.

The Queen of Sheba lives in folklore as the *reine pédauque*, a slightly sinister figure with one webbed foot. She has co-existed with the stately figures of medieval Renaissance, and Baroque art, and enjoys a sort of life even to this day. The *reine pédauque* is, of course, the European version of Talmudic and Islamic legend, and is therefore sub-Christian. Her history is a fascinating episode in itself.

Both the second *Targum* to the Book of Esther and Arabic legends relate how a hairy-legged Queen of Sheba came to visit Solomon. Versions of this probably circulated widely at an early date in Islam, in Byzantium, and in the Christian West. Several ecclesiastics of the twelfth century repeat a rumour that Solomon's visitor was curiously deformed. Thus in one manuscript datable between 1154 and 1159, the queen is termed 'lady of Sheba and also of Ethiopia, and a Sibyl, with goose-like feet and eyes shining like a star'. This characterization was repeated in the *De imagine mundi* by a certain Honorius, perhaps of Augsburg.

There is a considerable gap between an Eastern hairy-legged queen and a Western goose-footed one. The missing link is probably to be found in Byzantium. Both Western writers of the twelfth century deal with versions of the legend of the True Cross, itself a Greek fabrication; and they both characterize the queen as a sibyl, another sign of Byzantine influence. The goose-footed queen seems therefore to have entered Europe surreptitiously from Greece in a garbled version of the legend of the Cross.

The documented life of Sheba Goose-foot seems to have been restricted to Germany during the Middle Ages. The two twelfth-century writers just referred to were active in Bavaria and the Rhineland. From Nuremberg in the fifteenth century comes a manual for painters, in which is described the legend of the Cross and mention made of the queen's anserine deformity. The *Sibillien Boiche*, a

52. Ghiberti: *Solomon* panel from the Gates of Paradise, Baptistery, Florence

53. Apollonio di Giovanni: *cassone* panel (Museum of Fine Arts, Boston)

54. Tintoretto: *The Queen of Sheba*, panel, *c.* 1545 (Kunsthistorisches Museum, Vienna)

55. Sano di Pietro: *cassone* panel, *c.* 1450–60 (Metropolitan Museum of Art, New York)

popular devotional poem printed in 1513, describes in homely verse how the Queen of Sheba refused to traverse Solomon's bridge:

> She goes straight through the water in the stream
> Just to honour the wood and respect it
> That over the water was laid;
> And then, by God's good will,
> Was her goosefoot changed
> Into a man's foot just like the other
> Which pleased the Sibyl so . . .

It must be emphasized that these German texts are the only ones in the corpus of medieval writings on the legend of the Cross, a formidable mass of literature, to mention the goose's foot. Moreover, the queen is never represented in paintings of the legend as deformed, despite the instructions of the Nuremberg painters' manual. The texts document only the remarkable persistence of a rumour whose elements were like those of folk tales.

The goose-foot queen did appear fitfully in medieval art, but not in Germany. In several French churches of the twelfth century carved portal figures represented the Queen of Sheba in uncanonical guise. The principal piece of evidence for this tradition is a drawing of the portal of Saint-Bénigne at Dijon, made before its destruction in the late eighteenth century. At the extreme right beside King Solomon is a crowned queen whose left foot is webbed. The sculpture was probably carved in the late twelfth century. Documentary evidence indicates that similar web-footed queens adorned the church of St Pierre at Nevers and the Abbeys of Saint-Pourçain and Nesle-la-Réposte, as well as a church in Toulouse. All of these examples unfortunately have been destroyed.

We are left with a body of sculpture that offers limited evidence for the existence of a goose-footed queen. All of these examples came from Burgundy and southern France, not from the Ile-de-France where the great Gothic figures were carved. The churches can be securely placed in the twelfth century. It is likely, therefore, that the French version of Sheba Goose-foot was a local tradition of the early Middle Ages, derived no doubt from garbled texts of the German type. The type is unknown elsewhere in France, nor is the queen deformed in later Gothic art.

The portal figures of web-footed queens remained vivid in popular imagination long after their original purpose had been forgotten. In the sixteenth century, Rabelais mentioned parenthetically those 'who have such huge and ungainly feet, as geese do, and as the *reine pédauque* did at Toulouse once upon a time'. Rabelais probably was referring to a lost Romanesque statue which had become a familiar object, a proverb in stone.

Scholarly interest in the identity of the *reine pédauque* did not appear until more recent times. To the labours of Mabillon in the seventeenth century and Lebœuf in the eighteenth we owe our knowledge of the works of art before their destruction as well as a remarkable body of lore and conjecture on what they represented. Some who then believed that all regal portal figures represented French monarchs tried to place the *reine pédauque* in the Merovingian or Carolingian dynasties. One candidate was Bertha, the mother of Charlemagne, who according to medieval legends had one foot considerably larger than the other. In one Spanish romance Queen Bertha is web-footed. Thus the *reine pédauque* was confusedly identified with Bertha Big-foot.

The Abbé Lebœuf reported that the portal figures were called by some Princess Austris, reportedly converted to Christianity by Saint Sernin, a saint of Provence. Lebœuf argued convincingly that this princess was a pious fraud, and that 'Austris' was really a corruption of *Regina Austri*, queen from the south, the medieval epithet of the Queen of Sheba. The legend of the princess was a popular invention made to fit the ill-remembered name of a biblical queen. Lebœuf strengthened his argument by adducing the Jewish tales of the queen's deformity, thus proving that the *reine pédauque* was in truth the Queen of Sheba. Students of medieval iconography in the nineteenth and twentieth centuries have accepted and confirmed Lebœuf's deductions.

It is pleasant to report that the *reine pédauque* still survives. A sign board depicting the goose-footed queen plays a part in a delightful tale by Anatole France set in the eighteenth century and treating of a failed priest, a would-be-savant, and a cabbalist. *La rôtisserie de la reine pédauque* was first published in 1893 and has been translated into English several times. And the queen adorns the bottles of a fine Beaujolais produced in Aloxe-Corton in upper Burgundy, not far from where the Romanesque statues were.

The legend of Sheba Goose-foot is sub-Christian by virtue of its predominantly Oriental sources. As such, it prefigures the post-Christian Queen of Sheba, who is largely an invention of the nineteenth century. She was made possible by new disciplines of archaeology and Orientology which opened up sources of information (and misinformation) hitherto known only at second hand and in confused form in the West. The post-Christian Queen of Sheba is found in literature, rather than the visual arts. That literary tradition in turn has coloured present-day notions of the Queen of Sheba to an extraordinary extent.

The nineteenth century's image of the Queen of Sheba is best studied in the *Tentation de Saint Antoine* by Gustave Flaubert, a work first devised between 1846 and 1849, revised in 1856, and given final form in 1874. It is based on the legend of the hermit Anthony the Abbot, who was tormented by monstrous temptations in the Egyptian desert near Thebes. Flaubert used many sources for this, including medieval hagiography, the paintings of Bruegel and Bosch, and the discoveries of archaeology. Among the first nightmarish visions of the book is the advent of the

Queen of Sheba, who had tempted Solomon with hard questions. She comes riding to Saint Anthony's cell on a white elephant, 'on cushions of blue wool, cross-legged, with eyelids half-closed and well-poised head . . . so magnificently attired that she emits rays around her'. She tempts Anthony with the spices of Araby and the wealth of Orient. She offers him the wealth of Sheba itself, palaces, lakes, animals, diamonds and grottoes.

The final temptation is the queen's own body. For she is beautiful, clad only in gold and silver—'a chain of plate gold, passing under her chin, runs along her cheeks till it twists itself in spiral fashion around her head, over which blue powder is scattered; then descending, it slips over her shoulders and is fashioned above her bosom by a diamond scorpion, which stretches out its tongue between her breasts'. Her garments restrain a ravishingly sensuous body, a succession of mysteries proffered to Saint Anthony. She comes close to kiss him. He abruptly makes the sign of the Cross to save himself. The queen laughs scornfully, as a monkey lifts up her robe to reveal a deformed foot, and then departs.

Flaubert's glamorous prose is well matched by the lithographs of Odilon Redon, published as illustrations to the *Tentation de Saint Antoine* in 1888 and 1896. In the first, Redon suppresses the setting and portrays the queen as Flaubert had described her in her jewels, while a miraculous bird, a man-faced hoopoe, is about to alight on her shoulder (Ill. 61). The most striking aspect of the print is a contrast between the agitation of the bird and the calm of the queen. A further contrast between the subtle modelling of her figure and the abrupt rendering of the bird accentuates the mystery of Redon's lithograph. In his second version of Flaubert's Sheba in 1896, Redon presents only the head of the queen in profile like an Egyptian relief. Again she is introspective and yet menacing, for we see her through the eyes of the saint as she breathes 'Bring your lips near! My kisses have the taste of fruit that would melt in your heart.'

Flaubert's Queen of Sheba, so different from the virtuous pilgrim of the Christian tradition, is a substitute for the generalized figure of Luxury, usually a naked woman, who frequently assails Saint Anthony in religious art and literature. The notion of the Queen of Sheba as a temptress who had overcome Solomon was gleaned from Islamic sources made available by such early handbooks as Herbelot's *Bibliothèque orientale*. But Flaubert is more than a zealous antiquary, as his treatment of the hoopoe indicates. In Eastern legends, the bird is falcon-like and belongs to Solomon. Flaubert has given the diabolical creature to Sheba as a symbol of her potency. In the last analysis, Flaubert's Queen of Sheba is the product of a romantic imagination.

Flaubert's *Tentation* was not the only literary appearance of the new Queen of Sheba in the early nineteenth century. Queen Balkis is the heroine of *La fée aux miettes*, a rambling hallucinatory fantasy composed by Charles Nodier in 1832. His 'Belkiss' is a demonic witch who lures the narrator into a series of confused misadventures. A more coherent and compelling creation is the image of the queen in the work of Gérard de Nerval. In the *Aurélia*, for example, the poet paints her as the goddess of his dreams, like the Apocalyptic Woman described by St John, standing on a crescent moon, 'crowned with stars and coiffed with a turban of the hues of the rainbow . . . her dress was of the colour of hyacinths'.

For Gérard de Nerval the Queen of Sheba was a fatal obsession. She is the moving spirit of 'Histoire de la reine du matin et de Soliman prince des génies', a novel appended to his *Voyage en orient* of 1851. The story is woven together from the Old Testament, the Qur'an, the Talmud, and the occult lore of Freemasonry. As in Flaubert's *Tentation*, all is leavened by the writer's imagination. The story begins as the queen of the morning arrives in Jerusalem to marry Solomon. Accompanied by an innumerable throng, Queen Balkis shines forth; 'her face has the beauty of a sphinx, with black eyes like those of gazelles, and a mouth trembling between a smile and seduction'. When the queen greets the king, she is clad simply in a cloud of transparent gauze in contrast to Solomon's golden attire, 'like a lily strayed into a field of dandelions'. Nerval's imagery is superbly visual.

Nerval brought to the ancient legend the powers of a sensitive novelist and poet. His Balkis wins the king by subtle flattery, and then demolishes his wisdom by clever arguments. She comes alive as a woman of quick wit and high intelligence, far more interesting than the complacent and vain Solomon. He tries to win her by flattery, romantic ardour, and deceit. Her love, however, goes out to a kindred spirit, a marvellous artificer, Adoniram, master of the works of the Temple. Only his boldness and intellect are fit for Balkis. The queen sleeps with Adoniram, who gets her with child. They part at the end forever. Balkis flees back to Sheba, while Adoniram is assassinated on the orders of Solomon. This bare summary does no justice to the splendour of Nerval's descriptions or to the subtlety of his characterizations. Adoniram is a brooding titanic figure, part Faust, part Michelangelo. He and the queen are creatures of fire, who dare to overreach mortal bounds, while Solomon is fearful, despondent, and even melancholic. Nerval's 'Reine du matin' is less a re-telling of an old tale than a new invention with power and life of its own.

Gérard de Nerval once dreamed of writing an opera about the Queen of Sheba. That ambition was posthumously realized in January of 1862 when *La reine de Saba* was performed at the Opéra in Paris. The libretto, based on the 'Reine du matin', was by Jules Barbier and Michel Carré, the music by Charles Gounod. Unlike his *Faust* of 1859, Gounod's *Reine de Saba* was not a success. Part of the blame lies in the libretto, an over-simplified version of Nerval's story, which at once slights the poet's complex play of motives and yet is couched in overly abstract language. Moreover, the story was bowdlerized, so that the tragic passion of Adoniram and Balkis becomes merely a conventional affair, finished off by a bungled elopement.

The libretto is compensated for by several stirring choruses, one or two fine arias sung by the queen, and the events of Act II when volcanoes erupt and furnaces explode on stage.

More to nineteenth-century taste was *Die Königin von Saba* by Karl Goldmark, first performed in Vienna in 1875. The libretto was by Salomon Hermann von Mosenthal, and is yet another romantic triangle. The hero is a Jewish noble, Assad, who is betrothed to Sulamith, daughter of Solomon. Their love is destroyed by the Queen of Sheba, a demonic creature much like Flaubert's temptress. Assad is doomed when he spies the queen bathing in the woods of Lebanon:

> From crystal waves a swan-like body rises,
> It is a woman of celestial beauty!
> Dark raven hair her neck and bosom veils
> As ebony frames a bust of ivory;
> Two stars flash through the drooping lashes' night,
> Two roses keeping guard over glittering pearls,
> Two arms entwined into a wreath of lilies . . .
> She throws her lily arms around my neck!
> She draws me to her softly swelling bosom,
> Confused and half unconscious I kneel down
> Upon my knees before the fair enchantress.

The settings and the score rise to similar heights. The action takes place in oriental halls of vast scale, palaces and gardens of luxuriant splendour. The triumphal entry of the queen in the first Act is worthy of *Aida*, while the grand finale is a sandstorm in the Arabian desert. The music, which combines Wagnerian grandiloquence with motifs from Oriental melodies, has been characterized as 'highly spiced'. How far have we come from Handel's stately airs!

The British counterpart to these continental extravagances is in the realm of poetry, rather than the performing arts. Leaving aside the contributions of Lascelles Abercrombie (*Emblems of Love*) and John Freeman (*Balkis and Solomon*), we shall find new variations on nineteenth-century themes in the writings of Symons and Yeats.

In 1899 the poet and critic Arthur Symons published *The Lover of the Queen of Sheba*, a dramatic dialogue in verse. The characters are Solomon, the queen, and a youth of Sheba in love with his sovereign. Though he loves the queen, she has moved beyond passion:

> She, the one whiteness of the earth,
> For whom the ardent valley grows
> A flame, an odour, and the rose
> Finds in the world but wisdom worth
> The trouble of the soul's repose . . .

In Solomon the queen has found the wisdom she seeks. Yet the king has fallen out of love with knowledge and power,

> Love only is the eternal now,
> Being of our frailty piteous.
> When thou are I, and I am thou,
> Time is no more . . . Beloved, come
> Into the garden dim with spice;
> Let us forget that we are wise,
> And wisdom, though it be the sum
> Of all but love, is love's disguise.

Symons' poem owes much to nineteenth-century traditions, and yet deviates from them. The idea of an amorous triangle involving the Queen of Sheba had been exploited by Gérard de Nerval, whose work Symons much admired. But the English writer remains closer to the Old Testament than the French one: Sheba regains her 'Christian' identity as a virtuous seeker after wisdom, and Solomon's reputation is rehabilitated. The old story has now become a symbolic presentation of the paradoxical union of love and wisdom.

The problems raised by Symons' *The Lover of the Queen of Sheba* were treated anew by William Butler Yeats. In his *Solomon and Sheba* of 1919 he writes with lyrical directness:

> Sang Solomon to Sheba,
> And kissed her Arab eyes,
> 'There's not a man or woman
> Born under the skies
> Dare match in learning with us two,
> And all day long we have found
> There's not a thing but love can make
> The world a narrow pound'.

This simple-seeming singing ballad masks a number of knotty problems. Yeats paints his characters with economy; we know that Sheba is a dusky Arab, and that she and Solomon are wise. The pair becomes generalized, and also very personal, so that the reader is made to confront immediately the paradox that wisdom is love's disguise.

New dimensions appear in *On Woman*, also of 1919. Yeats begins playfully by asserting that Solomon grew wise only while talking to his queens. But wisdom is more than intellectual cognition,

> When Sheba was his lass
> When she the iron wrought, or
> When from the smithy fire
> It shuddered in the water:

> Harshness of their desire
> That made them stretch and yawn
> Pleasure that comes with sleep,
> Shudder that makes them one.

Sex was the moving ingredient of the nineteenth-century myth of Sheba, but only Yeats wrestled with the implications of sexual love. In his taut verse, cerebral and sensual at the same time, sexual union is forged into a species of mystical wisdom.

Of Yeats' 'Sheba' poems, *Solomon and the Witch* of 1921 is the most difficult. Its theme is sexual love, its images a mystical cockerel and a spider, and its form a dialogue between Solomon and the Arab queen. Love and hate are closely allied, yet passionate love only is the eternal now:

> Maybe the bride-bed brings despair
> For each an imagined image brings
> And finds an imagined image there
> Yet the world ends when these two things
> Though several, are a single light
> When oil and wick are burned in one;
> Therefore a blessed moon last night
> Gave Sheba to her Solomon.

This is perhaps the most occult and challenging manifestation of the post-Christian Sheba. The poetry of Yeats at the least also demonstrates the power of the old story, even in the twentieth century.

The popularity of the Sheba theme in the twentieth century is attested to by the British and American contemporaries of W. B. Yeats. Rudyard Kipling devoted one of his Just-So Stories, 'The Butterfly That Stamped', to King Solomon and Balkis the Most Beautiful Queen, 'Queen that was of Sheba and Sabie and the Rivers of Gold of the South—from the Desert of Zinn to the Towers of Zimbabwe', who is his principal wife and in charge of the other nine hundred. The story is a robust oriental fantasy. The Sheba legend was parodied in 1922 in *The Queen of Sheba, Her Life and Times* purportedly by Phineas A. Crutch. The queen is a flapper, Solomon a middle-aged roué, and the supporting characters are all addicted to dreadful puns. The *mise en scène* is vaguely Egyptian. The book parodies not only Gérard de Nerval and the Bible, but also the occasional pedantries of modern scholarship. An entirely different use of the story is in *Three Soldiers* of 1921 by John Dos Passos. A wounded soldier, Andrews, lies in hospital half-delirious; into his reveries floats the Queen of Sheba, or rather Flaubert's temptress, who on closer inspection is merely a nurse. Yet the vision of the Queen of Sheba functions in the novel as a romantic escapist symbol of a peaceful world.

Three Soldiers indicates the continuation of the nineteenth-century Queen of Sheba far into the twentieth. The same point is made by an art form which is indigenous to this century, the motion picture. There have been at least three versions of the story in the last fifty years. The first, *The Queen of Sheba*, was released in 1921 with Betty Blythe in the title role. Its plot, by Virginia Tracy, sounds like a parody of the operas of Gounod and Goldmark. The heroine is an obscure maiden who marries the usurper King of Sheba and then murders him on their wedding night in order to liberate her people. As the Queen of Sheba she visits Solomon, and they fall in love, much to the annoyance of Solomon's Egyptian wife Amrath. The film's quota of violence and sex included several battle scenes, a chariot race reminiscent of *Ben Hur* between Amrath and the Queen of Sheba, and the appeal of Miss Blythe. In the most recent version of the story, biblical accuracy is once more of secondary importance. *Solomon and Sheba* of 1960 presented armies clashing in the sand, architectural settings of no discernible period style, and the timeless and abundantly displayed charms of Gina Lollobrigida as the queen. The climax of the film was an artfully photographed bathing scene, perhaps a subconscious memory of Goldmark's *Die Königin von Saba*.

The Sheba theme has played a less sensational role in more traditional forms of the visual arts. Recent examples include a series of illustrations to the Bible made by Marc Chagall in 1956. Chagall, a Russian Jew, has returned to the account given in the Book of Kings. Solomon is a patriarchal crowned figure who welcomes a demure queen riding a camel to his palace. The etching is marked by an air of gentle whimsy, most apparent in the curlicues and carvings of Solomon's house. The scene becomes simple and artfully childlike.

The continuing heritage of the Queen of Sheba is apparent in the work of Romare Bearden, a painter resident in New York's Harlem who often does collages based on biblical themes. *She-ba* of 1970 (Ill. 62) presents a queen seated, with an attendant. The collage is like ancient Egyptian paintings in its stiff poses, hieratic gestures, and figural proportions. In a way the painting is thus a descendant of the fantasies of Redon, but made modern. This She-ba is black, as were the queens of Romanesque and Gothic art; moreover, the assemblage of bright textiles and patterned shapes evokes the folk art of West Africa. One level of meaning for this complex image is given by Bearden's title, She-ba, which is a deliberate pun; she is the focus of love for a particular woman, even as the Shebas of Yeats and Nerval were. *She-ba* also admits of a new, collective significance peculiar to America. This black African queen is relevant to a new black nationalism, black history, and even black mythology taking shape in the United States at this time. In several textbooks on Negro history the Queen of Sheba has been treated as a major culture heroine. Bearden's *She-ba* is a vivid and poetic symbol for the black community in the United States.

Bearden's Ethiopian queen and Yeats's dusky Arab show that the post-Christian Queen of Sheba is very much alive in the twentieth century. These widely divergent conceptions of the lady indicate that she, like her Christian predecessor, is an exotic

56. Unknown Italian, marriage salver, *c.* 1475 (Museum of Fine Arts, Boston)

57. Marcantonio Raimondi: engraving, *c.* 1518 (British Museum)

58. Paolo Veronese: *The Queen of Sheba offers gifts to Solomon*, before 1588 (Pinacoteca, Turin; Photo Alinari)

59. Hans Holbein the Younger, drawing, *c.* 1535 (Reproduced by gracious permission of
H.M. The Queen, Windsor Castle)

60. Claude Lorrain: *Embarkation of the Queen of Sheba*, 1648 (National Gallery, London)

61. Odilon Redon: 'And a large bird, descending from the sky', *Tentation de Saint Antoine*, 1888, lithograph

62. Romare Bearden: *She-ba*, 1970, collage (Wadsworth Atheneum, Hartford, Conn.)

63. The Sacred Bowl. Roman, green glass, 40 cm. across (Museo del Tesoro della Cattedrale, Genoa). According to the most ancient tradition which goes back to William, Bishop of Tyre, the bowl was part of the rich loot which the Crusaders brought back from Caesarea in 1101. Supposedly it had been given by the Queen of Sheba to King Solomon and was used by Jesus Christ during the Last Supper and by Nicodemus after the Crucifixion to collect Christ's blood. Archaeologists disagree as to its chronology: some believe it belonged to the first Imperial Period, some to a much later age, even after the foundation of the Eastern Empire. It is likely that the bowl was manufactured in some Syrian or Palestinian workshop where coloured glass was produced in imitation of precious stones. (With acknowledgement to C. Marcenaro)

symbol in which the artist may project what he wishes. But perhaps we should remember that this romantic Queen of Sheba is a reflection of the sober researches of biblical archaeology and scholarship. It is fitting, therefore, to let an archaeologist have the last word. In his memoirs Sir Leonard Woolley tells of a charming and daftly logical conversation with some Kurdish tribesmen who kept the memory of Solomon and Sheba green. 'How', they asked, 'do you think he communicated with her if he didn't have wireless, and how did he visit her if he didn't have aeroplanes?' George Sprod's cartoon in the Assyrian style is an appropriate answer (Fig. 15).

The quest for the significance of a very old story has not yet come to its end.

Fig. 15. George Sprod: 'Solomon Visiting Sheba', cartoon (from Sir Leonard Woolley, *As I Seem to Remember*, George Allen & Unwin Ltd, London 1962)

Conclusion

James B. Pritchard

HAVING reached the end of our examination of the Solomon and Sheba stories we must ask some 'hard questions' of the evidence we have presented. The starting point was a courtly tale out of the remote past—exactly how old it is we cannot say—that had been kept alive in writings sacred to a people for whom Solomon was a symbol of wisdom. And the figure of Solomon and the golden age that his wisdom had made possible, an era of peace and prosperity, were memories that served well to underpin Israel with hope in times of trouble. The breathless amazement at the wisdom and wealth of Solomon on the part of the queen of the fabulously wealthy kingdom of Sheba constituted sure documentation for the dream of past glory. What served man's need so well was not easily forgotten.

How often was the tale told? And to how many in the course of the centuries? Identifiable references to it appear in such influential books as the *Gospels*, the *Qur'an*, *Kebra Nagast*, the *Zohar*, the *Targum Sheni*, as well as in scores of other documents that have by chance been preserved. But beyond the written word the queen's visit to Solomon was depicted to those who entered the doors of the cathedrals at Chartres, Amiens, Rheims and Canterbury, or beheld the Gates of Paradise, cast by Lorenzo Ghiberti and installed at the Baptistery of Florence. Others were reminded of the famous meetings when viewing the paintings of Raphael, Veronese, Tintoretto, Holbein, Rubens, and many others, or upon listening to the oratorio *Solomon* by Handel. The tale from ancient Jerusalem has cast a long shadow through the ages and across the world.

What evidence in fact is there for the picture presented in the story for the extravagant magnificence of the Age of Solomon? In due course we have turned to archaeology for its evidence on the quality of life lived in the tenth century before Christ in Palestine. The so-called cities of Megiddo, Gezer, Hazor—all said to have been built by Solomon—Gibeon, the site of Solomon's holocausts, and Jerusalem itself, were in reality more like villages and surrounded by circumambulatory ramparts of roughly hewn stone. Within were relatively small public buildings and frequently poorly constructed dwellings with clay floors. Strewn on the floors and embedded in the debris were objects which reveal a material culture that, even by the standards of the ancient Near East, could not be judged sophisticated or luxurious. When compared to the Canaanite civilization of the preceding Late Bronze Age the material culture did not match the earlier standards in craftsmanship and art. And when compared with the culture which had long flourished in the neighbouring areas of Phoenicia, Assyria and Egypt, the 'magnificence' of the Age of Solomon is parochial and decidedly lacklustre. Such is the realistic picture that emerged from the cultural remains recovered in comparatively recent times by archaeology.

Such a view of the age and its wealth presented by archaeology does not tally with the impression gained from reading the chapters in I Kings describing the glories of the Solomonic age. The obvious gap between the two sources, archaeology and the biblical narratives, has been lessened, if not entirely removed, by the general conclusion of biblical scholars that the extant record of the wealthy and wise king is the product of an age far removed—even as much as three centuries—from the realities of the tenth century. Distant though it was from the age it sought to describe the record has, however, preserved, along with its exaggerations and legends, authentic information about events and the spirit of the times. By following 'tracks' left behind, in both archaeological remains and the written record, it is hoped, as Marc Block once wrote, we may be 'successful in knowing far more of the past than the past itself had thought good to tell us'. In short, the written sources for our knowledge of the Age of Solomon are indeed scanty, obviously biased in certain directions, but when used with sympathy and understanding they provide the basis for the recovery of an age which without them would have been completely forgotten.

In our search for information about Sheba, the locale in the Arabian peninsula from which the queenly visitor is said to have come, we have found the remains of a high culture that flourished through many centuries: buildings, statuary, irrigation systems, articles of everyday life, and inscriptions that attest the literacy of those who lived there. Yet, as Gus Van Beek has pointed out, it must be made clear that the evidence for constructing a detailed picture of Sheba's culture is for the most part from periods later than the tenth century BC. Only at Hajar Bin Humeid, a site located forty miles south of Marib, the capital of Sheba, have there been found as yet deposits that can be dated to the reputed time of the Queen of Sheba; and that material is scanty indeed. Yet, the very isolation of the ancient kingdom of Sheba throughout its entire pre-Christian history ensured a continuity of cultural traditions. The extrapolation backwards from better-known later periods of time to the tenth century is, in the absence of any concrete evidence, a method of reconstruction that commands some credibility. The deductive evidence, while admittedly not primary, provides a clue that should be afforded some weight in forming a conclusion to our search. To sum up, Sheba was inhabited in the tenth century BC; by the seventh century we know that a high culture flourished there and continued down to Christian times; the actual names of two queens who ruled in Arabia are known from Assyrian inscriptions; the region of Sheba was long famous for the production and export of the odiferous gums of frankincense and myrrh, widely used throughout the ancient Near East for incense, lotions and medicines; and caravan routes from Sheba to Palestine have been traced. Although this increment of archaeological and historical research does not provide positive support for the historicity of the event with which we are concerned, it casts no doubt on the *mise en scène* of the Arabian queen described in the biblical story.

What, then, is the verdict? Is there substantial evidence for a queen of Sheba who made a long journey with presents for the Israelite monarch? Was there an actual meeting between the two principals? We are forced to reply that, like so many happenings reported from the past, the factual basis for the story cannot be verified beyond the single witness we have to it, the few verses in the Book of Kings. The verdict in the last analysis must rest upon circumstantial evidence and a decision made on the basis of probability. Here two cases can be made.

In support of a decision for historical probability there are two arguments. The one has to do with Solomon's foreign policy. Unlike David, his father, who was frequently at war, Solomon is reported to have been on friendly terms with his neighbours. Hiram was his ally in maritime commerce as well as his principal supplier in a national building programme. He cemented his bonds with Egypt through marriage to the daughter of the Pharaoh. Throughout his long reign he was apparently free from the necessity of wars with neighbouring states, who in less happy times were the enemies of Israel. This picture of an era of peace sketched by the biblical narratives is consistent with what records we have of the neighbouring powers. Thus, the reign of Solomon seems, as best as can be established, to have been in a climate of amicable foreign relations; those so vividly described in our story as having existed between the King of Israel and the Queen of Sheba are consistent with the whole. The spirit of the visit would have been in keeping with the mood of the time.

The second argument for the probability of the event is the reality of a rich kingdom in the far-distant south—the famed kingdom of Sheba. The evidence is slight, to be sure, but sufficient to make plausible the background described in the story. Sheba is more than a shadow; too much of its past has been recovered to allow one to doubt its existence.

Yet the case for the opposing view must be summarized. The marks of folklore are unmistakably present in the narrative, such as the mention of a fantastic amount of gold. The four and a half tons of gold as part of the royal gift carried across the wastes of Arabia is a strain upon the credibility of those familiar with the level of culture that prevailed in the tenth century of the ancient Near Eastern world. There is, too, the improbability of a long journey of more than 1,400 miles across a rugged terrain for the sole purpose of satisfying the curiosity of a woman. There are indeed records of long treks across the ancient world, but these were generally for the purpose of military or economic expansion. Such a trivial purpose as the desire to propound riddles seems strangely out of place in a world where travel was both arduous and dangerous. Furthermore the main thrust of the story is clearly to emphasize the greatness and splendour of Solomon. Similar tributes to the great king are known to have been presented by his admirers in ages long after the more realistic accounts of his reign had been composed. Certainly the courteous and even pious speech of the pagan queen reads more like that of an admirer from an epigonous age than an actual report of her exclamation.

A final verdict on the historicity of the account may never be possible. Yet if archaeological investigation continues it is not unreasonable to expect more discoveries, and perhaps some will throw light on this puzzling problem. The final verdict will at least have to be suspended until more evidence has been accumulated. In the meantime the basis in fact for this tantalizing story will remain an open question.

Although our attempts to get at the origin of the famous story have not yielded proof for its basis in history, but only two options of probability, we are on firmer ground in tracing its wide diffusion. Whether fact or fiction, the story has run a long and winding course. What clues are there to be found in the records for the use of the story that may explain its popularity? Surely the grandiose picture of royal splendour—the ostentation of the court of Solomon and such luxuries as gold, precious stones, and spices—is of a king that delights the story-teller and invites embellishment. The mention of the queen's long journey from a traditionally fabulous land was bound to suggest imaginative detail. And Solomon's renown for wisdom provided a point of departure for subsequent sages who augmented the tradition with their own contribution to this genre of stories. Yet these elements alone cannot fully account for the widespread popularity of the tale.

Oddly enough it is in the Judaic tradition, where one would expect scrupulous transmission of the biblical story, that there are the greatest departures. The friendly Queen of Sheba, the propounder of riddles, was transformed in the passage of time into Lilith, queen of the demons. When we seek the reason for this radical change in the role of the queen we have only a hint of the nexus between these two antithetical concepts. Somewhere in the course of the transmission of this bit of ancient lore an imaginative spinner of tales, one with no concern for the chronology of the biblical history, made the Queen of Sheba the mother of Nebuchadnezzar, the Babylonian king responsible for the destruction of the Temple in Jerusalem. Who but a demon could have given birth to such an enemy of the Jewish people! Folk logic had triumphed over the more sober record of the past. The amiable queen from the south was eventually metamorphosed into the monster who, with the passage of time, became increasingly more ferocious and spread her evil influence even wider. To be sure, the record of the story's history is sketchy but hints here and there in a variety of sources suggest that this bizarre geneaology was the source for an unexpected *dénouement* of the story.

For the European Christian, to judge from the artistic record, the queen was cast in quite a different role. She was revered as a prototype of the Church, the bride of Christ. Jew and Christian, living side by side, had each inherited a tradition and had accepted it without question. As a stone-mason carved the statue of the Queen of Sheba for the portal of a cathedral dedicated to the Virgin, or a glass-maker fashioned a window depicting the celebrated visit, an equally devout Jew may have been making an incantation to conjure up the evil queen of the demons. Yet both reached back into the same tradition for the basic inspiration of his concept of the Queen of Sheba. Such is the course of ideas through different channels of history.

The course of the Sheba tradition in the Christian art of Europe is a fairly consistent one. The queen maintained her exalted role as the Church Fathers opened the door for introducing the themes found in the Old Testament into Christian theology by means of the device of typology. The queen was seen as a type of the Church; and her eagerness to visit Solomon prefigured the Church's desire for Christ. As the Magi brought their gifts from afar to Christ so had the visit to Solomon by the queen from the south been a symbolic precursor to this later event of homage. In their representations of the tale artists seized avidly upon the rich possibilities in the exotic background suggested by the wealth of Sheba and the grandeur of Solomon's court. And even when the patristic scheme of typology that linked the queen with the Church was abandoned in Europe the theme of Sheba–Solomon continued to be a favourite subject of artists as they reverted to a portrayal of the more classical biblical form of the story.

The story appears in the Qur'an as but an adumbration of the biblical narrative. Stripped of all but the characters of Solomon, the clever and wealthy king, and the woman who ruled in Sheba and paid him a visit, it was recast so as to become a quite different tale. The *dramatis personae* included djinn, the hoopoe bird, and the Devil; alien episodes and themes were woven into the older fabric, such as the conversion of the queen from the worship of the sun-god to that of the true God of Islam; the miraculous transfer of the queen's throne to Solomon; and the king's palace that was paved with glass, that appeared to the queen as a pool of water as she, with upraised garment, set foot on it. This embroidery had its source, as we have seen, either in the tradition current in Medina among the Jewish residents there in the time of Muhammad or in the fertile imagination of the Prophet's followers.

The richness of imagery and the further ramifications of the plot are woven about the ever-growing characters of the story. Long before modern science and technology enabled man to triumph over time and space, men marvelled at Solomon, the wise man, who had become a magician and whose djinn did his bidding. In forms bizarre to us, Islam proved to be a link between the wisdom of Near Eastern man—Sumerian, Egyptian, Greek, Persian, Jew and Christian—and those who lived in the vast area of the world which Islam came suddenly to occupy in the first century after its birth.

A part of the popularity of the narrative in Islamic tradition may be explained as due to geographical features. After all, Islam had been born in Arabia, the home of the famous queen. In the Islamic proliferation the biblical skeleton was filled out with imaginative details about her name, her appearance, and supplemented with traditions that satisfied a natural curiosity and delighted an audience of oriental listeners. The story was in its natural habitat. In that soil allusions made in the earlier narrative took root and grew.

The popularity of the story in Ethiopia is perhaps easiest to understand. With complete disregard for the chronology of history the Queen of Sheba became one with 'Candace queen of the Ethiopians', who was associated with the introduction of Christianity into Ethiopia. Sheba was equated with Ethiopia. While Solomon is given a new part, namely that of the seducer of his royal visitor, the queen, whose only offence was that she sought to satisfy her thirst for water after a heavily spiced meal, becomes the mother of the first of a long line of Ethiopian kings. To have become a part of a national tradition, accepted as a fact in the middle of the twentieth century AD, is indeed an impressive record for a story that reaches so far back into the past.

While the evidence for the historical documentation of the story—if it indeed exists—has not yet appeared, the proof for its wide diffusion in a variety of legends is ample and instructive. Its use through the centuries was in no way inhibited, as far as we can see, by doubts over its historical pedigree. As historical truth or as legend it was carried along through memory and writing to do service in a variety of ways to ideas and institutions, tying them firmly into the past and providing continuity and support without which they might have faltered and failed. Such is the record of the past three thousand years. One can only wonder what the future holds for the memory of a brief moment within the tenth century BC which has cast such a long shadow.

Bibliography

Introduction

John Bright, *A History of Israel*, Philadelphia, 1959.

Edward L. Curtis and Albert A. Madsen, *A Critical and Exegetical Commentary on the Books of Chronicles*, New York, 1910.

John Gray, *I & II Kings: A Commentary*, Philadelphia, 1963.

James A. Montgomery, ed. by Henry S. Gehman, *A Critical and Exegetical Commentary on the Book of Kings*, New York, 1951.

Jacob M. Myers, *I Chronicles: Introduction, Translation and Notes*, The Anchor Bible, New York, 1965.

Martin Noth, *Könige*, Biblischer Kommentar, Neukirchen, 1968.

R. B. Y. Scott, 'Solomon and the Beginnings of Wisdom in Israel', *Supplement to Vetus Testamentum*, vol. III, 1955, pp. 262–79.

Chapter I

G. A. Barrois, 'Chronology, Metrology, etc.', *The Interpreter's Bible*, vol. 1, Nashville, 1952, pp. 142–64.

John Bright, *A History of Israel*, Philadelphia, 1959.

William G. Dever, *et al.*, *Gezer I: Preliminary Report of the 1964–65 Seasons*, Jerusalem, 1970.

William G. Dever, *et al.*, 'Further Excavations at Gezer, 1967–1971', *The Biblical Archaeologist*, vol. 34, pp. 94–132.

John Gray, *I & II Kings: A Commentary*, Philadelphia, 1963.

R. S. Lamon and G. M. Shipton, *Megiddo I: Seasons of 1925–34, Strata I–V*, Chicago, 1939.

J. Liver, 'The Book of the Acts of Solomon', *Biblica*, vol. 48, 1967, pp. 75–101.

R. A. S. Macalister, *The Excavation of Gezer*, vols. 1–3, London, 1912.

Eugene H. Maly, *The World of David and Solomon*, Englewood Cliffs, N.J., 1966.

Benjamin Mazar, *et al.*, eds., *Encyclopaedia of Archaeological Excavations in the Holy Land* (in Hebrew), Jerusalem, 1970, vol. 1, pp. 158–170.

James A. Montgomery, ed. by Henry S. Gehman, *A Critical and Exegetical Commentary on the Book of Kings*, New York, 1951.

Martin Noth, *The Old Testament World*, Philadelphia, 1966.

Martin Noth, *The History of Israel*, London, 1958.

Martin Noth, *Könige*, Neukirchen, 1968.

Bezalel Porten, 'The Structure and Theme of the Solomon Narrative (I Kings 3–11)', *Hebrew Union College Annual*, vol. 38, 1967, pp. 93–128.

James B. Pritchard, ed., *Ancient Near Eastern Texts Relating to the Old Testament*, 3rd edition, Princeton, 1969.

James B. Pritchard, *The Ancient Near East in Pictures Relating to the Old Testament*, 2nd edition, Princeton, 1969.

R. B. Y. Scott, 'Solomon and the Beginnings of Wisdom in Israel', *Supplement to Vetus Testamentum*, vol. III, pp. 262–79.

D. W. Thomas, ed., *Archaeology and Old Testament Study*, Oxford, 1967.

Yigael Yadin *et al.*, *Hazor I*, Jerusalem, 1958.

Yigael Yadin *et al.*, *Hazor II*, Jerusalem, 1960.

Yigael Yadin *et al.*, *Hazor III-IV*, Plates, Jerusalem, 1961.

Yigael Yadin, 'The Fifth Season of Excavations at Hazor, 1968–1969', *The Biblical Archaeologist*, vol. 32, pp. 50–71.

Yigael Yadin, 'Megiddo and the Kings of Israel', *The Biblical Archaeologist*, vol. 33, pp. 66–96.

Yigael Yadin, 'New Light on Solomon's Megiddo', *The Biblical Archaeologist*, vol. 23, pp. 62–68.

Yigael Yadin, 'Solomon's City Wall and Gate at Gezer', *Israel Exploration Journal*, vol. 8, pp. 80–86.

Yigael Yadin, *Hazor* (the Schweich Lectures, 1970), 1972.

Chapter II

Anon., *The Periplus of the Erythraean Sea*, trans. and annot. by Wilfred H. Schoff, Longmans, Green, and Co., New York, 1912.

Richard LeBaron Bowen and Frank P. Albright, *Archaeological Discoveries in South Arabia*, The Johns Hopkins Press, Baltimore, 1958.

Gertrude Caton Thompson, *The Tombs and Moon Temple of Hureidha (Hadhramaut)*, Reports of the Research Committee of the Society of Antiquaries of London, XIII, Oxford, 1944.

Ray L. Cleveland, *An Ancient South Arabian Necropolis*, The Johns Hopkins Press, Baltimore, 1965.

Brian Doe, *Southern Arabia*, Thames and Hudson Ltd., London, 1971.

Adolf Grohmann, *Arabien*, Munich, 1963.

G. Lankester Harding, *Archaeology in the Aden Protectorates*, Her Majesty's Stationery Office, London, 1964.

Albert Jamme, *Sabaean Inscriptions from Mahram Bilqis (Marib)*, The Johns Hopkins Press, Baltimore, 1962.

Wendell Phillips, *Qataban and Sheba*, Harcourt, Brace and Co., New York, 1955.

Gus W. Van Beek: (1) *Hajar Bin Humeid:* Investigations at a Pre-Islamic Site in South Arabia, The Johns Hopkins Press, Baltimore, 1969; (2) 'Frankincense and Myrrh', *The Biblical Archaeologist Reader*, 2, Doubleday Anchor Book A250b, Garden City, New York, 1964; (3) 'A New Interpretation of the So-Called South Arabian House Model', *American Journal of Archaeology* 63, 1959; (4) 'South Arabian History and Archaeology', in G. E. Wright, ed., *The Bible and the Ancient Near East*, Doubleday, Garden City, New York, 1961; (5) 'Monuments of Axum in the Light of South Arabian Archaeology', *Journal of the American Oriental Society*, 87, 1967; (6) 'An Archaeological Reconnaissance in Hadhramaut, South Arabia—A Preliminary Report', *General Appendix to the Annual Report of the Board of Regents of the Smithsonian Institution*, Washington, 1963; (7) 'Prolegomenon', *Arabia and the Bible*, Ktav Publishing House, 1969.

Hermann von Wissmann and Maria Höfner, *Beiträge zur historischen Geographie des vorislamischen Südarabien*, Akademie der Wissenschaften und der Literatur, Abhandlungen der Geistes- und Sozialwissenschaftlichen Klasse, Mainz, 1952.

Hermann von Wissmann, *Zur Geschichte und Landeskunde von Alt-Südarabien*, Österreichische Akademie der Wissenschaften, Philosophisch-Historische Klasse, Sitzungsberichte 246, Vienna, 1964.

The major classical authors who discuss southern Arabia can be read in the Loeb Edition; they include: Pliny, *Natural History*; *The Geography of Strabo*; *Diodorus Siculus*; *The Geography of Claudius Ptolemy*; Celsus, *De Medicina*.

Chapter III

Y. Aviad, 'Ma'ase Malkath Sheba', (The Tale of the Queen of Sheba), in *Sefer Asaf* (Festschrift in honour of Simha Asaf), Jerusalem, 1953.

The Babylonian Talmud, Tractate Baba Bathra, London (Soncino Press), 1935.

W. Bacher, 'Lilith Königin von Smargad', *Monatschrift für Geschichte und Wissenschaft des Judentums*, XIX (1870).

R. Borger, 'Assyriologische und altarabistische Miszellen', *Orientalia* (n.s.), 26:1 (1957).

S. Buber, ed., *Midrash Mishle*, Wilna, 1893.

S. Buber, ed., *Midrash Tanhuma*, Wilna, 1885.

P. Cassel, *An Explanatory Commentary on Esther*, Edinburgh, 1888. The Second Targum is Appendix I. See as well, *Zweites Targum zum Buche Esther*, Leipzig, 1885; *Aus Literatur und Geschichte*, Berlin, 1885.

A. Chastel, 'La Légende de la Reine de Saba', *Revue de l'Histoire des Religions*, 119 and 120.

L. Dukes, *Rabbinische Blumenlese*, Leipzig, 1844.

Abr. Epstein, *Miqqadmoniot ha-Yehudim* (Beiträge zur Jüdischen Alterthumskunde), Erster Teil, Vienna, 1887.

S. Gelbhaus, *Die Targumliteratur, I: Das Targum Scheni*, Frankfurt a/M., 1893.

L. Ginzberg, *The Legends of the Jews*, III, IV, VI, Philadelphia, 1911, 1913, 1939.

M. Grünbaum, *Neue Beiträge zur semitischen Sagenkunde*, Leiden, 1893.

M. Grunwald, *Mitteilungen der Gesellschaft für Jüdische Volkskunde*, II (1898), V (1900).

W. Hertz, 'Die Rätsel der Königin von Saba', *Zeitschrift für deutsches Altertum*, XXVII; also in *Gesammelte Abhandlungen*, 1905.

M. Jastrow, *A Dictionary of the Targumin, the Talmud Babli and Yerushalmi, and the Midrashic Literature*, New York/Berlin and London, 1926.

Josephus, *Jewish Antiquities*, V–VIII, translated by H. St. J. Thackeray and R. Marcus, Cambridge (Mass.) and London, 1966.

J. Klausner, 'Shelomo ha-Melek u-Malkat Sheba', *Ha-Shiloah*, XIII (1904).

S. Krauss, 'Die Namen der Königin von Saba', *Festschrift Freimann*, Berlin, 1937.

S. Krauss, *Griechische und lateinische Lehnwörter im Talmud, Midrasch und Targum*, II, Hildesheim, 1964 (reprint).

J. Levy, *Chaldäisches Wörterbuch über die Targumim . . .*, Leipzig, 1881.

L. Munk, *Targum Scheni zum Buch Esther nebst Variae Lectiones nach handschriftlichen Quellen*, Berlin, 1876.

A. Roesch, *Die Königin von Saba als Königin Bilqis*, Leipzig, 1880.

G. Salzberger, *Die Salomo-Sage in der semitischen Literatur*, Berlin and Heidelberg, 1907.

S. Schechter, ed., *Midrash ha-Godol to Genesis*, Cambridge, 1902.

S. Schechter, ed., *Agadath Shir ha-Shirim*, Cambridge, 1896. (Reprint from *Jewish Quarterly Review*, old series.)

S. Schechter, 'The Riddles of Solomon in Rabbinic Literature', *Folklore: a Quarterly Review*, I, London, 1890.

G. Scholem, 'Peraqim hadashim me'inyane Ashmodai v-Lilit' (New chapters concerning Ashmodai and Lilith), *Tarbiz*, 19, Jerusalem, 1948.

L. H. Silberman, 'Unriddling the Riddle . . .', *Revue de Qumran*, 11, 3, 3 (1961).

M. Steinschneider, ed., *Alphabetum Siracidis*, Berlin, 1858. (Hebrew.)

A. Sulzbach, *Targum Scheni zum Buch Esther*, Frankfurt a/M., 1920.

A. Wünsche, *Die Rätselweisheit bei den Hebräern*, Leipzig, 1883.

The Zohar, translated by H. Sperling and M. Simon, London (Soncino Press), 1931–4.

Chapter IV

A. Bausani, 'Drammi popolari inediti persiani sulla leggenda di Solomone e della regina di Saba', Rome, 1960 (Accademia dei Lincei, no. 48).

André Chastel, 'La Légende de la Reine de Saba', *Revue de l'Histoire des Religions*, 119 (1939). 204–25; 120.27–44, 160–74.

W. A. Clouston, *Flowers from a Persian Garden*, 215ff.

Georg Graf, *Geschichte der christlichen arabischen Literatur*, Rome, 1944, etc., i. 210; refers to Migne, *Patrologia Graeca*, 122.1315–58 ('Testament of Solomon').

al-Kisa'i, *Qisas al-anbiya'*, 278ff.

al-Mas'udi, *Muruj adh-dhahab*, Paris (with French translation), iii. 152f., 173f.

Qur'an, 27:22–45 and commentaries.

Jalal-ad-din Rumi, *Mathnawi*, tr. Nicholson, iv. 563, 614, 653, 718, 764, 781, 799, 839, 859, 903, 1041.

D. Sidersky, *Les Origines des légendes musulmanes dans le Coran*, Paris, 1933.

ath-Tha'labi, *Qisas al-anbiya'*, 216–20.

Yaqut, *Mu'jam al-buldan*, i. 674; ii. 596; iii. 115, 640, 812; iv. 171 (chiefly about castles in the Yemen).

Chapter V

(A detailed bibliography will be found in Edward Ullendorff, *Ethiopia and the Bible* (Schweich Lectures of the British Academy), Oxford, 1968).

A. Bausani, 'Drammi popolari inediti persiani sulla leggenda di Salomone e della regina di Saba', in *Atti del Convegno Internazionale di Studi Etiopici*, Rome, 1960.

C. F. Beckingham and G. W. B. Huntingford, *The Prester John of the Indies*, 2 vols., Hakluyt Society, London, 1961.

C. Bezold, *Kebra Nagast*, Munich, 1905.

Sir E. A. Wallis Budge, *The Life and Exploits of Alexander the Great*, 2 vols., London, 1896.

Sir E. A. Wallis Budge, *The Queen of Sheba and her only son Menyelek*, London, 1932.

A. Caquot, 'La Royauté sacrale en Éthiopie', in *Annales d'Éthiopie*, ii, 1957.

E. Cerulli, 'La regina di Sicilia e la regina Saba' in *Studi in onore di Piero Meriggi*, Pavia, 1969.

E. Cerulli, 'La Regina Saba e la tradizione dei Trenta Denari', in *Rendiconti Accademia Nazionale dei Lincei*, Roma, 1968.

E. Cerulli, *Storia della letteratura etiopica*, 3rd edition, Milan, 1968.

C. Clapham, *Haile-Selassie's Government*, London, 1969.

C. Conti Rossini, 'La regalità sacra in Abissinia e nei regni dell'Africa centrale ed occidentale', in *Studi e materiali di storia delle religioni*, xxi, Bologna, 1948.

A. Dillmann, *Catalogus Codicum Manuscriptorum Bibliothecae Bodleianae Oxoniensis*, pars VII, Oxford, 1848.

M. Grünbaum, *Neue Beiträge zur semitischen Sagenkunde*, Leiden, 1893.

Guebre Sellassie, *Chronique du règne de Menelik II*, 2 vols., Paris, 1932.

I. Guidi, *Il Fetha Nagast* (Eth. text, Italian transl.), 2 vols., Rome, 1897 and 1899.

E. Haberland, *Untersuchungen zum äthiopischen Königtum*, Wiesbaden, 1965.

E. Hammerschmidt, *Symbolik des orientalischen Christentums*, *Tafelband*, Stuttgart, 1966.

D. A. Hubbard, *The Literary Sources of the Kebra Nagast*, as yet unpublished Ph.D. thesis, St. Andrews University, 1956.

A. R. Johnson, *Sacral Kingship in Ancient Israel*, Cardiff, 1967.

E. Littmann, *Deutsche Aksum Expedition*, Berlin, 1913.

E. Littmann, *The legend of the Queen of Sheba in the tradition of Axum*, Leiden, 1904.

E. Mittwoch, 'Dschanhoi—die amharische Bezeichnung für "Majestät"', in *ZA*, 1911.

J. A. Montgomery, *Arabia and the Bible* (1934 and 1969 re-issue).

F. Praetorius, *Die Amharische Sprache*, Halle, 1879.

F. Praetorius, *Fabula de regina Sabaea apud Aethiopes*, Halle, 1870.

G. Rösch, 'Die Königin von Saba als Königin Bilqis ', in *Jahrbuch für Protestantische Theologie*, vi, 1880.

S. Rubenson, 'The lion of the tribe of Judah, Christian symbol and/or Imperial title', in *JES*, iii. 2, 1965.

Bertrand Russell, 'The Queen of Sheba's nightmare', in *Nightmares of eminent persons*, Penguin, 1962.

G. Salzberger, *Die Salomo-Sage in der semitischen Literatur*, Berlin, 1907.

Edward Ullendorff, *The Ethiopians*, 3rd ed., Oxford Paperbacks, 1973.

Edward Ullendorff, 'The Biblical sources of the Ethiopian national saga' (in Hebrew), in *Sefer Tur-Sinai*, Jerusalem, 1960.

Edward Ullendorff, 'Bilkīs', in *Encyclopaedia of Islam*, 2nd. ed.

Edward Ullendorff, *Ethiopia and the Bible* (Schweich lectures; British Academy and Oxford University Press, 1968).

Edward Ullendorff, 'The Queen of Sheba', in *Bulletin of the John Rylands Library*, March 1963.

Edward Ullendorff, 'Candace (Acts VIII, 27) and the Queen of Sheba', in *New Testament Studies*, ii, September 1955.

J. Varenbergh, 'Studien zur abessinischen Reichsordnung (Šer'ata Mangešt)', in *ZA*, vol. 30, 1915.

I. Velikovsky, *Ages in Chaos*, London, 1953.

G. Weil, *Biblische Legenden der Muselmänner*, Frankfurt, 1845.

Chapter VI

J. Ph. Berjeau, *Geschiedenis van het heylighe Cruys: or, History of the Holy Cross*, C. J. Stewart, London, 1863.

Giovanni Boccaccio, *Concerning Famous Women*, translated and edited by Guido A. Guarino, George Allen and Unwin Ltd., London, 1963.

Pedro Calderón de la Barca, *El árbol del mejor fruto* in *Obras completas*, ed. Ángel Valbuena Prat, Áquila, Madrid, III, 1952, pp. 985–1009.

Pedro Calderón de la Barca, *La sibylla del oriente y gran reina de Sabá*, in *Las Comedias*, ed. J. J. Keil, Ernest Fischer, Leipzig, III, 1829, 200–218.

André Chastel, 'La Légende de la Reine de Saba', *Revue de l'Histoire des Religions*, 119, 1939, pp. 204–25; 120, 1939, pp. 27–44.

André Chastel, 'La Rencontre de Salomon et de la reine de Saba dans l'iconographie médiévale', *Gazette des Beaux-Arts*, series 6, XXXV 1949, pp. 99–114.

André Chastel, 'L'Épisode de la Reine de Saba dans la *Tentation de saint Antoine* de Flaubert', *The Romantic Review*, XL, 1949, pp. 261–7.

Sir Sidney Colvin, *A Florentine Picture-Chronicle*, B. Quaritch, London, 1898.

François Constans, 'Deux Enfants du feu: la Reine de Saba et Nerval', *Mercure de France*, CCCII, April 1948, pp. 623–32; CCCII, May 1948, pp. 43–54.

Phineas A. Crutch (pseudonym), *The Queen of Sheba, Her Life and Times*, G. P. Putnam's Sons, New York and London, 1922.

John Dos Passos, *Three Soldiers*, Modern Library, New York 1932.

Gustave Flaubert, *La Tentation de saint Antoine* in *Œuvres complètes*, Louis Conrad, Paris, III, 1924; English tr., *The Complete Works*, M. Walter Dunne, New York and London, VII, 1904, 1–170.

T. Fisher, *Ancient Allegorical, Historical, and Legendary Paintings in Fresco*, H. G. Bohn, London, 1838.

Anatole France, *La Rôtisserie de la Reine Pédauque*, Paris, 1893; English tr., by Mrs. Wilfrid Jackson, *At the Sign of the Reine Pédauque*, Everyman's Library, London, 1941.

Karl Goldmark, *The Queen of Sheba*, libretto by Salomon Hermann Ritter von Mosenthal, Hugo Pohle, Hamburg, 1881.

Charles Gounod, *La Reine de Saba*, libretto by Jules Barbier and Michel Carré, Paris, 1862.

Carroll Greene, *Romare Bearden: The Prevalence of Ritual*, Museum of Modern Art, New York, 1970.

J. L. Herr, 'La Reine de Saba et le bois de la croix', *Revue archéologique*, series 4, XXIII 1914, pp. 1–3.

W. Hertz, 'Die Rätsel der Königin von Saba', *Zeitschrift für deutsches Alterthum und deutsche Literatur*, XXVII, 1883, pp. 1–33.

158   *Bibliography*

Jacobus de Voragine, *The Golden Legend*, translated by Granger Ryan and Helmut Rippinger, Arno Press, New York, 1969.

Adolf Katzenellenbogen, *The Sculptural Programs of Chartres Cathedral*, W. W. Norton Co. Inc., New York, 1964.

Rudyard Kipling, 'The Butterfly That Stamped' (Just So Stories, 1902), *The Collected Works of Rudyard Kipling*, Ams Press, New York, XII, 1970, 197–217.

R. Köhler, 'Zur Legende von der Königin von Saba oder der Sibylla und der Kreuzholze', *Germania*, XXIX 1884, pp. 53–9.

Richard Krautheimer, in collaboration with T. Krautheimer-Hess, *Lorenzo Ghiberti*, Princeton University Press, Princeton, 2nd. ed., 1970.

P. Kristeller, *Biblia Pauperum: Unicum der Heidelberger Universitäts-Bibliothek*, B. Cassirer, Berlin, 1906.

J. Lebœuf, 'Conjectures sur la reine pédauque: où l'on recherche quelle pouvait être cette reine',*Mémoires de l'Académie des Inscriptions et des Belles-Lettres*,XXIII,1756, parte 1, pp. 227–34.

J. Lutz and P. Perdrizet, *Speculum Humanae Salvationis*, Karl W. Hiersemann, Leipzig, 1907, 2 vols.

H. Leclercq, 'La Reine Pédauque', *Dictionnaire d'archéologie chrétienne et de liturgie*, XIII, 1938, cols. 2927–28.

Wilhelm Meyer, 'Die Geschichte des Kreuzholzes vor Christus', *Abhandlungen der philosophisch-philologischen Classe der königlichen bayerischen Akademie der Wissenschaften*, XVI, part 2, 1888, pp. 103–66.

Gérard de Nerval, 'Histoire de la reine du matin et de Soliman prince des génies' (*Voyage en orient*, in *Œuvres*, ed. Henri Lemaître, Éditions Garnier Frères, Paris, 1958, II, pp. 565–676.

Anton Pigler, *Barockthemen*, Ungarische Akademie der Wissenschaften, Budapest and Berlin, 1956, 2 vols.

Quentin, 'Note sur la reine pédauque', *Bulletin monumental*, 2nd series, VIII, 1852, 359–63.

Gerhard Schmidt, *Die Armenbibeln des XIV. Jahrhunderts*, H. Böhlau, Graz and Cologne, 1959.

Laurie Schneider, 'The Iconography of Piero della Francesca's Dealing With the Story of The True Cross in The Church of San Francesco at Arezzo', *Art Quarterly*, XXXII 1969, pp. 23–45.

Elizabeth Soltesz, *Biblia Pauperum: The Esztergom Blockbook of Forty Leaves*, Corvina Press, Budapest, 1967.

Arthur Symons, 'The Lover of the Queen of Sheba', *Images of Good and Evil*, William Heinemann, London, 1899, 30–41.

Franz Unterkircher and Gerhard Schmidt, *Die Wiener Biblia Pauperum*, Oesterreichische Nationalbibliothek in Wien, Graz, Vienna and Cologne, n.d., 3 vols.

William Butler Yeats, *The Collected Poems*, The Macmillan Company, London & New York, 1963.

Index